Blockchain

Blockchain: A Hype or a Hoax? fills a gap in the book market to provide material that is not only technical but also caters to business readers. This book was written to keep in mind various stakeholders and the current gap in blockchain education as well as use case implementation.

This book reviews blockchain technology, discusses why proof of concept fails, offers examples of use cases that have been successful and that have failed and articulates a framework that should be used before deciding whether blockchain is the right technology for transformation. It uses strategic models and frameworks to assist organisations to see a fit score for their specific use cases.

This book provides guidance on how to create a blockchain strategy and a business case to pitch for the budget. It also includes a case study to apply the knowledge on practical use cases for blockchain and a technical overview of most of the blockchain use cases in the market including crypto, non-fungible tokens, decentralised finance, and decentralised autonomous organisations, as well as financial and non-financial industry use cases.

This book also provides a detailed overview of most of the mainstream blockchain products currently available in the market. It also offers guidance on how readers can best educate themselves on blockchain technology that is available through commercial and free resources.

It concludes with a clear direction on selecting blockchain to solve real-life use cases that are best fit. A financial and non-financial value-adding framework is discussed throughout this book to assist business leaders, programme managers, product managers and information technology leaders to make strategic choices, and business cases and develop strategies for digital transformation through the use of blockchain.

The distinctive feature of this book is the critical analysis of blockchain from a technology and business perspective. This is the first book to focus on business, technology and blockchain selection framework. The most unique feature of this book would be to apply Michael Porter's competitive advantage strategy theory on blockchain use cases and their impact on companies.

This book is aimed at technology students, technology professionals, blockchain and fintech consultant and business leaders. It will also be useful for readers who are building a business case to adopt blockchain into an organisation or are seeking to grow their knowledge of blockchain and improve their fintech strategy.

Blockchain
A Hype or a Hoax?

Kapil Sharma

CRC Press
Taylor & Francis Group
Boca Raton London New York

CRC Press is an imprint of the
Taylor & Francis Group, an **informa** business

First edition published 2023
by CRC Press
6000 Broken Sound Parkway NW, Suite 300, Boca Raton, FL 33487-2742

and by CRC Press
4 Park Square, Milton Park, Abingdon, Oxon, OX14 4RN

CRC Press is an imprint of Taylor & Francis Group, LLC

© 2023 Taylor & Francis Group, LLC

ISBN: 978-1-032-12657-9 (hbk)
ISBN: 978-1-032-12658-6 (pbk)
ISBN: 978-1-003-22560-7 (ebk)

DOI: 10.1201/9781003225607

Typeset in Sabon
by codeMantra

Dedication

This book is dedicated to my lovely wife Usha Sharma and my beautiful children Dhruv and Karina Sharma. My wife provided me with personal, moral, mental and motivational support and also put up with all my late nights and working weekends. I also dedicate this book to my late father Girdhari Lal Sharma and my mother Bimla Devi Sharma.

Contents

Acknowledgements   xv
Author   xvii

1 Blockchain: Is it a hype or a hoax?   1

Blockchain invention 1
  What is blockchain? 1
  Blockchain objectives 2
  Blockchain benefits and limitations 2
  Crypto (Bitcoin) evolution 2
    Who created Bitcoin? 2
    Features of Bitcoin 3
    Cryptocurrency overview 3
    Key layers of the cryptocurrency (CC) ecosystem 3
  Ethereum overview 5
    Ethereum smart contract overview 5
  Alternative currencies overview 5
  Overview of ICO 7
  How does blockchain work? 7
  Blockchain technology summary 8
  Types of blockchain (public/private/consortium/hybrid) 8
  Consensus algorithm 9
  Blockchain consensus algorithms 10
DeFi (Decentralised Finance) overview 12
  Most popular types of DeFi applications 15
  Examples of DeFi projects 16
  Use cases of DeFi 17
    Asset management 17
    Compliance and Know Your Transactions (KYTs) 17
    DAOs 17
    Data and analytics 17

Derivatives 18
DEXs 18
Gaming 18
Insurance 18
Lending and borrowing 18
Marketplaces 19
Payments 19
Prediction markets 19
Savings 19
Stablecoins 19
Synthetic assets 20
Tokenisation 20
Trading 20
Digital identity 20
Crowdfunding 20
How to get involved in DeFi? 21
Why invest time in dApps? 22
*How to develop dApps and launch them
onto the Ethereum network? 22*
How to get started with DeFi? 23
Try DeFi applications in real time 28
NFT overview 38
  What is an NFT? 38
  How do NFTs work? 39
  Current examples of NFTs 39
  Platforms to get involved in NFTs 40
CDBC revolution 41
  *Potential benefits and challenges related
to CBDC implementation 42*
Summary 46

2 **Blockchain products**   **47**

Blockchain products in the market 47
Blockchain product comparison 47
Cryptocurrency 51
Smart contract 51
Dynamic registry 52
Static registry 53
Payment infrastructure 53
Identity 54
DeFi and NFTs 54

Others 54
Comparison of top six platforms 55
Deep dive into successful products 55
  Bitcoin 55
    Use cases 55
  Ethereum 57
    Use cases 58
  Hyperledger 58
  Consensys Quorum 58
    Use cases 61
  R3 Corda 61
    Use cases 61
  Ripple 62
    Use cases 62

3 Blockchain: Is it hype?   63

Blockchain footprint in multiple sectors 64
  Financial services sector 64
  Capital markets 64
    Overview 64
    Blockchain footprint 64
    Use cases 66
  Trade finance 66
    Overview 66
    Blockchain footprint 67
  Insurance 69
    Blockchain footprint 69
  Supply chain 70
    Blockchain footprint 71
  Digital identity 73
    Blockchain footprint 73
  Agriculture 73
    Blockchain footprint 74
  Telecommunications 74
    Blockchain footprint 75
  Healthcare 75
    Blockchain footprint 75
  Healthcare data or EHR 75
  Monetising patient data 77
  Genomic data 78
  Healthcare cryptocurrency 79

Provenance and medical histories 80
Energy 80
  Blockchain footprint 80
Govtech 81
  Blockchain footprint 81
  Central Bank Digital Currency (CBDC) 82
Real estate 82
  Blockchain footprint 82
Education 83
  Use cases 83
Digital assets 84
  Blockchain footprint 84
Market value positioning based on Blockchain adoption 84
  Blockchain disruption 84
    Financial benefits 84
    Non-financial benefits 85
    Sector-specific benefits 85
Barriers to Blockchain adoption 88
Blockchain adoption to solve critical and
complex business problems 89
  Business problems 89
    Business problem #1 90
    Business problem #2 92
    Business problem #3 94
Summary 96

4 Blockchain: Is it a hoax?   **97**

Insights on cryptocurrencies 97
  Leverage 100
  Stablecoins 100
  Market sentiment 100
  Crypto fraud 101
Insights on ICOs 109
  Successful ICOs 110
  Unsuccessful ICOs including scams and fraud 111
    Dead coins 112
  Avoid ICO fraud and investment 112
    Disappearing with the investors' money 113
Educational and capability gap in blockchain technology 115
  Education gap 116
  University courses on blockchain 117

Training courses from private institutes 117
Online and offline resources by universities 119
Government support 125
Capability gap in business 126
   Partnership with universities to influence the syllabus 126
   Employee training programme 127
   Employee experience 127
   Resource capacity to support 127
   Process gaps 128
   Business knowledge gap 128
Use of blockchain for wrong business problems 129
   Key issues surrounding blockchain project failures 129
Summary 131

5 **Blockchain framework: A model to assess the Blockchain for Business use case**   **133**

Business problems 133
Questionnaire to assess maturity of the business process 140
Assess the gaps and recommendations 144
   Reference: A – Regulations 145
   Reference: B – Collaboration 146
   Reference: C – Technology 147
   Reference: D – Operating model 149
   Reference: E – Education 150
Framework to assess blockchain use case 152
   Blockchain technology usage – decision tree 152
      List of questions 152
   Type of blockchain – selection decision tree 158
      List of questions 158
   Type of consensus – consensus type decision tree 159
      List of questions 160
   Use of smart contract – smart contract decision tree 161
      List of questions 161
Conclusion with blockchain fit score 162

6 **Blockchain strategies**   **163**

Overview 163
Levels of strategies 163
   Corporate strategy 163
   Business strategy 164
   Functional strategy 164

Types of strategies 164
Michael Porter's generic strategy 164
  Generic strategy 164
  Cost leadership strategy 166
  Differentiation strategy 167
  Focus strategy 167
Selection of the strategy 168
Strategic models 168
  Michael Porter's five forces strategy model 168
  Porter's five forces 170
  Summary 172
PEST: political, economic, social and technological analysis 173
  Overview 173
  What are the areas assessed by PEST model? 173
  What are the additional areas assessed by PESTLE model? 174
  Application of PESTLE model to assess Blockchain use case 175
SWOT: strengths, weaknesses, opportunities and threats 179
  Overview 179
  Areas assessed by SWOT 179
  Application of SWOT on a company's blockchain use case 179
Blockchain strategy formulation 183
  Set up vision and mission 183
  Understand the external environment and our position 183
  Understand the internal environment and our position 184
  Articulate long-term objectives and goals 184
Strategy execution 184
  Strategy planning 184
  Communication of the objectives and goals 185
  Create strategic and transformational
  programmes aligned to the strategic plan 185
  Define the operating model 186
  Program and milestone governance 186
  Realignment of human resources to strategic programmes 187
  Capability uplift 189
  Establish Centre of Excellence 191
  Requirements for CoE 191
  Steps to establish CoE 192
  Benefits of CoE 193
  Evaluation of strategy execution 193
  Steps for strategy execution evaluation 194
Assess the Blockchain strategy 195

Use of the strategic model to assess
the blockchain business value 195
Blockchain sandbox 197
Conclusion 199

7 **Blockchain business cases: A framework to produce a business case for blockchain**   **201**

Features and elements of a good blockchain business case 201
Problem statement 201
Stakeholders 202
Alignment to strategy 203
Approach 204
Financial acumen 204
Business benefits 204
Risks 205
Leadership 205
Options 205
Timelines 206
Governance 206
Framework to draft a blockchain business case 207
Framework template 207
Approval process of the blockchain business case 208
Execution of a blockchain business case 209
Steps 209
Recommendations 211
Conclusion 213

8 **Blockchain case study: Apply concepts on practical use case**   **215**

Case study 1: Create a platform for a digital art marketplace 215
Background 215
Strategy execution phases 215
Problem statement 216
IOSpeed potential strategic outcomes 216
Strategic outcomes 216
Organisation analysis for strategy formulation 217
Organisation analysis 217
SWOT: strengths, weaknesses, opportunities, and threats 217
Overview 217
Areas assessed by SWOT on IOSpeed 217

Strategy formulation 221
  Setup vision and mission for IOSpeed 221
  Understand the external environment and our position 221
  Understand the internal environment and our position 222
  Articulate long-term objectives and goals 223
  Prospective solutions 223
  Advantages of the third-party NFT platform 224
  Disadvantages of the third-party NFT platform 225
  Recommendations 225
  Architecture diagram 226
  Advantages of the IOSpeed-owned NFT platform 229
  Disadvantages of the IOSpeed-owned NFT platform 229
  Recommendations 230
  Architecture diagram 230
  Solution selection 230
  Strategy sign-off 232
Strategy execution 232
  Strategy planning 232
  Communication of the objectives and goals 233
  *Create strategic and transformational
  programmes aligned to the strategic plan 234*
  Realignment of human resources to strategic programmes 234
  Capability uplift 235
  Establish Centre of Excellence (COE) 235
  Programme and milestone governance 236
  Define the operating model 237
  Evaluation of strategy execution 238
  Lessons learnt 241
Summary 241

9 Conclusion   243

Is blockchain a hype or a hoax? 243
  Why blockchain is not a hoax? 244
  Why blockchain is not a hype? 244
*Best practices to adopt blockchain and
gain a competitive advantage 246*
Summary 247

References   249
Index   259

Acknowledgements

Special thanks to Angelos Stefanidis (Dean of AI and Advanced Computing at Xi'an Jiaotong-Liverpool University, China) for reviewing my book proposal and providing guidance.

I thank CoinDesk (https://www.coindesk.com/layer2/2022/09/26/best-universities-for-blockchain-2022/) for providing permission to use its fantastic work on university rankings providing blockchain education.

Author

Kapil Sharma is a global technology transformation executive with more than 23 years of extensive management experience (C-Suite level) in large globally distributed investment banking and consulting environments, with a proven track record of initiating and delivering multiple global strategic initiatives.

Kapil has worked for tier 1 banks in London on technology strategy, complex technology transformation, innovation and education. Kapil is an experienced leader with a proven record of formulating technology strategy, service management, cost models, delivering strategic initiatives, globally complex technology and regulatory programmes, private and public cloud strategy/execution, blockchain, AIOps, product development, mentoring and team management.

Kapil has been a visiting lecturer at the University of Westminster and Bournemouth University since 2001. His latest assignment with Bournemouth University included designing and teaching a postgraduate module called 'Blockchain & Digital Futures'. Kapil is the author of four technology books published by Wiley (previously Wrox Press). Kapil has an MBA degree from Bayes Business School, London (formerly Cass Business School) specialising in finance and strategy.

Kapil is also a founder of the IOSpeed Limited (https://iospeed.com) company in the United Kingdom. IOSpeed provides blockchain consulting and education to corporates.

Chapter 1

Blockchain: Is it a hype or a hoax?

BLOCKCHAIN INVENTION

Blockchain was originally created to support a cryptocurrency called Bitcoin. Bitcoin was the first example of cryptocurrency and also the most successful.

Bitcoin had tremendous success since then and had a market cap of about $1.2 trillion as of writing in April 2021. The Bitcoin system enables payments to be sent between users without passing through a central authority, such as banks or payment gateway. They are created and held electronically.

What is blockchain?

Blockchain technology is a distributed ledger, which allows permanent and immutable recording of data with value addition of providing complete transparency and immutability of the records or blocks. Blocks are linked together to form a chain of blocks, i.e., a blockchain.

Blockchain is also sometimes referred to as distributed ledger (DLT), which is the fundamental technology behind it.

Although there are various attempts to explain blockchain in simple terminology, the following is my favourite.

- The simplest way to explain blockchain complex concepts is to think about globally distributed teams using a giant shared Microsoft Excel spreadsheet. Blockchain technology is like a shared spreadsheet where anyone can make updates to the spreadsheet, and not one person is the owner. Each time the spreadsheet is updated, the change is visible to all; however, the change is only committed to a final spreadsheet when 51% of the project team members approve. The record once approved is committed and becomes immutable (the shared spreadsheet is updated with the approved record and all members of the project team can download the updated spreadsheet on their local computers).

DOI: 10.1201/9781003225607-1

Blockchain objectives

Blockchain can be used to create value for multiple industries. The following is a summary of what blockchain can do:

- **Establish digital identity:** Cryptography is an important force behind the blockchain as it provides a platform to digitally verify a person's identity.
- **Serve as a system of record:** Blockchains are an innovation in information registration and distribution. It can store data in an unencrypted, encrypted and hashed format.
- **Prove immutability:** Blockchain provides a system of record as the transaction cannot be reversed (immutable).
- **Serve as a platform:** Blockchain technology provides a platform with three technologies: Private key cryptography, P2P network and Protocol to exchange an asset globally through smart contracts.

Blockchain benefits and limitations

The following table provides an overview of Blockchain benefits and limitations.

Benefits	Current limitations
• Provides a simple, secure way to establish trust for any kind of transactions • Quick and simple movement of money internationally • The transparency of blockchain has real value for regulators. The regulators and lawmakers are still working to resolve questions about standardisation, stability and other legal issues. • Use of blockchain can automate and simplify the manual processes within Business. However, companies might be reluctant to bear the costs and risks of new technology like blockchain.	• Although blockchain is protected by business-grade cryptography, no technology is 100% secure. • When large sums of money are involved, hackers will try to follow • Limitation on the speed of transaction processing – blockchain (Public blockchain used for Bitcoin) can only process five to eight transactions a second. Emerging blockchain software companies are working on solutions for credit card networks that already process nearly 10,000 times the volume processed by existing blockchain networks.

Crypto (Bitcoin) evolution

Who created Bitcoin?

Bitcoin was created by a pseudonymous software developer named Satoshi Nakamoto who proposed Bitcoin in 2008. The idea was to produce a means of exchange, independent of any central authority, which could be transferred electronically in a secure, verifiable, and immutable way. To this day, no one knows who Satoshi Nakamoto really is.

Features of Bitcoin

- **Decentralisation:** Bitcoin is decentralised. No single institution controls the Bitcoin network as it is maintained by a group of volunteer coders and run by an open network of dedicated computers around the world. With Bitcoin, the integrity of the transactions is maintained by a distributed and open network, owned by no one.
- **Limited supply:** Fiat currencies (dollars, euros, pounds, etc.) have an unlimited supply, i.e. central banks can issue as many as they want and can attempt to manipulate a currency value relative to others. However, for Bitcoin, the supply is tightly controlled by the underlying algorithm. A small number of Bitcoin comes into the network every hour until a maximum of 21 million has been reached. If the demand grows and the supply remains the same, the value will increase.
- **Pseudonymity:** Since there is no central validator, users do not need to identify themselves when sending Bitcoin to another user. When a transaction request is submitted, the protocol checks all previous transactions to confirm that the sender has the necessary Bitcoin as well as the authority to send them to others.
- **Immutability:** Bitcoin transactions cannot be reversed, unlike electronic fiat transactions. It also means that any transaction on the Bitcoin network cannot be tampered with.
- **Divisibility:** The smallest unit of Bitcoin is called a Satoshi. It is one hundred millionth of a Bitcoin. This could enable microtransactions, unlike traditional electronic money.

Cryptocurrency overview

As of 15 November 2021 (Coinmarketcap, 2021), there are about 14,131 cryptos with a market cap of ~$2.87 trillion. The two dominant cryptos making up the market cap of $1.6 trillion are Bitcoin (43.3%) and Ethereum (19.4%) (at the time of writing on 15 November 2021).

Key layers of the cryptocurrency (CC) ecosystem

- **Miners or mining:** Cryptocurrencies are mined by individuals using computers to process transactions and earn a CC reward
- **Wallets:** Wallets store CCs and can come in many forms including online wallets (App- or browser-based). Examples: Coinbase, Crypto.com, Blockchain.info, etc.
- **Exchanges:** CCs can be bought or sold on exchanges. Most exchanges allow trading for CCs for fiat currencies.
- **Processors:** They provide services and tools for merchants to accept CCs as a form of payment. Examples are stripe, Shopify, Braintree, Coinbase, etc. (Figure 1.1).

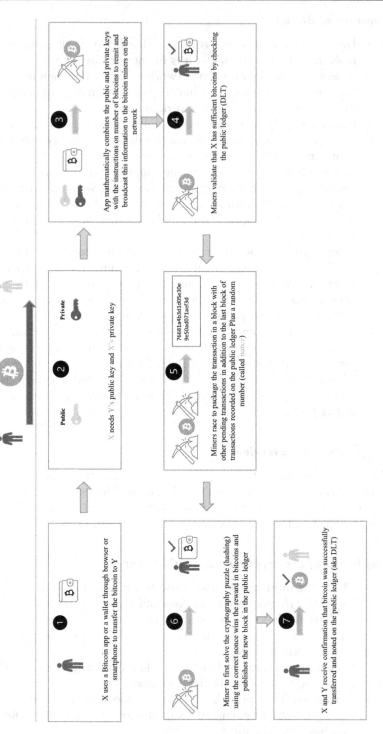

Figure 1.1 How Bitcoin works?

Ethereum overview

- Ethereum is a blockchain platform for transacting anything. Its native currency is Ether.
- Ethereum is considered a decentralised platform for applications, enforced by smart contracts.
- Ethereum framework includes 'smart contracts' (code) embedded in the blockchain that gets executed once certain transaction conditions are met.
- These contracts are executed by miners in exchange for a reward of Ether.

Ethereum smart contract overview

- Smart contracts help you exchange money, property, shares, or anything of value in a transparent, conflict-free way while avoiding the services of a middleman.
- You can use smart contracts for all sorts of situations that range from financial derivatives to insurance premiums, breach contracts, property law, credit enforcement, financial services, legal processes, and crowdfunding agreements.

Alternative currencies overview

Alternative currencies are also called 'Altcoins'. In essence, they are any form of cryptocurrencies that are other than Bitcoin and now even Ethereum (Eth) because of their market value. Some Altcoins share the same characteristics as Bitcoin, but most of them are also different in terms of consensus, platform, the project behind them, etc.

As of November 2021, there are over 14,131 cryptocurrencies including Bitcoin and Ethereum; however, Bitcoin ($1.1 trillion market cap) and Ethereum ($521 billion market cap) account for nearly 60% of the total market cap of the total cryptocurrency market in November 2021.

The following is a list of some of the most successful and with the highest market cap Altcoins (as of 21 November 2021):

- **Binance Coin (BNB):** market cap of $98.8 billion
- **Tether (USDT):** market cap of $73 billion
- **Solana (SOL):** market cap of $65.9 billion
- **Cardano (ADA):** market cap of $62.5 billion
- **Ripple (XRP):** market cap of $51 billion
- **Polkadot (DOT):** market cap of $40.8 billion
- **SD Coin (USDC):** market cap of $36 billion
- **Avalanche (AVAX):** market cap of 30.7 billion
- **Dogecoin (DOGE):** market cap of $30.3 billion
- **Dhibu INI (SHIB):** market cap of $25 billion (Figure 1.2)

#	Name	Price	24h %	7d %	- Market Cap	Volume(24h)	Circulating Supply
1	Bitcoin BTC Buy	$59,791.67	^3.66%	^6.27%	$1,129,919,407,627	$25,927,742,733 433,218 BTC	18,879,450 BTC
2	Ethereum ETH Buy	$4,393.77	^3.78%	^3.09%	$521,581,027,674	$14,251,720,389 3,236,065 ETH	118,432,723 ETH
3	Binance Coin BNB Buy	$592.32	^2.23%	^8.19%	$98,881,118,860	$2,222,227,702 3,748,644 BNB	166,801,148 BNB
4	Tether USDT Buy	$0.9996	^0.23%	^0.06%	$73,114,625,605	$68,424,821,127 88,396,540,486 USDT	73,086,543,702 USDT
5	Solana SOL	$217.76	^4.48%	^6.10%	$65,924,790,115	$1,626,038,230 7,492,718 SOL	303,778,734 SOL
6	Cardano ADA	$1.88	^0.13%	^6.91%	$62,546,915,032	$1,260,072,075 671,129,698 ADA	33,313,246,915 ADA
7	XRP XRP	$1.08	^1.22%	^7.76%	$51,054,069,319	$2,148,588,202 1,984,664,856 XRP	47,158,974,920 XRP
8	Polkadot DOT	$41.59	^3.42%	^8.05%	$40,823,509,035	$1,018,888,172 24,648,368 DOT	987,579,315 DOT
9	USD Coin USDC	$0.9987	^0.04%	^0.06%	$36,108,281,212	$3,199,264,687 3,204,137,502 USDC	36,163,277,899 USDC
10	Avalanche AVAX	$136.99	^11.73%	^47.25%	$30,739,101,805	$3,338,265,631 23,923,116 AVAX	220,286,577 AVAX
11	Dogecoin DOGE	$0.2306	^1.87%	^11.94%	$30,361,420,177	$766,324,420 3,336,958,671 DOGE	132,208,763,907 DOGE

Figure 1.2 Alternative currency overview.

Overview of ICO

- An initial coin offering (ICO) is the cryptocurrency industry's equivalent of an initial public offering. ICOs act as a way to raise funds, where a company is looking to raise money to create a new coin, app, or service by means of launching an ICO.
- Interested investors can buy into the offering and receive a new cryptocurrency token issued by the company. This token may have some utility in using the product or service the company is offering, or it may just represent a stake in the company or project.
- Some of the sites to track the ICO statistics are:
  - https://icodrops.com/category/active-ico/
  - https://www.crypto-rating.com/ico-rating/

How does blockchain work?

1. Blocks are chained together through each block containing the hash digest of the previous block's header.
2. If a previously published block were changed, it would have a different hash.
3. This in turn would cause all subsequent blocks to also have different hashes since they include the hash of the previous block.
4. This makes it possible to easily detect and reject altered blocks.
5. This makes it possible to create a chain of connected blocks, i.e., blockchain (Figure 1.3).

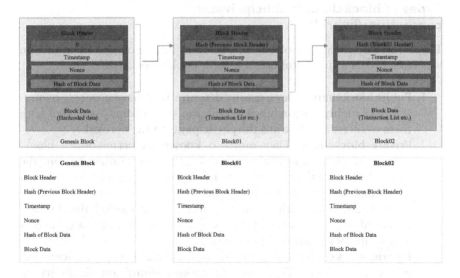

Figure 1.3 How does blockchain work?

* Hashing is a method of applying a cryptographic hash function to data, which calculates a relatively unique output (called a message digest, or just digest) for an input of nearly any size (e.g., a file, text, or image).

Blockchain technology summary

- Shared Ledger
    o History of all transactions
    o Append only with immutable history
    o Distributed and replicated

- Cryptography
    o Integrity of shared ledger
    o Authenticity of transactions
    o Privacy of transactions
    o Identification of participants

- Consensus
    o Decentralised protocol
    o Transaction validation
    o Network Integrity

- Shared Contract
    o Embedded login within the ledger
    o Self-enforcing 'smart contracts'

Types of blockchain (public/private/consortium/hybrid)

There are four categories of blockchains that have emerged since Bitcoin was launched as a successful use case for a public blockchain:

1. **Public blockchain:** They are fully decentralised, have no single ownership, are highly censorship-resistant and have tokens associated with them to incentivise/reward the participants in the network.
2. **Private blockchain:** They are also known as permissioned blockchains. In these blockchains, participants need consent to join the network, transactions are private and are only available to ecosystem participants. They are more centralised.
3. **Consortium blockchain:** They are like private blockchains but are governed by a group rather than a single entity. They can be treated as a sub-category of private blockchain.
4. **Hybrid blockchain:** These chains combine features of a private and public blockchain. This gives businesses significant flexibility to choose what data can be made public and what data they want to keep private (Figure 1.4).

	Public	Private	Consortium	Hybrid
Network Structure	Decentralised	Centralised	Partly Decentralised	Partly Decentralised
Access	Permissionless	Permissioned	Permissioned	Mix of Permissioned and Permissionless
Performance	Slower (~10 minutes)	Faster as number of participants are limited	Vary by number of participants nodes in the network	Vary by number of participants nodes in the network
Consensus	Proof of Work, Proof of Stake	Pre-approved	Proof of Stake, Proof of authority	Proof of Stake, Proof of authority
Identity	Anonymous	Known identities	Known identities	Known identities
Use cases	Cryptocurrencies	Confidential documents audit	Supply chain, Trade Finance	Land registry for assets
Current examples	Bitcoin, Ethereum	R3 Corda, Quorum, Multichain	R3 Corda, Hyper Ledger	R3 Corda, Hyper Ledger

Figure 1.4 Types of blockchain.

Consensus algorithm

Consensus is a mechanism to reach an agreement in a group. A consensus algorithm (also known as a consensus mechanism or consensus protocol) is a digital method by which a decision can be reached in a decentralised environment. In theory, an attacker can compromise consensus by controlling 51% of the network. Consensus mechanisms are designed to make a '51% attack' unfeasible or difficult.

In order to understand consensus, it is essential to learn more about the 'Byzantine Generals' Problem'.

Situation and Task:

There is a group of Byzantine generals. They want to attack a city in a coordinated fashion as that is the only way to win.

Problem:

- The generals and their armies are scattered and far away, so centralised authority is impossible. This makes it difficult to support coordinated attacks.
- The city has a huge army and the only way to win is if they attack together at once.

Solution:

In order to make a coordinated attack, the armies on the left of the castle need to send a messenger to the armies on the right of the castle with a message that says 'ATTACK WEDNESDAY'.

However, if the armies on the right are not prepared for the task and say, 'NO ATTACK FRIDAY' and send back the messenger through the city back to the armies on the left.

This is where they face a problem.

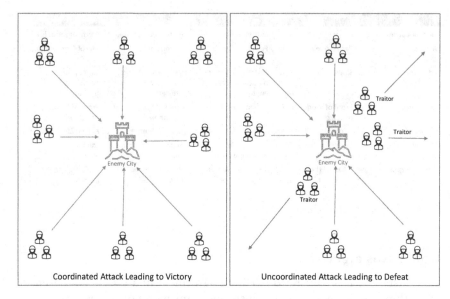

Figure 1.5 Byzantine general problem.

A number of things can happen to the messenger and effectively to the actual message. He could get captured, compromised, killed, and can be replaced by another messenger by the city. This would lead to the armies getting tampered-with information which may result in an uncoordinated attack and prospective defeat. The Byzantine generals' problem can be solved using consensus mechanisms which can make sure their army can actually carry out an attack as a unit.

Now let us apply the above Byzantine generals' problem to the blockchain as it has clear references to the blockchain as well. For instance, if you want to send cryptocurrency like 1 Bitcoin to someone in a huge decentralised network, how would you trust the other party and make sure someone has not tampered with the transaction to change it from 1 to 10 Bitcoin? (Figure 1.5).

Blockchain consensus algorithms

- **Proof of Work (PoW)**
    - o PoW is used by the Bitcoin network. Miners solve cryptographic puzzles to 'mine' a block for it to get added to the blockchain.
    - o This process requires a lot of computational power and energy.
    - o When a miner solves the puzzle, they present their block to the network for verification.
    - o Once the block has been verified, it gets added to the blockchain.
    - o Miners get awarded a % of Bitcoin to solve the puzzle. One of the disadvantages of PoW is that it takes an immense amount of

power and energy consumption to solve the puzzle. This in effect costs a lot of investment; hence, the big players acting as mining pools control the highest % as miners. Therefore, in theory, these big mining pools can simply team up with each other and launch a 51% attack on the Bitcoin network.

- **Proof of Stake (PoS):** PoS uses the concept of validators rather than miners. Validators will start validating the blocks. The creator of the new block is chosen in a deterministic way, and it depends on their wealth, i.e. stake, which is locked up in a wallet while you are staking (funds cannot be moved while you are staking). The PoS validator takes the transaction fees rather than an award. However, if you attempt to cheat by proposing or validating invalid transactions, you will lose a portion or all of the reserved stake. PoS is fast and cost-effective as compared to PoW. Ethereum 2.0 is planning to migrate from PoW to PoS.
- **Proof of Authority (PoA):** In PoA, the right to generate new blocks is awarded to nodes that have proven their authority to do so. These nodes are also referred to as validators. They run software that allows them to put transactions in blocks. PoA consensus leverages the value of identities which effectively means they are not staking coins but their own reputation on the network instead. PoA is also secured by the trust in selected identities.
- **Delegated PoS (dPoS):** The Delegated PoS (dPoS) consensus algorithm comes with a voting system where stakeholders vote for a few delegates who will be responsible for achieving consensus during the generation and validation of new blocks. dPoS algorithms are faster than PoW or PoS algorithms.
- **Practical Byzantine Fault Tolerance (PBFT):** We have already gone through the Byzantine general problem. This concept of Byzantine general problem facilitated the innovation PBFT algorithm mechanism. This consensus mechanism is being used by Hyperledger Fabric.
- **Proof of Elapsed Time (PoET):** The PoET consensus algorithm is also known as PoET. This consensus mechanism is often used on permissioned blockchain networks. It is based on the principle of a fair lottery system where every single node is equally likely to be a winner. The PoET consensus mechanism is based on spreading the chances of winning fairly across a huge possible number of network participants. In PoET, each participant node in the network is required to wait for a randomly chosen time period. The first one to complete the designated waiting time wins the new block. The winning node then commits a new block to the blockchain and broadcasts the necessary information to the whole peer network. The PoET concept was invented by Intel in 2016. PoET is used by Hyperledger Sawtooth.

- **Proof of Reputation (PoR):** The PoR consensus algorithm model depends on the reputation of the participants to keep the network secure and safe. It is similar to PoA. A company that would like to join the network needs to prove its reputation and pass verification. A network participant must have a reputation high enough, and if they attempt to cheat the system, they face significant financial and brand consequences.
- **Proof of History (PoH):** PoH is a high-frequency verifiable delay function. A verifiable delay function requires a specific number of sequential numbers of sequential steps to evaluate; however, it produces a unique output that can be efficiently and publicly verified.

  For instance, when you take a photograph with the cover of a newspaper front page (*Guardian* cover page), you are creating proof that your photograph was taken after the newspaper was published. Using PoH, you can create a historical record that proves that an event has occurred at a specific moment in time. Solana blockchain uses PoH.
- **Directed Acyclic Graph (DAG):** The DAG consensus algorithm is popular for high scalability due to its unique structure. In DAGs, blocks are added parallelly rather than in a linear way like any other blockchain system. For instance, in any other blockchain, there is a linear structure whereby transactions/blocks are added one by one. However, DAGs add the blocks/transaction, parallelly making it a very scalable solution.

  DAGs are used by projects such as IOTA, Hashgraph and Nano, to name a few.

Figure 1.6 shows some of the famous and most used consensus algorithms.

DEFI (DECENTRALISED FINANCE) OVERVIEW

DeFi is a short form for 'decentralised finance'. It is also known as 'open finance'. It is an umbrella term for a variety of financial applications (also called dApps) geared towards disrupting financial intermediaries. It is here to disrupt every financial service you use today like savings, loans, trading and insurance, to name a few. The main value add of DeFi is that they are accessible to anyone with a smartphone and internet connection.

Currently, Ethereum is the leading blockchain technology to drive DeFi applications because of the inbuilt smart contract feature. Decentralised finance is here to unlock the opportunities for the financial ecosystem by providing financial security and transparency and unlock liquidity and growth opportunities through the use of blockchain (Figure 1.7).

The following are some of the Ethereum principles that are being appreciated by DeFi dApps:

Algorithms	Advantages	Disadvantages	Use cases
Proof of Work (PoW)	• Stable • Tested since 2009	• Huge Energy consumption • Slow • Not good for environment	Bitcoin, Ethereum, Litecoin, Dogecoin
Proof of Stake (PoS)	• Energy efficient • Fast • More expensive to attack than PoW	• Bit centralised. • Participants with high stakes can vote themselves in to become a validator	EOS, Lisk, ARC
Proof of Authority (PoA)	• Energy efficient • Fast	• Bit centralised • Usually used in permissioned private Blockchains	VeChain
Delegated Proof of Stake (dPoS)	• Energy efficient • Fast	• Pre-approved	Proof of Stake, Proof of authority
Proof of Elapsed Time (PoET)	• Low cost of Participation • Simple verification of the leader	• Use of specialised hardware • Suitable for permissioned Blockchains	Hyperledger Sawtooth
Proof of Reputation (PoR)	• Energy efficient • Fast	• Usually used in permissioned private Blockchains	GoChain
Proof of History (PoH)	• Fast • High Throughout • Low Fees • Scalability	• Centralised • Fewer DAppS compared to Ethereum dApps	Solana
Byzantine Fault Tolerance	• Fast • Scalable	• Usually used in permissioned private Blockchains	Hyperledger Fabric, Steller, Ripple
Directed Acyclic Graph (DAG)	• Highly Scalable • Fast • Every Efficient	• Smart contracts implementation can only be possible using Oracles	IOTA, HashGraph, Nano

Figure 1.6 Blockchain consensus algorithms.

Feature	DeFi	Traditional Finance
Ownership	You are in charge and hold your money	Your money is held by other companies like intermediators or Banks
Control	You are in control over your own money including how it is transferred and how it is spent	Other companies control the management of your money. You need to trust them.
Payment latency	Transfer of funds can happen in minutes rather than days	Transfer of funds can take days due to administration and multiple parties' involvement
Identification	Financial transaction activities is pseudonymous depending on the region you are in. It means your identification is hidden and does not need to be disclosed to other parties.	Financial transaction activities are tightly connected to your identity due to tight financial regulations
Access	Open to anyone globally as long as they have internet connection and access to technology like laptop or desktop	You need to apply to use and be part of financial services
Availability	DeFi markets do not sleep. They are open 24/7 globally	Financial markets close as per their region. They are reliant on banks, stock exchange and employees etc.
Transparency	DeFi core architecture is based on full transparency of historical records to anyone around the globe. Anyone can look at transactions, product data and also inspect how the DeFi application works.	Traditional financial institutions are closed books. Their products are propriety (mostly patented). They however must disclose the financial activity to regulators.

Figure 1.7 DeFi and traditional finance comparison.

- **Programmability:** DeFi uses smart contracts (one of the core features of Ethereum) to provide an automated smart contract for various use cases across the financial ecosystem. It provides a highly programmable smart contract to automate execution and enable the creation of new financial instruments and digital assets.
- **Immutability:** It uses the immutability feature of blockchain to tamper-proof, immutable audit and transparency across decentralised architecture to increase security and auditability.
- **Interoperability:** It provides a common software stack and standard whereby dApps applications can integrate and complement one another. DeFi developers have the flexibility to build on top of existing protocols, customise interfaces and integrate third-party applications.
- **Transparency:** It uses the core feature of public blockchains like Ethereum whereby anyone can see the audit of all transactions.
- **Permissionless:** DeFi is defined by its open and permissionless access. Anyone with a crypto wallet and internet connection globally can access DeFi applications.
- **Self-custody:** DeFi market participants keep custody of their crypto assets and have control of their personal data. It cuts the various intermediatory and bureaucracy.

Some of the main features of DeFi are as follows:

- The operation of these use cases built through dApps is not controlled by a single institution or its employees; instead, it is controlled by smart contracts and automation with multiple business rules.
- Code is transparent on the blockchain for anyone to audit.
- dApps are global from the start; however, local regulations may apply to them.
- They are decentralised and permissionless where anyone can create and use them. Users interact directly with the smart contracts from their crypto wallets.
- dApps provide a flexible user experience where anyone can change the user interface or use a third-party interface.
- dApps are interoperable, whereby anyone can combine other DeFi products, e.g. stablecoins, decentralised exchanges and prediction markets, to form entirely new products.

Most popular types of DeFi applications

- **Decentralised exchanges (DEXs):** These are online exchanges where users can exchange crypto with other cryptocurrency or crypto with Fiat currencies. For example, US dollars for Bitcoin or Ethereum for Bitcoin. In DEX exchanges, users can directly trade cryptocurrencies with one another without a need for any intermediaries.

- **Stablecoins:** These are types of cryptocurrencies that are tied to an asset or fiat currency (USD or Euro or GBP) outside of cryptocurrency to stabilise the process.
- **Lending platforms:** These platforms are automated through smart contracts to replace the intermediaries such as banks to provide loans etc. to the users directly through the platform.
- **Predictive markets:** This is a DeFi platform that provides markets for betting on the outcome of future events like elections or football matches etc., without any intermediaries.
- **Yield farming:** Using these platforms, users can scan through various DeFi tokens to search for opportunities for larger returns.
- **Composability:** As mentioned before, dApps are open sources and as such can be used to compose new apps with the code as building blocks.
- **Money Legos:** DeFi apps are like Lego blocks (children's games from Lego) where you can build a new toy by combining various Lego blocks. To put this in perspective, users can combine various DeFi apps to create new financial products.

Examples of DeFi projects

There are thousands of DeFi projects mostly on the Ethereum blockchain. We will go through some of the famous ones in this section.

- **Maker:** Maker is an Ethereum-based decentralised autonomous organisation (DAO) that allows anyone to lend or borrow cryptocurrencies. It is a stablecoin project whereby each stablecoin is pegged to US dollars, and it is backed by collateral in the form of crypto. Therefore, in essence, Maker offers some security in the form of collateral and has a lower risk than other cryptocurrencies like Bitcoin or Ethereum.
  Website: https://makerdao.com/en/
- **Compound:** Compound is a blockchain-based borrowing and lending dApp. You can lend your cryptocurrencies out and earn interest on them or you can borrow real money (fiat currency) through the security of crypto on the platform. The compound platform provides various borrowers and lenders and automatically matches them through a contract. The contract adjusts the interest rates based on demand and supply.
  Website: https://compound.finance
- **Uniswap:** Uniswap is a cryptocurrency exchange like Coinbase. It is entirely based on smart contracts, letting customers trade popular tokens directly from its wallet. It provides an innovative mechanism known as an automated market, enabling one to automatically settle trade near the market price.
  Website: https://uniswap.org

- **Augur:** Augur is a decentralised prediction market protocol. It provides the functionality to vote on the outcome of events by attaching a monetary value to your vote.

  Website: https://augur.net
- **PoolTogether:** PoolTogether is a platform where participant deposit stablecoin into a common pool. At the end of each month, one lucky participant wins all the interest earned on that cryptocurrency pool and everyone gets their initial deposits back. It is a no-loss game platform.

  Website: https://pooltogether.com

Use cases of DeFi

Asset management

Through the use of crypto wallets like Metamask, you own your own data and custody of the digital assets. You can interact with various decentralised applications to carry out transactions like buying, selling and transferring crypto to earn interest on your digital assets.

Compliance and Know Your Transactions (KYTs)

In the traditional financial ecosystem, there is a requirement to know your customer (KYC) to comply with anti-money laundering (AML) and counter the financing of terrorism. In the DeFi space, Ethereum decentralised technology enables compliance analysis around participants' wallet addresses rather than participant identity. This compliance of transaction (KYT) mechanism helps compliance against fraud and financial crimes in real time.

DAOs

DAO stands for a decentralised autonomous organisation that cooperates according to transparent rules within Ethereum blockchain technology. It eliminates the need for a centralised administrative entity. Products like Maker and Compound have launched DAOs to fundraise, manage financial operations and decentralise governance to the community.

Data and analytics

DeFi offers a great range of transparency around data and network activity. DeFi protocols offer great advantages for data discovery, analysis and decision-making around financial opportunity and risk management. DeFi Pulse and Codefi Data are a few examples of applications that help users to unlock the value of DeFi protocols, assess platform risk and compare yield and liquidity.

Derivatives

DeFi enables Ethereum-based smart contracts to enable the creation of tokenised derivatives whose value is derived from the underlying assets, in which the counterparty agreements are hardwired in the code. DeFi derivatives are able to represent real-world assets such as fiat currencies, bonds, commodities and also cryptocurrencies.

DEXs

DEX stands for decentralised exchange. DEXs are cryptocurrency exchanges that operate without a central authority. It allows users to transact peer-to-peer and maintain control of their funds. DeXs reduce risks of price manipulation by a central authority as well as theft and hacking activities because crypto assets are never in the custody of the exchange itself.

DEXs also provide an advantage in that token projects can have access to liquidity without any listing fees through decentralisation. The traditional crypto exchanges used to charge millions of dollars to get tokens listed on a centralised exchange.

Some of the popular DEXs in the DeFi space include AirSwap, Liquality, Mesa, Oasis and Uniswap.

Gaming

Ethereum-based games have evolved under DeFi because of their built-in economies and innovative incentives. For instance, PoolTogether is a no-loss audited savings lottery that enables users to purchase digital tickets. You have to deposit the DAI stablecoin in order to participate. These get pooled together and lent to the compound money market to earn interest.

Insurance

Several insurance use cases are trying the use of DeFi to offer traditional insurance alternatives to help users buy coverage and protect their holdings. Nexus Mutual provides a smart contract-based cover that protects against unintended uses of a smart contract code.

Lending and borrowing

DeFi offers opportunities to users to earn interest on their crypto assets. For instance, Compound is an algorithmic, autonomous interest rate protocol that integrates with several DeFi platforms including PoolTogether, Argent and Dharma. The compound smart contract automatically matches borrowers and lenders and also calculates interest rates based on the demand and supply of crypto assets.

Marketplaces

DeFi protocols provide functionalities for online marketplaces to allow users to exchange products/services globally and peer-to-peer. Some examples are freelance coding gigs, digital collectibles, real jewellery and apparel.

Payments

Peer-to-peer payments are nothing new in the blockchain ecosystem. DeFi payment solutions further establish an open economic system for under-banked and unbanked users. It also helps large traditional financial institutions to streamline market infrastructure and better serve retail and wholesale customers.

Prediction markets

Multiple applications in the DeFi ecosystem are growing to harness the prediction of an event and trade value on the outcome of an event. Augur is a popular DeFi betting platform where users can bet on the prediction of the outcome of an event like a sports game, economic events, election results and many more.

Savings

Defi protocols like Compound offer users to earn interest by putting their crypto assets into the pool to prospectively earn more interest than traditional savings accounts. Some of the popular applications on the DeFi platform are Argent, Dharma and PoolTogether. They offer no-loss saving games in which participants get their original money back whether they win or not. They also offer high interest rates on Yoru cryptocurrencies for staking them on the platform.

One of the innovative mechanisms is called yield farming where users move their idle crypto assets around in different liquidity protocols to maximise their returns.

Stablecoins

The new phenomenon that has been in the lime lite is called stablecoin. Stablecoin is any cryptocurrency that is pegged to a stable asset like fiat currency, gold or other cryptocurrencies. The stablecoin concept is being used now across the DeFi space for remittance payments, lending and borrowing platforms and also the upcoming use cases like Central Bank Digital Currency (CBDC).

Synthetic assets

Synthetic assets are crypto assets that provide exposure to other assets like gold, fiat currencies and cryptocurrencies. They are collateralised by tokens that are locked into Ethereum-based smart contracts. It uses an Ethereum-based smart contract to offer built-in agreements and incentive mechanisms. The synthetic protocol implements a 750% collateralisation ratio to help the network to absorb process shocks.

Tokenisation

Tokenisation is one of the core features of DeFi and also a native functionality of the Ethereum blockchain. A token is a digital asset that can be created, issued and managed on a blockchain. Tokens are secure and instantly transferrable. They are also can be programmed inside a smart contract to transfer value for multiple use cases. One of the examples of use cases whereby tokens can be used is fractionalised property ownership, payments, and digital alternative to access, trade and store value.

Trading

DeFi offers an extensive list of benefits for trading from derivatives trading, margin trading and token swaps. Crypto traders benefit from decentralised exchanges whereby they benefit from lower exchange fees, faster transaction settlements and full custody of their assets without a need for intermediaries.

Digital identity

DeFi can offer a portable self-sovereign identity with security and privacy as core features. The traditional approach to a person's identity and creditworthiness is defined by one's income or accumulated assets. With a DeFi-paired digital identity, it is possible to take into account other factors like financial activities or professional reputation. Blockchain-based digital identity systems are already getting a lot of traction. Combining these systems with DeFi protocols will provide a global ecosystem for all privileged as well as unprivileged people of society.

Crowdfunding

Ethereum is one of the best platforms for crowdfunding dApps. It provides a global platform for funders and fundraisers to raise money for a project with security, transparency and complete automation. Fundraisers can prove how much money has been raised as well as anyone can trace how the funds are being spent later down the line after the successful fundraising. Fundraisers can also set up automatic refunds if there is a specific deadline and the minimum amount is not met.

How to get involved in DeFi?

We have explained a high-level overview of DeFi along with top projects within DeFi that are getting a lot of traction. Let us get into the practical side of DeFi as to how to get involved in it before it is too late.

I think the very first step for any great investment or adventure is to do some research and analyse the market.

The following sources provide live information on the DeFi projects and $ value locked into them:

- **DeFi Pulse** (Figure 1.8):
    - **Website:** https://defipulse.com
- **DeFi Prime** (Figure 1.9):
    - **Website:** https://defiprime.com

Figure 1.8 DeFiPulse screenshot.

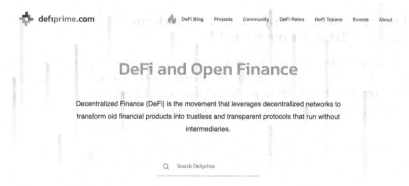

Figure 1.9 DeFi Prime.

Why invest time in dApps?

As we are moving toward the adoption of Web3, Ethereum has innovated a platform to assist and make it simple for anyone to start the development of decentralised applications for multiple use cases. I have tried to articulate the most important reasons why you should invest your time in learning to use and develop dApps.

- **Zero downtime:** There is no downtime for dApps as once the smart contract has been deployed on the Ethereum Blockchain, the Ethereum network as a whole will always be able to serve clients looking to interact with the contract.
- **Resistance to censorship:** There is no censorship to using the Ethereum network. There is no single entity on the network that can block users from submitting transactions, deploying dApps or reading data from the Blockchain.
- **Built-in payments:** Ethereum blockchain provides the benefit of a built-in payment currency called ETH. dApps built using the Ethereum blockchain can readily use this payment method.
- **Privacy:** As a developer or user of dApps, you do not need to provide a real-world identity to deploy or interact with dApp.
- **Data integrity:** One of the best features of the blockchain is data immutability. This is the same case for Ethereum-based dApps. Any data stored on the Ethereum blockchain through dApps is immutable and indisputable. Malicious actors or parties cannot forge transactions or any other data that has been committed to the blockchain.
- **Trustless, decentralised and verifiable:** Ethereum blockchain is fully decentralised, trustless and verifiable. For instance, smart contracts can be analysed and guaranteed to execute in a predictable way as designed in the first place. There is no need to trust a central authority. All committed transaction in the blockchain is fully transparent to all users of the network.

How to develop dApps and launch them onto the Ethereum network?

Anyone with internet access can get involved in the development of dApps. To start with, have a look at the following site with lots of resources to get you started with Ethereum platform dApps and more.

Website: https://ethereum.org/en/developers/

How to get started with DeFi?

In order to start getting your hands dirty with DeFi, we will need a few things that are dependencies to get started. Let us walk through the steps in this section.

1. **Get an Ethereum wallet:** There are so many wallets these days with multiple features; however, I still like the simplicity and features of the Metamask browser extension. You can check the variety of available wallets at: https://ethereum.org/en/wallets/find-wallet/
2. **Make sure to have Chrome/Firefox/Brave/Edge as a browser:** Download the Metamask extension on your desktop/laptop. By the way, you can also download an app for Metamask on your mobile phone. We will use a browser extension for this demonstration.

   This is the website to download the Metamask extension for your browser: https://metamask.io/download/
3. **Create a new wallet:** Once you have installed the Metamask extension, you will be asked to create a new wallet. Go ahead to follow the instructions on the screen and create a new wallet. Please note that if you already had a wallet previously, you can also import the old wallet as listed within the options below.

 METAMASK

New to MetaMask?

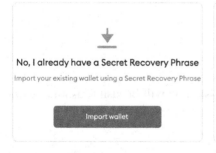

No, I already have a Secret Recovery Phrase

Import your existing wallet using a Secret Recovery Phrase

Import wallet

Yes, let's get set up!

This will create a new wallet and Secret Recovery Phrase

Create a Wallet

If it is the first time you are creating a wallet, it will ask you to set up a password and then it will share with you a secret backup phrase. It will then ask you to confirm the same secret phrase. Once successfully confirmed, you have a working wallet. Please never share this phrase with anyone else; they will be able to take your Ether forever.

 METAMASK

Congratulations

You passed the test - keep your Secret Recovery Phrase safe, it's your responsibility!

Tips on storing it safely

- Save a backup in multiple places.
- Never share the phrase with anyone.
- Be careful of phishing! MetaMask will never spontaneously ask for your Secret Recovery Phrase.
- If you need to back up your Secret Recovery Phrase again, you can find it in Settings -> Security.
- If you ever have questions or see something fishy, contact our support here.

*MetaMask cannot recover your Secret Recovery Phrase. Learn more.

4. **Use Metamask wallet:** Metamask now will be visible as an extension in your Chrome browser.

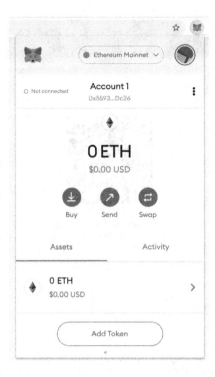

5. **Metamask internals:** By now, you would have already known about public/private keys. Your wallet shows you a public key as highlighted in the figure 1.13. My public key looks like: *0x559316c4cB374933eC7aBd9675617AD20295Dc26*

You can check all transactions using this public key on https://etherscan.io as it is one of the Ethereum blockchain explorers.

The private key on the other hand is like a key to your vault which must be always kept secret from others. You can export the private keys to secure them safely within the wallet as listed below.

With the Metamask wallet, go to account details as shown in the figure.

Now you can either save the QR code for your public key in a document and also export the private key and keep it safe. Private keys can be exported using the Export Private Key button. It will ask for your Metamask password to access them. Once confirmed, you will be shown your private key. Please note that if you lose your private key, you will lose access to your wallet and all cryptocurrency within it.

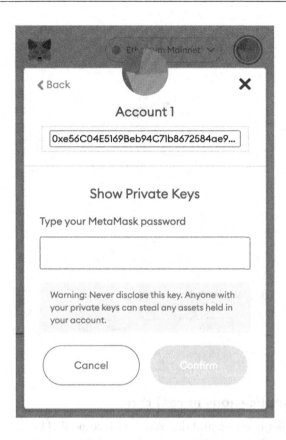

6. Get some ETH 'Ethereum currency': Now in order to get involved with DeFi, you need some Ether. You can buy it using fiat currency from crypto exchanges like Bittrex.com or Coinbase.com. Fiat currency is a real currency like US dollars or British pounds. When you click on the Buy button under the Metamask screen, it will also give you a few options to buy or deposit it if you have already bought it from the exchanges.

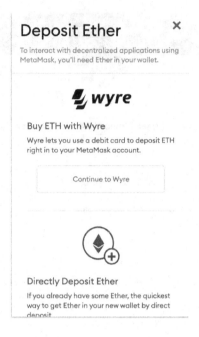

Try DeFi applications in real time

Once the wallet is set up and deposited with some ETH, we can try a suitable dApp to taste the power of DeFi. Let us follow the following steps:

1. Go to the website https://defi.instadapp.io/.
   On this website, you can see some of the top dApps and interact with them to get a loan as well as get involved in providing liquidity to the market and earn interest as a reward (Figure 1.10).
2. Let us try to buy some 'Inst pools' and earn interest. We will use a simulator mode and an Ethereum test net as an exercise. Click on the Connect button at the top right corner of the screenshot.
   You will be shown a window to select which wallet you want to connect with. In our case, we will select Metamask (Figure 1.11).
   If you have multiple wallets within Metamask, then select an appropriate wallet to connect with (Figure 1.12).

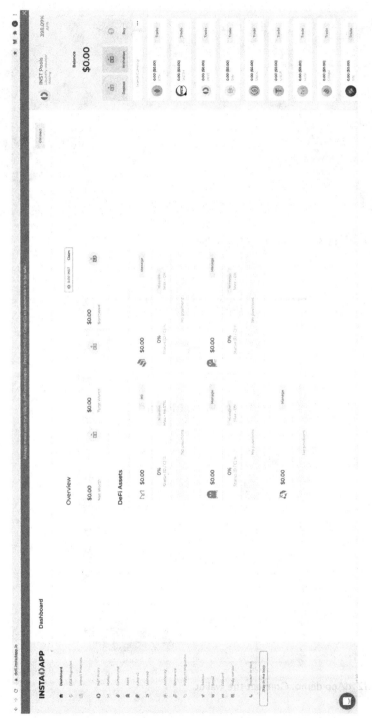

Figure 1.10 dApp demo 1.

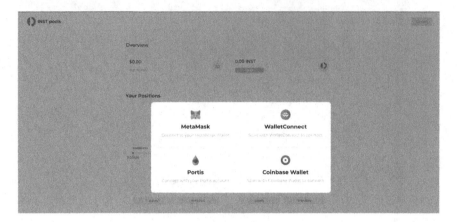

Figure 1.11 dApp demo. Connect the wallet.

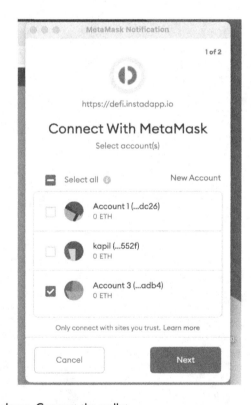

Figure 1.12 dApp demo. Connect the wallet.

Read and review the final message and click on the Connect button (Figure 1.13).

3. Now, we have just connected our Metamask wallet with InstPools DeFi Dapp. As we do not have an account, it will allow us to create a new account (Figure 1.14).

4. We will select the 'Try in simulation mode' option on the right-hand side.

5. You will get an acknowledgement to remind you that it is a simulated account and 100ETH has been deposited in your wallet to test (Figure 1.15).

6. Now we will buy some INST tokens through trading ETH. Therefore, let us buy INST worth 1 ETH (Figure 1.16).

7. Once the transaction has been successful, we will see the balance in our wallet as shown in Figure 1.17.

8. Now let us see if we can supply some liquidity to the market (Figure 1.18).

Figure 1.13 dApp demo. Connect the wallet.

Figure 1.14 dApp demo. New account.

The application is running in simulation mode.

Following are the things to take into consideration:

- Your Metamask wallet is updated with 100 ETH to test.
- Token swaps may have high price impact in this environment than Mainnet as we don't consider all exchanges.
- Automation feature is not supported in this environment.
- Loading might be a little slower than the Mainnet.

Acknowledged

Figure 1.15 dApp demo. New account.

Figure 1.16 dApp demo. Buy Inst tokens.

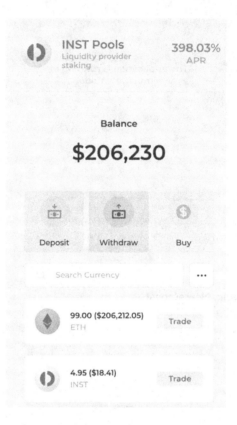

Figure 1.17 dApp demo. Buy Inst tokens.

As you can see, we have a position and we supply some liquidity to the market and will earn up to 398.02% APR as a reward that is not possible with any of the banks.

9. You can also play with another dApp called Maker and take a loan from the DeFi market. Let us run through it as an example in the simulation mode.

10. Click on Maker on the left-hand side of the screen. You will see a screen as shown in Figure 1.19.

11. Click on the 'Deposit & Borrow' option on the right-hand side of the screen. Once clicked, you will see the following screen. Please note the interest rate for the loan. It is still cheaper than high street banks.

12. It calculates the risk based on its criteria of maximum liquidity of 66.67% of an asset. We will go for 4.5 Ether and take a loan of 5,000 DAI tokens (Figure 1.20).

13. In a matter of minutes, we borrowed USD 5,000 by depositing $9,551.25 worth of Ethereum based on the current market price.

Figure 1.18 dApp demo. Supply liquidity to the market.

Figure 1.19 dApp demo. Maker.

Figure 1.20 dApp demo. Maker.

14. When you do not need a loan, you can simply settle it in one transaction by clicking on the 'Payback & Withdraw' button (Figure 1.21).

I hope you are now getting on well with some practical experience in the world of DeFi. The whole ecosystem is moving so fast, it is important to learn at the same pace as well.

In the next section, we will start our journey with another newly launched technology called non-fungible token (NFT). Hold tight...

Figure 1.21 dApp demo. Maker.

NFT overview

There has been a lot of talk about NFTs recently. NFTs are now touted as a digital answer to collectibles. In this section, we will unveil the reality of NFTs, their use cases and some critical analysis of the technology and end-use cases.

What is an NFT?

NFT stands for non-fungible token. For instance, in economic terms, a fungible asset is something that can be measured and readily interchanged like money or an office building. Another example is to purchase a physical painting in exchange for money. This painting will have value and can be touched and felt as an asset.

NFTs are assets in the digital world that can be exchanged like any other fungible assets, but they have no tangible properties. In other words, NFTs can be thought of as digital certificates of ownership of virtual or physical assets that cannot be tampered with or copied.

NFTs can be used for anything digital like digital art, digital music, digital scripts, tweets and pictures.

NFTs allow you to buy and sell the ownership of unique digital assets with full transparency on ownership visible to anyone on the blockchain.

How do NFTs work?

On a high level, most NFTs are part of the Ethereum blockchain. NFTs can use the inbuilt cryptocurrency called ETH and also can benefit from the use of smart contracts.

Let us take the example of artwork. Traditional artworks/paintings such as the 'Mona Lisa' are one of a kind and valuable. The 'Mona Lisa' painting's digital copies can be easily duplicated.

With NFTs, any artwork can be tokenised to create a digital certificate of ownership that can be bought and sold.

NFSs records are immutable and cannot be forged. As NFTs use Ethereum blockchain technology, they can integrate the smart contract feature to automate the buying and selling of the NFTs without any intermediatory or middleman intervention.

Current examples of NFTs

Although it might seem crazy and unbelievable, the following are real examples of NFTs that have been sold for unprecedented amounts so far:

- Beeple's video sold for $6.6m. Although the ownership of the art is unique, anyone can copy the image and reproduce it. However, the original is only owned by the true owner of the art and can easily be identified through a blockchain ledger.
- Beeple's art was also sold for $69m on Christie's platform for online auctions. (https://onlineonly.christies.com/s/beeple-first-5000-days/beeple-b-1981-1/112924)
- Someone paid over $170k for a kitten image. There is a portfolio of images that can be traded on the platform https://www.cryptokitties.co. It is a gaming platform where players can trade virtual cats, play games and create collections to earn rewards.
- An animated Gif of Nynan Cat (a 2011 meme of a flying pop tart cat) was sold for more than $645,948. (https://foundation.app/@NyanCat/foundation/219)
- Gucci Ghost Gif was sold for $3,600 (https://niftygateway.com/marketplace/item/0x4140783cc1ba30653a0777126b122931e23 3ba14/1300010027)

- Musician Grimmes sold some of her digital music for more than $3.8m on the Niftygateway platform. (https://niftygateway.com/collections/warnymphvolume1)
- Twitter's Co-founder Jack Dorsey sold his first-ever tweet for just nearly $3m through a NFT platform called Valuables by cent. https://v.cent.co/tweet/20. The winning bidder was Sina Estavi – CEO of a blockchain company called Bridge Oracle.
- Nike has achieved to get a patent to verify the authenticity of the shoe through the use of blockchain-based sneakers authenticity verification called 'Cryptokicks'. The patent outlines a system whereby blockchain technology can be used to attach cryptographically secured digital assets to physical products. Patent link: https://patents.google.com/patent/US10505726B1/en

Platforms to get involved in NFTs

- Valuables by CENT (https://v.cent.co) is a platform to buy and sell Twitter tweets
- Opensea (https://opensea.io) is the world's first and largest NFT marketplace. You can literally sell or buy anything digital here.
- Rarible (https://rarible.com) is another online marketplace to exchange digital collectibles through NFTs.
- Superare (https://superrare.com) is a digital art NFT marketplace where you can buy and sell NFTs from the world's top artists.
- Foundation (https://foundation.app/about) is a platform whereby digital art creators can use Ethereum blockchain BFT technology to sell their digital art and collectors can buy them.
- AtomicMarket (https://wax.atomicmarket.io) is a shared liquidity NFT market smart contract. It offers a unique feature in terms of shared liquidity. This means that everything that is listed in one market also shows the same listing in all other markets.
- BakerySwap (https://www.bakeryswap.org) is a NFT marketplace for digital artworks and Gamification NFTs.
- EnJin (https://enjin.io/software/marketplace) provides a platform to create next-gen NFTs as well as a marketplace to buy and sell one.
- Portion (https://portion.io/app.html) is another marketplace to buy and sell digital art through NFTs and also physical art.
- Async (https://async.art) is an online platform to buy and sell digital art and music through NFT technology.
- Niftygateway (https://niftygateway.com) – It is a marketplace to buy and sell digital art called Nifties on the platform.
- KnownOrigin (https://knownorigin.io) is another NFT platform to discover digital art and collect NFTs.
- Cryptocurrency exchange Binance (https://www.binance.com/en/nft) has also launched the NFT marketplace.

- Crypto.com (https://crypto.com/nft) has recently also launched the NFT marketplace on top of a successful crypto wallet and exchange.

CDBC revolution

Over the past few years, we have seen a lot of technological revolutions in the financial industry, e.g. mobile banking, and mobile payment solutions from tech giants like Apply Pay, Google Pay, PayPal and Amazon, to name a few. There also has been some disruption in online payments and e-wallets as a substantial portion of traditional banking are now carried out through mobile and digital payments. One of the major advancements has been advancements in the acceptance of Bitcoin currency as an asset class by fund managers who insist that it belongs in any balanced portfolio.

One of the upcoming disruptions that would be the most revolutionary is the creation of government digital currencies, which can provide a facility for people to deposit funds directly with a central bank bypassing conventional lenders.

As per *The Economist* (https://www.economist.com/), these 'govcoins' are a new incarnation of money. They promise to make finance work better but also to shift power from the individual to the state, alter geopolitics and change how capital is allocated. They are to be treated with optimism and humility.

Government or CBDCs seem to be setting the stone of the digital financial world; however, they come with a twist. CBDC would ultimately centralise power in the state government rather than spread it through various payment networks and/or conventional banks.

Imagine a possibility whereby instead of holding an account with a retail bank, customers can directly open an account with a central bank through an interface similar to apps such as Apple Pay, Alipay etc. Another possibility might be that customers can directly deal with the central bank for any transaction discrepancy support, rather than calling Barclays's support, saving commission usually charged by retail banks or intermediaries like Mastercard/VISA. Rather than paying by a credit card or cheque, customers would be able to use the central bank application and also have more security as their money would be backed by a government guarantee.

The above hypothesis looks unreal; however, it is already underway. Over 50 monetary authorities are exploring central bank digital currencies.

The following are some of the initiatives that have been kicked off or are already established and in use.

- The Bank of England & HMRC in the UK published a discussion paper on 12 March 2020 about opportunities, challenges and design. The discussion paper can be accessed using the link: https://www.bankofengland.co.uk/research/digital-currencies
- On 19 April 2021, the Bank of England and HM Treasury announced the joint creation of a CBDC Taskforce to coordinate the exploration of a potential UK CBDC.

- The Bank of England published a discussion paper on *New Forms of Digital Money and Summarises Responses to the 2020 Discussion Paper on Central Bank Digital Currency*. The Bank of England accepted feedback until 7 September 2021 on the paper. Paper link: https://www.bankofengland.co.uk/paper/2021/new-forms-of-digital-money.
- The European Central Bank (ECB) published a report on the digital euro on 10 October 2020. This report (https://www.ecb.europa.eu/paym/digital_euro/report/html/index.en.html) examines the issuance of a CBDC or a digital euro from the perspective of a Eurosystem.
- On 14 July 2021, the governing council of the ECB decided to launch the investigation phase of a digital euro project.
- The Central Bank of The Bahamas launched a Sand Dollar (https://www.sanddollar.bs) as a CBDC nationwide on 20 October 2020 and became the world's first country to adopt CBDC. Sand Dollar is the digital version of the Bahamas dollar (B$).
- The National Bank of Cambodia (NBC) officially launched its CBDC (project named Project Bakong) on 28 October 2020. Its blockchain-based payment and money transfer platform will help promote the use of local currency over the US dollar.
- The People Bank of China released a paper in July 2021 about the CBDC. China has already started trials of digital Yuan across Mainland China and also trying cross-border use of digital Yuan trials in Hong Kong.
- The Monetary Authority of Singapore (MAS) launched a global challenge for retail CBDC solutions (called Global CBDC Challenge) on 28 June 2021 (https://www.mas.gov.sg/news/media-releases/2021/mas-partners-imf-world-bank-and-others-to-launch-global-challenge-for-retail-cbdc-solutions). MAS launched it in partnership with International Monetary Fund, World Bank, Asian Development Bank, United Nations Capital Development Fund, United Nations High Commission for Refugees, United Nations Development Programme, and the Organisation for Economic Co-operation and Development.

There are various other projects that are in some form of pilot maturity. The full list is shown in Table 1.1.

Potential benefits and challenges related to CBDC implementation

The following is a list of potential benefits and challenges related to CBDC implementation and adoption (Table 1.2).

Table 1.1 CBDC projects

CBDC project name	Country	Status	Insights	Website
Sand Dollar	Bahamas	Launched for the public on 20 October 2020	World's first country to adopt CBDC for all residents	https://www.sanddollar.bs
Bakong	Cambodia	Launched on 28 October 2020	Aim to promote transactions in Cambodia Riels over US Dollars	https://bakong.nbc.org.kh/
DC/EP (digital Currency/Electronic Payment)	Mainland China	Advanced level of Trail	Preparing for widespread domestic use of DC/EP during the Beijing 2022 Winter Olympics.	N/A
E-hryvnia	Ukraine	NBU (National Bank of Ukraine) is still evaluating the possibility of CBDC issuance	E-hryvnia should be technically feasible, but there are doubts over its process disruption and financial stability benefits	https://bank.gov.ua/admin_uploads/article/ Analytical%20Report%20on%20E-hryvnia. pdf?v=4
e-peso	Uruguay	Successful pilot but issues are still under consideration	Banco Central del Uruguay (BCU) is still considering full-scale issuance of public e-peso	https://www.bis.org/events/eopix_1810/ licandro_pres.pdf
E-Krona	Sweden	Under review that is expected to complete by November 2022	Sweden is seeking to implement a retail digital currency to replace Swish	https://www.riksbank.se/en-gb/ payments--cash/e-krona/
E-Won	Korea	Around the end of 2022 post successful testing	High possibility of the issuance of CBDC in 2022	https://www.bok.or.kr/portal/bbs/B0000232/ view.do?nttId=10062867&menuNo=200725

Table 1.2 Potential benefits and challenges

CBDC benefits	CBDC challenges	Additional insights
CDBC could lower costs associated with providing and managing cash.	Banking-sector disintermediation: There can be a risk of people withdrawing their deposits from commercial banks if they decide to hold CBDC in significant volumes. This would force banks to raise more expensive and runnable wholesale funding or somehow retain customers by raising the interest rate on their deposits. This would effectively compress banks' margins and they would try to raise money by charging higher interest rates on loans and mortgages.	I think governments would take a mixed approach initially by offering options to customers to adopt CBDC and maintain existing channels like retail bank accounts, credit cards and cash.
Financial inclusion. CDBC has the potential to provide safe and government-backed means of payment to the public even those who do not have a bank account.	'Run risk': In the time of pandemic or economic crisis, bank customers can flee from deposits to CBDC as CBDC is viewed as safer and more liquid. CBDC is also backed by the government to provide further security.	It would be beneficial for the public that does not and could not have a bank account due to various reasons. I think the government should support unbanked and people with low credits to have an option to get included in the financial systems and improve financial inclusion.
Stability of the payment system: CDBC can enhance the resiliency of the payment system and also reduce the concentration of the payment systems in the hands of very large companies.	Central bank balance sheet and credit allocation: In the case of the high adoption of CBDC, the central bank balance sheet could grow substantially. Central banks may need to provide liquidity to banks that have experienced large funding outflow. Due to these factors, central banks would take credit risks and decide on the allocation of funds across banks. This could lead to open doors for political interference.	CBDC can enhance financial system resiliency. Governments need to have tight governance and protection, so there is no favouritism and political interference in the credit allocation.
Market contestability and discipline: CDBC can potentially improve competition for large payment companies and cap the commission they can charge.	International implications: CBDC could lead to currency substitution ('dolarisation') in countries with high inflation and volatile exchange rates.	CBDC could further improve competition in the financial markets and let the market derive the commission rates.

(Continued)

Table 1.2 (Continued) Potential benefits and challenges

CBDC benefits	CBDC challenges	Additional insights
Countering new digital currencies: CDBC can provide healthy, safe government-backed digital currencies that can create competition against privately issued digital currencies. It can also provide more regulated digital currency markets and reduce/prevent the adoption of privately issues currencies that may be difficult to regulate.	Costs and risks to the central bank: central banks would have to bear the costs of offering CBDC and could pose risks to their reputation if there are any glitches, system failure, instability or unavailability of the platform offering CBDC. Offering full-fledged CBDC would require central banks to invest and further maintain the whole digital ecosystem of CBDC that includes DLT, front-end wallets, monitoring transactions, governance and policies supporting cyber, KYC, AML etc., to name a few.	I think governments need to take a collaborative approach. The government should have tight regulations and establish partnerships with tech companies, and financial banks to run part of the CBDC ecosystem. I also think CBDC is the way to go forward with digital currencies that are guaranteed by the government like existing fiat currencies, e.g. dollar and pound.
Support Distributed Ledger Technology (DLT): Some central banks have a view that the adoption of DLT-based CBDC will proliferate the DLT-based asset market as well. CBDC adoption will improve the automated supply chain further through the use of smart contracts, cross-border payments and digital asset transfer.	Same as the above point on establishing, maintaining, and supporting the CBDC ecosystem by the Government.	Same point as above.
Monetary policy: Academics and economists have a view that CDBC adoption can enhance the transmission of monetary policy. Monetary policies can be quickly implemented digitally to provide an economic response to macroeconomic events or pandemics like COVID-19.	Existing financial stakeholders like banks and intermediaries need to adopt the policies. The central government also need to take feedback from the financial market key stakeholders before enforcing monetary policies. There can also be a risk of political influence if the central government can enforce the policies without taking feedback from stakeholders in the financial industry.	There needs to be tight governance to adopt monetary policies without any political interference.

SUMMARY

In this chapter, we walked through the introduction of blockchain technology and how does it work technically as well as in business terms. This chapter also provided us with a deep understanding of all the use cases of blockchain including DeFi, DAO, Smart Contacts, ICOs, NFTs and CBDC. We also went through a practical guide to exchanges and dApps where you can start the journey to get involved with Crypto, NFTs, DeFi etc.

In the next chapter, we will do a deep dive into all the famous products available for blockchain including blockchain platforms, products, crypto and much more.

Chapter 2

Blockchain products

By now, you have a great bit of information about blockchain technology and some of the successful use cases including cryptocurrencies like Bitcoin and Ethereum. There are thousands of real-life use cases utilising and appreciating blockchain technology to make them simpler, transparent and secure. In this chapter, we will walk through some of the most adopted blockchain technologies used by multiple organisations to solve complex business use cases.

BLOCKCHAIN PRODUCTS IN THE MARKET

There has been an influx of blockchain products; however, there are only a handful of products which are successfully adopted by organisations and have been established for production use. Table 2.1 is a point-in-time matrix (as of the time of writing) of the blockchain products along with their technology stack.

BLOCKCHAIN PRODUCT COMPARISON

There has been a tremendous amount of activity within the blockchain space, especially with regard to product and platform development. However, there are only a handful of products that have been able to establish themselves within financial, supply chain, payments, digital identity and many more industries. We will walk through those top products in this section. We will also go through their features and the differentiation that has allowed them to succeed in specific areas (Table 2.2).

DOI: 10.1201/9781003225607-2

Table 2.1 Blockchain product matrix

Blockchain technology name	Consensus algorithm	Type of network	Licence type	Adoption type	Project website
Bitcoin	PoW	Public	Open-source with % of Bitcoin to miners as a reward	Most usable cryptocurrency by market share. Best use case of payments as peer-to-peer payments	https://bitcoin.org/en/
Ethereum	PoW	Public with smart contract feature	Open-source with transactional cost in the ether as a gas price	Digital currency, payments, NFTs, DiFi (decentralised finance)	https://etbereum.org/en/
Ethereum 2.0	PoS	Public/Private	Open-source	Enterprise-grade adoption in payments, supply chain and trading	https://etbereum.org/en/eth2/
R3 Corda	Validity consensus, Uniqueness consensus	Consortium	Corda – Open-source Corda Enterprise – Licences	Open source as well as an enterprise-grade blockchain platform for financial services and many other industries	https://www.r3.com
Consensys Quorum	PoA	Public and/or Private	Open-source	Enterprise-grade Ethereum blockchain for business	https://consensys.net/quorum/
IBM blockchain	PoA, PoS	Hybrid	Licensed	Based on Hyper ledger. Enterprise-grade solutions for multiple industries	https://www.ibm.com/uk-en/blockchain
Hyperledger Fabric	Pluggable	Hybrid	Open-source	Enterprise-grade blockchain for multiple industries	https://www.hyperledger.org/use/fabric
Hyperledger Indy	Zero Knowledge Proofs	Hybrid	Open-source	Enterprise-grade blockchain software for decentralised digital identity	https://www.hyperledger.org/use/hyperledger-indy
Hyperledger Sawtooth	Pluggable	Hybrid	Open-source	Modular design to develop enterprise-grade smart contacts for multiple industries	https://www.hyperledger.org/use/sawtooth

(Continued)

Table 2.1 (Continued) Blockchain product matrix

Blockchain technology name	Consensus algorithm	Type of network	Licence type	Adoption type	Project website
Hyperledger Iroha	Yet Another Consensus (aka YAC)	Hybrid	Open-source	Enterprise-grade blockchain software for IOT use cases	https://www.hyperledger.org/use/iroha
Hyperledger Quilt	Pluggable	Hybrid	Open-source	Enterprise-grade blockchain software for payments	https://www.hyperledger.org/use/quilt
Hyperledger Transact	Pluggable	Hybrid	Open-source	Enterprise-grade library to execute smart contracts	https://www.hyperledger.org/use/transact
Hyperledger URSA	Pluggable	Hybrid	Open-source	Enterprise-grade library to provide cryptographic implementation	https://www.hyperledger.org/use/ursa
Hyperledger ARIES	Pluggable	Hybrid	Open-source	Enterprise-grade library to provide secure secret management and decentralised key management functionality	https://www.hyperledger.org/use/aries
Hyperledger BESU	PoW, PoA	Consortium	Open-source	Enterprise-grade Ethereum client	https://www.hyperledger.org/use/besu
Ripple	Ripple Protocol consensus algorithm (RPCA)	Permissioned/Private	Open-source	High-performance global payments business through Ripplenet. XRP as a digital currency that can be used as an asset	https://ripple.com
Steller	Stellar Consensus Protocol (SCP)	Public/Private	Open-source	Stellar is an open network for storing and moving money. Stellar makes it possible to create, send, and trade digital representations of all forms of money: dollars, pesos, Bitcoin, pretty much anything.	https://www.stellar.org/?locale=en
NEO	dBFT consensus mechanism	Permissioned/Private	Open-source	All in one blockchain solution with multi-language support, performance, interoperability, use of delegated Byzantine Fault Tolerance consensus	https://neo.org

(Continued)

Table 2.1 (Continued) Blockchain product matrix

Blockchain technology name	Consensus algorithm	Type of network	Licence type	Adoption type	Project website
Monero	PoW (RandomX)	Private (confidential and untraceable)	Open-source	Cryptocurrency asset symbol – XMR	https://www.getmonero.org
EOS	dPoS (Delegated PoS)	Public permissioned	Open-source	Decentralised operating system that enables the development, hosting, and execution of commercial-scale decentralised applications (dApps) on its platform	https://eos.io
Cardano	PoS and Ouroboros	Public	Open-source	Cardano is being built to accommodate a broad range of use cases, solving problems across multiple industry verticals. The Most Environmentally Sustainable Blockchain Protocol	https://cardano.org
Chainlink	PoS	Public	Open-source	Chainlink's decentralised oracle network provides reliable, tamper-proof inputs and outputs for complex smart contracts on any blockchain	https://chain.link
Openchain	Partitioned consensus	Private	Open-source	Organisations wishing to issue and manage digital assets in a robust, secure and scalable way	
Multichain	Round robin validation scheme	Permissioned	Open-source and licensed	https://blockchain.oodles.io/blog/overview-multichain-blockchain-use-cases/	https://www.multichain.com
Blocknet	Pluggable	XRouter, XBridge	Open-source	Blocknet is a decentralised network that connects blockchains, similar to how the internet connects computers	https://blocknet.co

Table 2.2 Matrix of the use cases of successful products

Reference	Use case/product	Bitcoin	Ethereum	Hyperledger	Ripple	R3 corda
A	Crypto Currency like Bitcoin, Ether, Litecoin	Yes	Yes	No	Yes	No
B	Automation through smart contracts like insurance claim payout	No	Yes	Yes	No	Yes
C	Dynamic registry like Fractional investing	No	Yes	Yes	No	Yes
D	Static registry like a land registry	No	Yes	Yes	No	Yes
E	Payment infrastructure like cross-border payments	No	Yes	Yes	Yes	Yes
F	Identity	No	Yes	Yes	User	Yes
G	DiFi, NFTs (multiple use cases)	No	Yes	No	No	No
H	Others (like ICO, blockchain as a service)	Enabler	Enabler	Enabler	Enabler	Enabler

Cryptocurrency

We are already aware by now about cryptocurrencies and how they have disrupted the financial market through blockchain technology. It all started with one of the most successful use cases and the very first practical example of blockchain technology called Bitcoin. At the time of writing this book, the Bitcoin market capitalisation was $744 billion. There are about 6,000 cryptocurrencies being traded on exchanges as of the writing of this book, and I believe there will be more influx of initial coin offering (ICO) and cryptocurrencies in the crypto ecosystem.

Some of the examples of crypto by market capitalisation are listed in Table 2.3.

Smart contract

The invention of the smart contract was one of the niche use cases of blockchain technology. Ethereum invented the smart contract, and it is the only blockchain that has it inbuilt along with its own cryptocurrency called ETH. There are other blockchains as well within that you can develop smart contracts in various languages and plug them inside the ecosystem like R3 Corda, Hyperledger etc.

Table 2.3 Examples of crypto by market capitalisation

Crypto name	Crypto sign	Price in USD ($)	Market capitalisation	Circulating supply (volume in units)
Bitcoin	BTC	39,610	$744b	18.77m
Ethereum	ETH	2,638	$310b	117m
Tether	USDT	1	$61.9b	61.9b
Binance Coin	BNB	333.7	$56b	168m
Cardona	ADA	1.32	$42.6b	32b
Ripple	XRP	0.74	$34.6b	46b
USD Coin	USDC	1	$27.4b	27.4b
Dogecoin	DOGE	0.20	$26.7b	130.6b
Polkadot	DOT	18.36	$18b	980m
Uniswap	UNI	22.92	$13.4b	587m
Binance USD	BUSD	1	$12b	12b
Chainlink	LINK	23.56	$10.4b	443m
Bitcoin Cash	BCH	548	$10.3b	18.8m
Litecoin	LTC	142	$9.5b	66.7m
Solana	SOL	33.75	$9.2b	272.6m

All data is as of writing on 2 August 2021.

The following are some of the use cases of smart contacts and how they can disrupt the business landscape through automation by removing any manual intervention.

Smart contracts are like any legal contracts but are defined through a software code. They are a set of conditions recorded on a blockchain that gets triggered automatically with self-executed actions when these pre-defined conditions are met. Some of the use cases are as follows:

- Supply chain contracts
- Music royalties
- Insurance claim payout
- Equity trading
- Mortgage drawdown
- Trade finance.

Dynamic registry

You might have already realised that the blockchain technology niche is a distributed ledger called DLT, which is immutable but depending on the use case can be used to record static as well as dynamic transactions. A dynamic registry is a dynamic database (ledger) that updates as assets are exchanged on the digital platform. DiFi a.k.a. decentralised finance is the upcoming horizon using this technology through something called dApps (decentralised apps). Some of the use cases of the dynamic registry are as follows:

- Fractional investing like buying pies of crypto or real digital assets on an exchange or P2P I (peer to peer)
- Supply chain transactions.

Static registry

A static registry is a classic example of blockchain technology. Once recorded on the ledger, it remains there as immutable. Some of the examples of static registry (within DLT) are as follows:

- Land registry, whereby ownership of the assets, i.e., properties, are recorded as unique records. It is similar to the existing land registry database that can be searched, but any amendments to them are governed and can only be appended within the existing record as new ownership by a government department.
- Patents as a unique record of the ownership of intellectual property.
- Food origin to know where it originates from as part of the supply chain.

Payment infrastructure

Payments are one of the other best use cases that thrive on the blockchain. One of the new disruptive technologies that shape the faster and cross-border payment ecosystem is Ripple Net. There are multiple use cases of payments that are being watched and created by multiple big organisations using blockchain technology to cut the time for payment transfer, cut the intermediaries and ultimately make it easier, secure, transparent, quicker and cheaper for the customers to make payment transactions. Some of the use cases for payment infrastructure utilising blockchain are

- cross-border peer-to-peer payment
- insurance claim settlement.

Identity

Digital identity has become a de facto standard enabling whole DeFi and other blockchain use cases to work within the ecosystem of the regulatory environment. Some of the use cases of digital identity within the blockchain world are

- Know your customer (KYC)
- Identity fraud solutions
- Civil registry and identity records like Passports/National Insurance number
- Digital voting.

DeFi and NFTs

Although DeFi and non-fungible tokens (NFTs) have been discussed in this book before, it is essential to refer to them as a use case again. DeFi and NFTs predominantly use Ethereum blockchain because of its integrated smart contracts, own currency and other features; there are other blockchains like Binance (BNB) which has recently launched a NFT platform using its own currency as well as ETH to offer NFTs.

Others

There are hundreds of use cases utilising and appreciating blockchain technology. This category is used as a catch for them. Some of the examples or use cases that could not be fitted under other categories are listed below:

- **Blockchain as a service platform:** With the influx of blockchain technology and various use cases, businesses have started appreciating the value addition of blockchain technology. It offers transparency, security, potentially long-term low cost, quick time to market etc., to name a few advantages. Having said that, setting up a blockchain platform is very expensive and comes up with challenges like accountability, cost, skilled employees and regulatory impact. This complexity derived start-ups and consulting companies to offer blockchain as a service platform whereby customers can utilise the pre-built platform and use consulting provided by skilled and experienced subject matter experts to transform their business use cases.
- **ICO:** It is similar to the initial public offering (IPO), a classical route for a company to go public to raise money by offering its stocks (units of ownership) to anyone who can afford to buy the shares or stocks.

ICO is backed by an idea to deliver a project. ICO's goal is to raise money through a digital platform by offering its coin as a utility. Some of the examples of successful ICOs are:

- o **Ethereum:** The only blockchain that offers inbuilt smart contacts and its own currency called ETH.
- o **IOTA:** IOTA offer a unique offering that combines elements from the internet of things (IoT) and blockchain technology to conduct transactions.
- o **NEO:** NEO is a Chinese open-source blockchain project that is sometimes known as 'China's Ethereum'.
- o **Stratis:** The Stratis platform is compatible with multiple programming languages and enables businesses to create, test and deploy custom applications without having to set up or maintain their own infrastructure.
- **EOS:** EOS is a full-fledged operating system that provides application developers with databases, account permissions, scheduling, authentication and internet-application communication tools. Its comprehensive ecosystem allows developers to operate seamlessly without worrying about advanced cryptography implementations.

COMPARISON OF TOP SIX PLATFORMS

See Table 2.4.

DEEP DIVE INTO SUCCESSFUL PRODUCTS

Bitcoin

We have already gone through an overview of Bitcoin in Chapter 1. I will go through some more insights in this section about Bitcoin and how it can be used for business purposes. As you already know, Satoshi Nakamoto published the Bitcoin whitepaper in January 2009. Satoshi's identity is still mysterious, and no one knows his real identity until now. Bitcoin offers a peer-to-peer version of electronic cash without any control by a central authority like the Bank of England. It is the first and still the best use case of blockchain technology.

Website: https://bitcoin.org/en/

Use cases

Businesses can use the Bitcoin decentralised platform for a quick, secure and transparent way to transfer electronic cash in the form of Bitcoin cryptocurrency called BTC.

Table 2.4 Comparison of top six Blockchain platforms

Platform/features	Bitcoin	Ethereum	Hyperledger	Consensys quorum	R3 corda	Ripple
Consensus Mechanism	PoW	PoW	Pluggable (depends on the framework being used)	PoA	Pluggable (Validity consensus, Uniqueness consensus)	Ripple Protocol consensus algorithm (RPCA)
Consensus energy consumption	High	High	Depends on the Consensus used	Low	Low	Low
Smart contracts	No	Yes	Yes	Yes	Yes	No
Decentralised apps (dApps)	No	Yes	No	No	No	No
Decentralised Finance (DiFi)	No	Yes	No	No	No	No
Transaction fees	Yes	Yes	No	No	No	No
Website	https://bitcoin.org/en/	https://ethereum.org/en/	https://www.hyperledger.org	https://consensys.net/quorum/	https://www.r3.com/corda-platform/	https://ripple.com

Table 2.5 Bitcoin exchanges and platforms

Platform	Type	Website	Wallet included	KYC requirement
Coinbase	Exchange	https://www.coinbase.com	Yes	Yes
Bittrex	Exchange	https://global.bittrex.com	Yes	Yes
Binance	Exchange	https://www.binance.com/en	Yes	Yes
CashApp	App – Peer-to-Peer Money transfer systems using Bitcoin	https://cash.app	Yes	Yes
Bisq	Exchange	https://bisq.network	Yes	No
Etoro	Trading platform	https://www.etoro.com	Yes	Yes
Huobi	Exchange	https://www.huobi.com/en-us/	Yes	Yes
Kraken	Exchange	https://www.kraken.com	Yes	Yes
Kucoin	Exchange	https://www.kucoin.com	Yes	Yes
Bitfinex	Exchange	https://www.bitfinex.com	Yes	Yes
Gate	Exchange	https://www.gate.io	Yes	Yes
Bitstamp	Exchange	https://www.bitstamp.net	Yes	Yes
Gemini	Exchange	https://www.gemini.com/uk	Yes	Yes
Blockchain. com	Exchange	https://www.blockchain.com/ explorer	Yes	Yes
Bittylicious	Exchange	https://bittylicious.com	Yes	No

There are multiple businesses that are now supporting Bitcoin currency to buy and sell products and services.

Multiple investment banks now offer Bitcoin futures as well as trade Bitcoin. There are hundreds of exchanges and platforms that offer buy and sell of Bitcoin cryptocurrencies. Some famous ones are listed in Table 2.5:

Ethereum

Ethereum is a community-run blockchain technology with unique features like its own cryptocurrency (ETH), smart contract, open-source and a platform to build dApps. After Bitcoin, Ethereum is the largest cryptocurrency as per the market capitalisation.

Ethereum was first proposed in 2013 by a programmer named Vitalik Buterin. In 2014, money was raised through crowdfunding and then the Ethereum platform network went live in July 2015.

Currently, a major upgrade is in progress to launch Ethereum 2.0. Ethereum 2.0 will provide better transaction throughput using sharding and use the proof-of-stake (PoS) consensus mechanism.

Website: https://ethereum.org/en/

Use cases

- Digital identity
- Any use cases that can benefit from automation through smart contracts (insurance, payments, supply chain, financial trading etc.)
- ICO to raise money to develop and launch a real digital product/platform
- NFTs
- DeFi

Hyperledger

Hyperledger is an open-source community-driven open-source blockchain technology. It provides a suite of stable frameworks, tools and libraries for enterprise-grade blockchain deployments for real-life use cases.

Hyperledger is supported by hundreds of software companies, financial institutions and blockchain consulting providers. Some of the premier members are

- JP Morgan
- IBM
- Accenture
- Consensys
- DTCC
- Fujitsu
- Hitachi

Hyperledger has been continuously evolving and is under the umbrella of The Linux Foundation (https://www.linuxfoundation.org/projects). There are various projects that are actively being developed or have been already implemented for multiple real-life use cases. The following is a list of all projects under Hyperledger (Table 2.6):

Website: https://www.hyperledger.org

Consensys Quorum

JP Morgan Chase (JPMC) initiated the Quorum project to enable Ethereum products to enterprise grade and make them usable for financial services. JPMC took the open-source codebase of Ethereum and made efforts to make it enterprise-grade for financial services. On 25 August 2020, JPMC sold it to Consensys.

JPMC launched Quorum in 2016. JPMC and Consensys have collaborated to make Ethereum a platform so that enterprises can utilise it to build a secure, scalable and customisable business network.

Table 2.6 List of projects under Hyperledger

Project name technology name	Project type	Description	Use cases	Adoption examples
Hyperledger Fabric	Distributed Ledger software	Blockchain software to develop applications or solutions with a modular architecture	Supply chain, loyalty programme, KYC, data security, Regulatory reporting	Honeywell aerospace created an online parts marketplace with Hyperledger Fabric https://www.hyperledger.org/learn/publications/honeywell-case-study
Hyperledger Indy	Digital identity software	Enterprise-grade blockchain software for decentralised digital identity	Digital identity	Kiva launched Africa's first national decentralised ID System https://www.hyperledger.org/learn/publications/kiva-case-study
Hyperledger Sawtooth	Distributed Ledger software	Modular design to develop enterprise-grade smart contacts for multiple industries	Smart contract, consensus (including practical Byzantine fault tolerance and proof of elapsed time [PoET])	BondEvalue launched the world's first Fractional Bond exchange with Sawtooth https://www.hyperledger.org/learn/publications/bondevalue-case-study
Hyperledger Iroha	Distributed ledger software	Enterprise-grade blockchain software for infrastructural or IOT projects	CBDC, IOT	The National Bank of Cambodia launched CBDC (Central Bank Digital Currency) to boost financial inclusion using Iroha. https://www.hyperledger.org/learn/publications/soramitsu-case-study
Hyperledger Quilt	Software Library	Enterprise-grade blockchain software for payments, Java implementation of the Interledger protocol, enabling payments across any payment network – fiat or crypto.	Payments	Various https://www.hyperledger.org/use/quilt

(Continued)

Table 2.6 (Continued) List of projects under Hyperledger

Project name technology name	Project type	Description	Use cases	Adoption examples
Hyperledger Transact	Software Library	Enterprise-grade library to execute smart contracts	Smart contract execution engine that is separated from distributed ledger implementation	Various https://www.hyperledger.org/use/transact
Hyperledger URSA	Software Library	Enterprise-grade library to provide cryptographic implementation	Cryptography and security solutions	Various https://www.hyperledger.org/use/ursa
Hyperledger ARIES	Software Library	Enterprise-grade library to provide secure secret management and decentralised key management functionality	Secure secret management and decentralised key management functionality.	Various https://www.hyperledger.org/use/aries
Hyperledger BESU	Distributed Ledger software	Enterprise-grade Ethereum client	Ethereum client designed to be enterprise-friendly for both public and private permissioned network use cases	Poste Italiane launched a customer loyalty programme using Besu https://www.hyperledger.org/learn/publications/posteitaliane-case-study
Hyperledger Caliper	Tool	Blockchain Benchmarking tool	Performance testing before going live in production. It supports performance testing of Hyperledger Besu, Ethereum, Hyperledger Fabric, Hyperledger Iroha and Hyperledger Sawtooth.	Various https://www.hyperledger.org/use/caliper
Hyperledger Cello	Tool	Operational dashboard for managing blockchain.	Blockchain as a service	Various https://www.hyperledger.org/use/cello
Hyperledger Explorer	Tool	Web-based tool to view, invoke, deploy or query blocks, transactions and associated data, network information and any other relevant information stored in the ledger.	Administration of blockchain platform	Various https://www.hyperledger.org/use/explorer

Consensys is a leading blockchain software company. Consensys provides a full range of products, services and post-quorum acquisitions and also provides full support for Quorum to facilitate enterprise-grade Ethereum products.

Website: https://consensys.net/quorum/

Use cases

- Supply Chain
- Financial services
- Healthcare
- NFT
- DeFi
- Many more

R3 Corda

R3 developed a Corda product from scratch by taking into account financial service requirements of privacy, scalability and security. Although the perception of Corda offering seems like is only adopted by financial services, Corda is being utilised for multiple sectors like supply chain, digital identity, voting and many more.

R3 offers two variants of the Corda product:

1. **Corda:** It is an open-source product available to all, but it comes with some limitations. Corda is community-driven and supported by R3.
2. **Corda Enterprise:** Corda Enterprise offers all features of Corda along with the additional functionalities and features like 24/7 support, software updates/released roadmap, high availability and industry-standard enterprise database support.

Website: https://www.r3.com

Use cases

- Banking
- Capital markets
- Digital assets
- Digital identity
- Energy
- Govtech
- Healthcare
- Insurance
- Real estate
- Supply chain
- Telecommunications
- Trade finance

Ripple

Ripple was founded in 2012 and since then has sold its cryptocurrency (XRP) to incentivise market maker activity to increase XRP liquidity. The cryptocurrency behind Ripple is XRP which can be traded on various exchanges around the globe.

The current market position of XRP liquidity is:

- XRP held by Ripple – ~$5.6bn
- XRP distributed through crypto exchanges – ~$50bn
- XRP placed in Escrow – ~$44.3bn

Note: The above is current as of 23 October, 2022 (Source: https://ripple.com/xrp/market-performance/)

Ripple is one of the best payment solutions with quick transfer of payments and provides a secure, transparent and quick solution for cross-border payments. The Ripplenet payment network is a high-performance global payment business solution.

Use cases

- Santander Bank (https://ripple.com/customer-case-study/santander/) used Ripple to bring faster, cheaper cross-border payment solutions to millions of its retail and commercial customers.

Chapter 3

Blockchain: Is it hype?

The blockchain journey started from the time when a person named Satoshi Nakamoto, whose true identity is still unknown, released a whitepaper called Bitcoin: A peer-to-peer electronic Cash System in 2008. This chapter discussed technology and a roadmap for the 'peer-to-peer version of electronic cash' known as Bitcoin. Shortly after releasing a whitepaper on Bitcoin, it was offered to the open-source community in 2009.

As we have already discussed how Bitcoin works and how it has been disrupting various industries around the globe.

Bitcoin was the first and the best use case of blockchain technology. Since then, hundreds of practical use cases around various sectors have been implemented and the journey is still ongoing.

There are many perceptions supporting blockchain and why/how it is disrupting businesses around the globe. Some experts have an opinion that it might be hype. In this section, we will walk through the facts and try to solve this complex puzzle that becomes more complex by views and opinions without any facts like fake stories in media.

In my view, blockchain is not hype. Although there have been multiple hurdles and challenges to its adoption, it still has multiple opportunities to solve real business problems.

Blockchain technology and its use in business appear to be hype due to the fact that a lot of senior management members would like to use blockchain as a technology to either influence the board/investors or increase the company's stock price. Another angle is to use blockchain predominantly as a buzzword to become more competitive in the market. There is also a theme to copy your competitors like if Competitor A is using blockchain why can't we do the same without even thinking about whether the use case is fit for purpose!!

The million-dollar question is if blockchain is really disrupting the business and providing business value for investors, customers and more importantly employees, over and above the existing cryptocurrency fever.

In the next section, we will walk through the blockchain footprint, successful use cases in multiple sectors, challenges, business value, competitive advantage and much more. So put your seat belts on and enjoy the exciting journey of blockchain.

DOI: 10.1201/9781003225607-3

BLOCKCHAIN FOOTPRINT IN MULTIPLE SECTORS

In this section, we will do a deep dive across blockchain footprints in various sectors. Each section is categorised by its sector and multiple sub-sectors have been included within its parent sector. One of the dynamic sectors is of course financial sector that is trying to use blockchain to disrupt its businesses.

Financial services sector

It is a building block of modern society without which the economy cannot *function*. It is like an engine of the economy. The following are subcategories within the financial sector.

Capital markets

Overview

Capital markets term in financial services refers to markets where funds are exchanged between suppliers and users of the capital. The suppliers of the capital can be banks and investors who would like to utilise their capital for investments in the hope to grow it. The users of the capital can be businesses, governments and individuals who seek capital to grow business, government investments like constructions (building bridges, town centres, houses, roads etc.) and individuals who want to buy a house etc.

The most common capital markets are stock and bond markets to raise capital for various purposes.

In summary, capital markets are venues where funds/capital can be exchanged between suppliers of the capital and those who seek capital.

There are two kinds of capital markets: primary capital market and secondary capital market.

1. **Primary capital market:** markets where new securities (stocks and bonds) are issued like the stock market to raise capital from the public (IPO – Initial Public offering)
2. **Secondary capital market:** Markets where already issues in securities are traded between investors through exchanges like the London stock exchange (LSE), the New York Stock Exchange (NYSE), Nasdaq, etc.

Blockchain footprint

As of Q3, 2022, the global stocks are worth about $111 trillion.[*] There has been also an IPO boom with some of the biggest IPO have had their debut. Some of the biggest debuts were Snowflake and Airbnb IPO which took the 2020 IPO to a record level of $175 billion in the USA.

---

[*] Source: https://www.sifma.org/resources/research/research-quarterly-equities/

Capital markets have grown into a complex global network of interconnected banks and intermediaries to enable the flow of capital across borders globally. Due to the nature of complex global transactions and capital flow through multiple banks and intermediaries; the probability of errors increases. Each bank and intermediaries maintain its own data in a silo. This leads to high costs and settlement delays due to duplication of the data entry and unnecessary reconciliation errors.

Blockchain has a real potential to solve most of the capital markets' existing issues as defined below:

- **Cost:** Reduce the cost substantially by simplifying the process, ruling out multiple intermediaries, reducing human reconciliation/data entry errors and minimising duplication.
- **Transparency:** Provide transparency across all parties that are part of a private blockchain network.
- **Speed:** Provide faster cross-border transactions globally through the blockchain network. Using Smart contracts within the blockchain consortium could automate the whole end-to-end flow of most of the transactions.
- **Security:** Blockchain implementation to replace siloed traditional ledgers maintained by multiple banks and intermediaries with single distributed ledgers with full security and transparency.
- **Resilience:** Blockchain technology provides distributed and immutable ledger (DLT), that provides a copy of approved transactions or blocks. Each participant within the blockchain network keeps a full copy of the ledger making the whole network resilient from a single point of failure – infrastructure failure, data corruption or hacking.
- As per the PWC paper (https://www.pwc.co.uk/financial-services/fintech/assets/blockchain-in-capital-markets.pdf), over $1bn was invested in blockchain companies since the technology's creation in 2009, with a 59% increase in the last year.

There are various use cases in Proof of Concept (POC) or live across capital markets globally. The following is the categorisation of them across the capital markets ecosystem:

- Debt markets
  o Digital bond issuance platform
  o Distributed order book for bond trading
- Equity markets:
  o Blockchain-based platform for digitalisation of existing post-trade infrastructure
  o Equity token issuance on the blockchain
- Securitised products
  o Blockchain-based end-to-end platform for securities origination, securitisation and servicing
  o Tokenisation of loans on a blockchain platform to facilitate services and data management

- Derivatives
  - o Blockchain-based platform for OTC (Over the Counter) derivatives post-trade lifecycle
  - o Blockchain-based platform for exchange-traded derivatives trade lifecycle
  - o Blockchain-based platform to manage collateral for cleared derivatives
- Security financing
  - o Blockchain-based platform for repurchase agreements and security swaps across collateral pools
- Asset management
  - o Blockchain-based fund distribution and register platform
  - o Platform for end-to-end fund distribution, administration and servicing
  - o Blockchain-based end-to-end platform for tokenised funds
- Others (Enablement/Facilitation/Enablers)
  - o Platform for digital asset issuance
  - o Blockchain-based platform to facilitate wholesale payments
  - o Platform to facilitate capital market digitalisation
  - o Platform to facilitate digital asset issuance

Use cases

- **FundsDLT** (https://www.fundsdlt.net): Blockchain platform to digitalise fund distribution
- **Project Jasper:** As stated in the new release on 12 October 2018 – Payments Canada, the Bank of Canada, TMX Group, Accenture and R3 have published a feasibility report on clearing and settlement of securities using DLT. This initiative proved that DLT technology can enable equity settlement.

Trade finance

Overview

As the name suggests, trade finance is a term used for facilitating international trade through the use of various financial instruments and products. It enables importers and exporters to compete in end-to-end international trade through financial instruments as per the agreement or contract.

There are various parties involved in trade finance. The following are the main parties, to name a few:

- Banks
- Trade finance companies (third parties providing financial solutions including brokers or intermediaries)
- Importers and exporters (Figure 3.1)

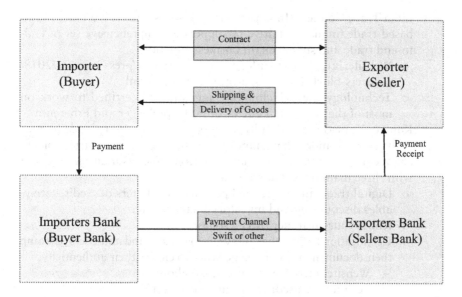

Figure 3.1 Trade finance workflow.

Blockchain footprint

There have been multiple POCs/MVPs in the trade finance sector. The section below will go through some of the successful implementations.

- **Contour:** Contour is a global network to create a decentralised global trade finance network enabling everyone to collaborate on a common platform. It was formed collaboratively by leading banks, corporates and trade partners.
  - Website: https://contour.network
  - Technology used: R3 Corda
- **Skuchain:** Skuchain provide multiple products including blockchain-based applications and platforms. One of the products called EC3 (Enterprise Collaborative Commerce Cloud) is a blockchain-based platform that provides an end-to-end solution for supply chains. EC3 links procurement and contract management, financing arrangements, corporate payments, inventory tracking and much more to provide a seamless and secure end-to-end supply chain solution.
  - Website: https://www.skuchain.com/ec3/
  - Technology used: Hyperledger fabric
- **eTradeConnect:** eTradeConnect is a trade finance consortium based in Hong Kong, China, and operated by Hong Kong Trade Finance Platform Company Limited (HKTFPCL).
  - Website: https://www.etradeconnect.net/Portal
  - Technology used: Hyperledger fabric

- **India Trade Connect (Infosys Finacle):** Infosys Finacle is a blockchain-based trade finance initiative to support a comprehensive set of end-to-end trade and supply chain business functions.
  - o **Website:** https://www.infosys.com/newsroom/press-releases/2018/pioneers-blockchain-based-trade-network.html
  - o **Technology used:** Technology agnostic and certified to work on most of the vendors like R3 Corda, Hyperledger and Ethereum.
- **Komgo:** Komgo is a live, fully decentralised commodity trade finance network with more than hundreds of banks, intermediaries, blockchain companies etc. on the platform. Komgo offers multiple products with three main ones that stand out:
  - o Digital trade finance-related products like letters of credit, receivables discounting and inventory financing etc.
  - o Know your customer (KYC) solution
  - o Certification feature that allows Komgo users and non users to stamp their documentation on the network to ensure their authenticity.
    - – Website: https://www.komgo.io/about
    - – Technology used: Quorum blockchain
- **Marco Polo TradeIX:** Marco Polo TradeIX network consists of about 30+ banks, 30+ Corporates and 10+ Technology partners to have a global reach in trade finance. The main aim of the platform is to facilitate working capital finance solutions through distributed trade finance platform.
  - o **Website:** https://www.marcopolonetwork.com
  - o **Technology used:** R3 Corda
- **Minehub:** Minehub is a digital supply chain platform for the mining and metals industry. Minehub platform supports:
  - o The end-to-end digital platform for mining and supply chain participants
  - o Real-time visibility and collaboration of upstream and downstream supply chains
    - – Website: https://minehub.com
    - – Technology used: Hyperledger fabric
- **TradeFinex:** TradeFinex is a peer-to-peer decentralised platform for trade finance. It can be described as a hybrid blockchain that can connect to multiple platforms by operating as a blockchain agnostic solution. TradeFinex supports receivables (invoices), letters of credit, guarantees and bills of landing, to name a few.
  - o **Website:** https://www.tradefinex.org
  - o **Technology used:** XDC protocol (https://www.xinfin.org/xdc-protocol.php)
- **TradeWaltz:** TradeWaltz is a blockchain-based trade finance platform. It was built by NTT DATA to enable an open and global trade ecosystem that will enable all participants to share information and deliver new value to all users.
  - o **Website:** https://www.tradewaltz.com/en/
  - o **Technology used:** in-house development

- **UAE Trade Connect (Etislat):** UAE Trade Connect (UTC) is a national trade finance platform wholly owned by Etisalat Group. The main purpose of the Blockchain-based platform is to de-risk trade finance transactions in the financial sector. As of the date of writing (23 August 2021), UTC had seven leading banks in the UAE to make a consortium.
  - o **Website:** https://www.etisalatdigital.ae/en/uae-trade-connect.jsp
  - o **Technology used:** Hyperledger fabric
- **we.trade:** we-trade is a Europe-based trade finance platform based on blockchain. It is Europe's largest consortium of 16 banks and growing fast. we.trade offers an end-to-end trade finance platform with multiple services and some of them are live including automation of payments based on pre-agreed conditions through smart contracts, bank payment undertaking (BPU), BPU financing and invoice financing.

  In summary, it offers the following services to make it even more attractive:
  - o Event-based automatic payment triggers through smart contacts
  - o Invoice financing
  - o Real-time trade settlement on one platform for all parties
  - o Bank payment undertaking (BPU)
  - o Track and trace for over 426 countries
  - o Identification of unknown counterparties i.e. all clients on we.trade platform are KYC'd
    - – **Website:** https://we-trade.com
    - – **Technology used:** IBM Blockchain platform (Hyperledger fabric)

Insurance

In simple terms, insurance is a contract between an individual/business and an insurance company against unforeseen risks. Individuals/businesses buy an insurance policy to protect themselves against a risk under a contract to get reimbursement as defined in the insurance policy in case risks actually occur. Insurance company pools the client or customer risks to make the insurance policy premium affordable.

There are multiple types of insurance policies:

- Life insurance
- Home insurance (buildings and content insurances)
- Automobile insurance
- And many more

Blockchain footprint

- **Ryskex:** Ryskex is a technology company providing a blockchain-based platform to insurance companies to assess and handle risks accurately.
  - o **Website:** https://ryskex.com
  - o **Technology used:** Consensys Quorum Blockchain

- **Fidentiax:** Fidentiax is a blockchain-based platform to trade insurance policies. It was launched in 2018 with a brand name called ISLEY (Your insurance buddy) for insurance policies. It allows customers to store, view and receive alerts for their insurance portfolios. It also allows the portfolio to be shared with designated loved ones to support beneficiary payout after death.
  o **Website:** https://www.fidentiax.com/isley-1
  o **Technology used:** Undisclosed
- **Lemonade:** Lemonade is a blockchain and artificial intelligence (AI)-based platform to offer insurance to renters and homeowners. Lemonade is operated in the USA to offer digital insurance for renters and homeowners with a simple and automated process to buy insurance policies online and also settle claims in minutes through their online AI and a blockchain-based platform. Lemonade also has a presence in some of the European countries and has an expansion plan to increase its presence in Europe.
  o **Website:** https://www.lemonade.com/
  o **Technology used:** Undisclosed
- **Black:** Black.Insure provides a platform as a service offering to insurance players with multiple unique features including creating and managing their risk portfolio, processing claims, generating insurance premiums and underwriting real-time using machine learning technology.
  o **Website:** https://black.insure
  o **Technology used:** Undisclosed
- **Etherisc:** Etherisc is a blockchain-based platform offering multiple insurance products and solutions. Its motto is to make insurance fair and accessible to anyone. Some of the products being offered by Etherisc technology solutions are
  o Crop insurance – Live
  o Flight delay insurance – Live
  o Hurricane protection – In progress
  o Crypto wallet insurance – In progress
  o Collateral protection for crypto-backed loans – In progress
  o Social insurance – In progress
  Some of the products listed above are live and others are being designed. Another unique feature of Etherisc is that they are community driven as well. Anyone can request a new product if it does not exist in their portfolio yet.
  o **Website:** https://etherisc.com/
  o **Technology used:** Ethereum

Supply chain

In simple and layman's terms, a supply chain is all about producing a product by suppliers and then distributing the final product to the buyer/customer. Obviously, there are multiple parties and processes involved during this chain of events. The main goal of supply chain management is to maximise value from all activities to gain competitive advantages. The core areas are people, processes and systems.

The best way to understand the supply chain and its management is to read about Michael Porter's value chain model (https://www.isc.hbs.edu/strategy/business-strategy/Pages/the-value-chain.aspx).

As per Porter's Value chain model,

> *A company's value chain is typically part of a larger value system that includes companies either upstream (suppliers) or downstream (distribution channels), or both. This perspective about how value is created forces managers to consider and see each activity not just as a cost, but as a step that has to add some increment of value to the finished product or service.* [emphasis added]

The following diagram visualises the end-to-end supply chain activities (Figure 3.2).

Blockchain footprint

- **Aero Blockchain Alliance – SITA:** SITA is the world's largest specialist in air transport communications and information technology. SITA launched MRO Blockchain Alliance comprises leading organisations in the Maintenance, Repair and Overhaul (MRO) chain.

  It is the air transport's first industry-wide blockchain implementation to track, trace and record aircraft parts.
  - **Website:** https://www.sita.aero/pressroom/news-releases/sita-joins-industry-partners-to-launch-mro-blockchain-alliance/
  - **Technology used:** Undisclosed

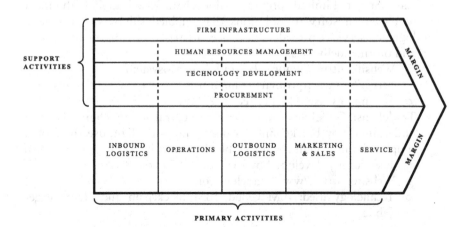

Figure 3.2 End-to-end supply chain activities.

- **Calista:** Calista is a global supply chain blockchain platform that is transforming the physical, compliance and financial activities of cargo logistics on a digital ecosystem. The blockchain solution improves efficiencies, facilitates trade, and provides a seamless experience of moving your cargo to market.
  - o **Website:** https://calista.globaletrade.services/CALISTAWEB/cus-Login/login.cl
  - o **Technology used:** Undisclosed
- **China-Europe E-Single Link:** The Sichuan province capital of Chengdu launched a Blockchain-based platform to cater to cross-border trade between China and Europe that involves multiple modes of transportation. The blockchain platform will make it simple and seamless to monitor logistics supply chains.
  - o **Website:** https://www.chinabankingnews.com/2019/10/30/chengdu-launches-blockchain-cross-border-trade-platform-to-connect-china-and-europe/
  - o **Technology used:** Undisclosed
- **DP World (Avanza Innovations):** DP World is a multinational logistics company based in Dubai and is a leading enabler of global trade. It has adopted a blockchain-based digital container logistics platform called TradeLens. TradeLens was jointly developed by A.P. Moller and IBM.
  - o **Website:** https://www.dpworld.com/news/releases/dp-world-joins-with-tradelens-to-digitise-global-supply-chains/
  - o **Technology used:** IBM Blockchain
- **Global Shipping Business Network (Cargo Smart):** The global shipping business network (GSBN) is a trade data utility platform powered by Blockchain. It enables supply chain participants to work collaboratively to accelerate the digital transformation of the shipping supply chain. GSBN solution is provided by CargoSmart Limited. CargoSmart Limited provides Blockchain-based global shipment management software solutions that enabled shippers, consignees, logistics services providers and ocean carriers to improve planning and on-time deliveries.
  - o **Website:** https://www.gsbn.trade/our-ecosystem
    https://www.cargosmart.com/en-us/
  - o **Technology used:** HyperLedger Fabric
- **TradeLens:** TradeLens is an open and neutral supply chain platform underpinned by blockchain. Its main aim is to digitalise the global supply chain through the use of blockchain. The TradeLens platform has been jointly developed by IBM and GTD Solution Inc.
  - o **Website:** https://www.tradelens.com
  - o **Technology used:** IBM Cloud, IBM Blockchain and HyperLedger Fabric

Digital identity

Digital identity is nothing more than a digital version of a person's unique identity. The existing ways of the identities are government-issued identity documents like the passport, driving licence etc. In other terms, digital identity is a trusted and secure way to prove a person's identity to prove that they are whom they claim to be.

- **Decentralised identity:** A decentralised identifier (DID) is a pseudo-anonymous identifier for a person, a company or an object. DID works on the public/private key principles. DID for an entity is secured by a private key that is unique to that entity. Only a private key owner can prove their identity. One person can have multiple DIDs associated with different activities in their life.
- **Self-sovereign identity:** Self-sovereign identity (SSI) is used to enable people and businesses to store their own identity data on their own devices and are in full control to share full or part of the information without a need for a central database of identity data controlled by the government or corporates.

Blockchain footprint

There are many companies now that are offering digital identity solutions for various sectors. Some of the ones are listed below along with their value add to the business around the globe.

- **WeTrust:** WeTrust provides various products to improve financial inclusion through the use of blockchain technology. One of the products is WeTrust Identity. WeTrust Identity provides a platform to build, share and manage your digital identity securely.
  - o **Website:** https://www.wetrust.io
  - o **Technology used:** Ethereum
- **Civic:** Civic is one of the comprehensive digital identity solutions. It provides SaaS-based offerings as well as customised solution meeting business requirements. Some of its use cases are KYC and identity verification.
  - o **Website:** https://www.civic.com
  - o **Technology used:** Undisclosed

Agriculture

Agriculture is the practice of cultivating plants and livestock. It is essential for humans to feed themselves and also trade for surplus plants or livestock to exchange for other items like farming tools or other necessities.

Blockchain footprint

- **AgriChain:** AgriChain is a blockchain-based platform to connect all stakeholders within the agriculture supply chain. The platform allows the stakeholders to make data-backed informed decisions, eliminate unnecessary paperwork, reduce supply chain inefficiency, provide transparency for end-to-end transactions and much more.
  - Website: https://agrichain.com
  - Technology used: Undisclosed
- **AgriDigital:** AgriDigital provide a simple blockchain-based platform to manage the end-to-end supply chain life cycle of Grain commodity. It provides a simple solution to buy, sell, move, store and report on Grain.
  - Website: https://www.agridigital.io
  - Technology used: Undisclosed
- **Etherisc:** Etherisc provides various insurance products built on blockchain technology. One of the products is called crop insurance. It offers crop insurance directly to the farmers based on your crop and the location of the field. The whole insurance lifecycle is automated through smart contracts.
  - Website: https://etherisc.com/
  - Technology used: Ethereum
- **Ripe:** Ripe is a blockchain-based platform to provide transparent and reliable information on the end-to-end journey and quality of food from its origin to delivery through a single interface.
  - Website: https://www.ripe.io
  - Technology used: Undisclosed
- **TE-FOOD:** TE-FOOD provides a solution to apply identification on most of the food and livestock items to provide end-to-end traceability throughout the supply chain.
  - Website: https://te-food.com
  - Technology used: Undisclosed

Telecommunications

Telecommunications has become an essential part of human society now. There have been multiple disruptions within the telecommunication sector from telephone, pagers, mobile phones and the internet. The major players in this sector are telephone (wired and wireless) operators, satellite companies, cable companies and internet service providers. You must have heard of the major players as listed below:

AT&T Inc, Verizon Communications Inc, Nippon Telegraph and Telephone Corp. (NTTYY), Deutsche Telekom AG (DTEGY), T-Mobile US Inc (TMUS), Vodafone Group Plc (VOD), Telefonica SA (TEF), British Telecom (BT) and Virgin Media.

Blockchain footprint

Multiple major telecom providers have initiated and now even using blockchain technology for internal as well as externally for their customers. AT&T, T-Mobile, Telefonica, China Mobile and Verizon are some of the major players that are using blockchain (combined with the Internet of things [IoT]/AI technologies) for supply chain, customer solutions, security, privacy etc.

Healthcare

Healthcare in simple terms is caring for human health through providing diagnostics, prevention and treatment of diseases, illness, injury and also physical and mental impairments.

It is one of the main necessities of human beings.

Through continuous scientific improvements, inventions and technology disruption in the healthcare sector, the human average living age has increased.

Blockchain footprint

There are hundreds of start-ups and corporates that have launched POC/minimum viable product (MVP) and have gone live with useable products using blockchain. In this section, we will go through some of them.

Healthcare data or EHR

Blockchain is one of the technologies that has been an enabler and continuously provides a disruption to the healthcare sector. One of the use cases is how to provide transparency and simplicity and make it more secure when it comes to confidential data. It has also become more important and critical now to comply with the regulations like Health Insurance Portability and Accountability Act (HIPPA), General Data Protection Regulation (GDPR), etc.

- **Humanscape:** Humanscape is a blockchain-based health data platform to make health data sharing more secure and simple. This platform's aim is to help increase the sharing of diagnostic and research data that would accelerate treatment and reduce the occurrence of disease.
    - o **Website:** https://humanscape.io/en/index.html
    - o **Technology used:** Undisclosed
- **Azaad health:** Azaad Health provides a Blockchain-based online HIPAA-compliant platform to allow healthcare providers and patients to share medical information securely and with confidence.
    - o **Website:** https://www.azaadhealth.com
    - o **Technology used:** Undisclosed

- **Consilx:** It is a blockchain-based platform designed to facilitate clinical trial participants to have better and easy trial experiences. It also provides pharmaceutical companies with a unified clinical trial management system with simplicity, transparency and security as the core features.
  - o **Website:** https://www.consilx.com
  - o **Technology used:** Undisclosed
- **MediBloc:** MediBlock is a blockchain-based healthcare data platform to centralise all patients' health data into a single place and redistribute the ownership of that data back to the owners i.e. patients.
  - o **Website:** https://medibloc.co.kr/en/
  - o **Technology used:** Undisclosed
- **Iryo:** Iryo is an online digital healthcare software based on blockchain technology that provides features like storing and sharing medical data and a customer relationship management (CRM) system to manage interactions with patients' security and transparently.
  - o **Website:** https://www.iryo.io
  - o **Technology used:** Undisclosed
- **Open Health Network:** Open Health Network is based on Blockchain technology to provide a data sharing platform to ensure patients have control over their medical data and also are able to monetise it. It offers HIPAA-compliant data sharing capability to various stakeholders within the healthcare ecosystem including healthcare providers, medical researchers, pharmaceutical companies and health insurers.
  - o **Website:** https://www.openhealth.cc/home
  - o **Technology used:** Undisclosed
- **MedBlox:** MedBlox is a decentralised platform based on blockchain to exchange digital health information securely. The MedBlox online platform enables collaboration between various healthcare stakeholders including healthcare providers, health systems, researchers and patients on a local and global scale.
  - o **Website:** https://medblox.io
  - o **Technology used:** Undisclosed
- **Gainfy:** Gainfy is a blockchain-based platform that uses AI, and machine learning to provide preventive care, restoration of health and well-being lifestyle to provide the best healthcare options to customers. It provides solutions like scheduling healthcare, telemedicine, digital payments, identity verifications and electronic medical records management, all from one seamless and secure portal.
  - o **Website:** https://gainfy.com
  - o **Technology used:** Various
- **Solve:** Solve.Care is a blockchain-based platform with a mission to simplify access to care, reduce bureaucracy to reduce administration costs, speed up payments to healthcare providers globally and ultimately provide simple, secure and cost-effective medical services to the customers.

o Website: https://solve.care
o Technology used: Undisclosed
- Medchain: MedChain is creating a new healthcare ecosystem enabling a secure dApp (Decentralised Application) infrastructure for health record storage. Some of the features of the platform are to provide up-to-date information to the customer (patients) including medical test results, medical history and documentation that patients are entitled to under HIPAA and EMR guidelines.
  o Technology used: Ethereum, Hyperledger
- Etheal: Etheal is a blockchain-based decentralised medical professional's reputation platform. It is creating a global network of vetted and reviewed physicians to provide simple, secure and cost-effective access to patients globally. The mission is to use AI and blockchain to show the best medical treatment in any country for anyone globally with safety, service and cost in mind.
  o Website: https://etheal.com/
  o Technology used: Ethereum

Monetising patient data

Finally, it is high time that big corporates and businesses, with a high amount of wealth, share some financial benefits with the customers for making money through their data. Blockchain has provided the technology and enablement to make it happen. In the following section, we will go through some of the current use cases of how end users can be monetised by corporates sharing their personal data but also having full control of their data.

- Betterpath: Betterpath provides a blockchain platform and software to enable EHR and data sharing.
  o Technology used: Undisclosed
- Citizen health: Citizen health is a society with an aim to provide affordable and better healthcare options to the citizens in need. It uses blockchain technology to connect physicians and patients directly and incentivise the patients to pursue healthy lifestyles.
  o Website: https://citizenhealth.io
  o Technology used: Undisclosed
- CoverUS: CoverUS uses blockchain technology to secure all its data. It uses blockchain technology to help users to monetise their data by giving consent to share it.
  o Website: https://coverus.health
  o Technology used: Undisclosed
- MediChain: MediChain uses blockchain to help patients store their own medical data locally and have full control of it. MediChain aim is to give its users full control of their data and allow them to share it anonymously with scientists working to develop treatments and cures.

Patients get rewarded by pharmaceutical companies, researchers and insurers when they provide consent to share their data anonymously.

- o **Website:** https://medichain.online
- o **Technology used:** Hyperledger
- **Bowhead Health:** They provide an encrypted wellness tracker and personalised heat app to individuals who want to take control of their health data and outcomes. They get rewarded through tokens for healthy lifestyles and sharing the data with interested parties and researchers.
  - o **Website:** https://bowheadhealth.com
  - o Technology used: Undisclosed

Genomic data

Due to the social impact and younger population, more and more people are cautious about their ancestors and their background. There has been a lot of traction surrounding online websites like 23andMe.com and Ancestry.com recently to provide details on individuals' family origins. This can only be possible through scientific innovations, i.e. genomics. Blockchain provides a solution to secure individual genetic profiles and kept them under their control rather than providing the whole data to a centralised institution. There have been a lot of start-ups providing solutions through the use of blockchain in this space. We will discuss some of the famous ones in this section.

- **DNAtix:** DNAtix uses blockchain to not only protect genetic data but also provide a safe place to store ad share it anonymously. It provides a platform to share genetic data with approved partners and for research purposes anonymously.
  - o **Website:** https://www.dnatix.com
  - o **Technology used:** Undisclosed
- **Zenome:** Zenome is a distributed genomic market based on blockchain and uses a P2P network to connect individuals willing to share their genetic data and researchers/corporates who would like to use the data. They use smart contracts and tokens to enforce fairness and drive participation in genomic data exchanges. The platform's aim is to put users in control of their genetic data and also be able to monetise it security and fairly. In this model, all participants on the network can be financially rewarded.
  - o **Website:** https://zenome.io
  - o **Technology used:** Undisclosed
- **Nebula Genomics:** Nebula Genomics is a human genome sequencing and health big data company with an aim to ensure users maintain full control of their data and are compensated for its use. They use Blockchain to securely store genetic data and anonymously share the data with researchers/companies on the platform. Users of the platform have a choice to keep their genetic data private securely or able to share it securely and anonymously with medical researchers in exchange for monetary benefit.

○ Website: https://nebula.org/whole-genome-sequencing-dna-test/
○ Technology used: Undisclosed

- **EncrypGen:** EncrypGen is yet another P2P marketplace to buy and sell genomic data. It also provides a platform to buy and sell health science products and services. They use blockchain to securely store genomic data and allow people to share it securely and/or anonymously with researchers in exchange for financial benefit. One of the main features of the platform is to give users full control of their data.
  ○ **Website:** https://encrypgen.com
  ○ **Technology used:** Ethereum

Healthcare cryptocurrency

As discussed in the previous section about financially rewarding customers to share their personal data, one of the missing pieces was how to facilitate it!! Blockchain provides technology and functionality to enable rewarding customers automatically, safely and ethically. Cryptocurrency enables customers who have provided consent to share their data, to be rewarded automatically through cryptocurrencies.

- **Dentacoin:** Dentacoin (DCN) is a start-up with an aim to streamline the global dental industry through the use of a cryptocurrency reward scheme. They have launched an Ethereum-based utility token (symbol DCN) that can be used for rewards, payments, and exchanges within and beyond the dental industry. They also have launched Dentacoin Assurance, a smart contract-based dental assurance plan.
  ○ **Website:** https://dentacoin.com
  ○ **Technology used:** Ethereum
- **Mosio Clinicoin:** Mosio Clinicoin is a decade-old healthcare software company that has recently appreciated Blockchain technology through the launch of its own cryptocurrency called Clinicoin. Clinicoin is a blockchain-based open-source Patient Engagement Platform with an aim to improve global health and wellness by connecting patients, providers and developers. The platform is further enhanced by a token-based rewards ecosystem, wherein it pays users for healthy behaviours and also increases their engagement with healthcare practitioners and organisations.
  ○ **Website:** https://www.mosio.com/about-clinicoin/
  ○ **Technology used:** Various
- **Well:** Well provides a mobile app, web portal and health devices to encourage people to be healthy and track their progress. Users can share the data with clinics, medical professionals and other interested companies. Users are in control of their data and get rewards in tokens or coins for their healthy lifestyle. They also get rewarded in coins that can be redeemed to buy goods and services on their marketplace.
  ○ **Website:** https://www.joinwell.io
  ○ **Technology used:** Ethereum

Provenance and medical histories

In the current paradigm, it is very difficult for health professions to trace back their patients' medical history along with the history of treatment they have received. It becomes more difficult if they have been to different territories and countries. Blockchain provides a solution to track the whole medical journey end-to-end even if it is global through a single interface.

- **BlockMedx:** BlockMedx is a blockchain-based software to provide a secure, HIPPA-compliant, end-to-end solution to digitalise Drug Enforcement Administration-controlled drug prescriptions. It provides next-generation blockchain-based technology to send and receive electronic prescriptions, track those prescriptions and predict at-risk patients.
  - o **Website:** https://www.blockmedx.com
  - o **Technology used:** Undisclosed
- **Spiritus:** Spiritus is using blockchain technology to track the maintenance of vital medical support devices. The solution is offered through a mobile app, web portal and cloud to provide a secure, transparent and immutable maintenance record of devices so that patients can be confident in the devices they rely on.
  - o **Website:** https://www.spirituspartners.com
  - o **Technology used:** Azure AI and Blockchain suite

Energy

The energy sector has been an important driver of industrial evolution and growth. Energy companies can be classified by the way they produce energy like non-renewable (fossil fuels) and renewable like solar.

An energy sector is a group of companies involved in the exploration/development of oil and gas reserves. Some examples are power utility companies including nuclear power, generating power through fossil fuels and also renewable energy like solar/wind power.

Blockchain footprint

- **Sympower:** Sympower offers multiple software products to provide flexibility in energy utilisation. The software balances energy supply with demand, hence unlocking energy efficiency. The software along with hardware devices can control the demand side of things by switching on and off equipment as per the demand of the energy.

  The end result of the supply and demand synergy is to reduce the strain on the electric grid and also give the consumer the ability to turn their big energy users into value-generating energy assets.

o Website: https://sympower.net
o **Technology used:** Undisclosed

- **LO3Energy:** LO3Energy is a US-based start-up using blockchain to create a peer-to-peer network to share energy from neighbour to neighbour. They have come up with a brand called Pando to enable utility companies and retailers to share a unique energy marketplace. It enables all members of the community to trade energy in order to achieve both personal and community energy goals.
  o **Website:** https://lo3energy.com
  o **Technology used:** Undisclosed

Govtech

As the economy and society are adapting to the digital age, governments have the accountability to transform their services for their citizens as well. Some of the ways that are transforming economics through government interventions/support are listed below:

- Deliver essential services through digitalisation such as income tax returns, voting, social benefits, healthcare registration, identity documents, land registry and support services.
- Partner with private companies to provide digital experience to its citizens to utilise the services in an efficient and secure way.

Blockchain footprint

- **Estonia government digitalisation:** Estonia is one of the best examples of digital government services through the use of technology, political support and an innovative mindset. Estonia has 99% of public services are offered as e-services.

  Estonia has managed to digitalise multiple essential government services to provide the best services to its citizens and reduce administrative costs and quick delivery by reducing bureaucracy and paperwork. They have managed to finally provide secure, transparent and one of the best experiences to citizens, visitors, companies and entrepreneurs. Some of the examples of services that are using blockchain are digital ID, i-Voting, Mobile ID, e-Health, e-Tax, e-School and e-Residency.
  o **Website:** https://e-estonia.com
  o **Technology used:** Various

- **Singapore digitalisation:** Singapore is another best example that is appreciating the technology and using it to provide a simple, secure and faster experience for its government services.
  o **Website:** https://www.tech.gov.sg
  o **Technology used:** Various

- **Dubai 'Smart Dubai':** 'The Smart Dubai initiative was founded following the vision of His Highness Sheikh Mohammad bin Rashid Al Maktoum, Vice President and Prime Minister of the UAE and Ruler of Dubai, to make Dubai the happiest city on earth. Participation from all city stakeholders – residents, visitors, business owners, parents and families – is a cornerstone of our strategy'. – https://www.smartdubai.ae
    Dubai is extensively investing to make the whole city smart by leveraging emerging technologies such as blockchain, AI and IoT, as well as Data Science capabilities. The initiative's aim is to make everyday experiences more personalised, seamless, efficient and impactful for residents and visitors.
    o **Website:** https://www.smartdubai.ae
    o **Technology used:** Various

Central Bank Digital Currency (CBDC)

Multiple governments are harnessing the power of blockchain to launch their own digital currency. CBDC will be crucial for the digital ecosystem. Please refer to Chapter 1, the section 'CDBC Revolution', for more details on CBDC.

These are some of the examples of blockchain footprint within government services. Obviously, there are many more examples whereby governments are either going through a POC or using the blockchain for various services.

Real estate

Real estate is a term used for intrinsic physical assets like buildings and land. It is one of the major assets class in the financial world. Some of the examples of real estate are:

- Shopping malls
- Business buildings including office spaces
- Entertainment avenues like casinos, leisure centres and gyms

Blockchain footprint

- **Rentberry:** Rentberry is a real estate platform that offers a fully digital rental journey. They offer a decentralised rental platform to provide transparency, automation and reduction in costs. It brings together landlords and tenants. It uses smart contracts to provide a simple, seamless and secure rental journey and ensure that the rights of both parties are safeguarded.
    o **Website:** https://rentberry.com
    o **Technology used:** Undisclosed
- **SmartRE:** SmartRE is a decentralised real estate platform that enables investors globally to invest in the US real estate sector. The platform allows homeowners to sell a fraction of their home equity instead of

borrowing. It also allows investors to buy a fraction of the property as an investment asset. The platform also offers customised insurance as an extra safety measure.

- o **Website:** https://smartre.io
- o **Technology used:** Undisclosed

- **Propy:** Propy provides a platform and software to automate the closing process for all participants of the real asset transactions. It makes transaction closing faster, simple and more secure. Propy's aims are to provide products like Propy Registry to store land registry records securely and Propy smart contract to automate the whole lifecycle of real estate transactions. The product will reduce delays and bureaucracy as with the traditional real estate legacy process and system.
  - o **Website:** https://propy.com/browse/
  - o **Technology used:** Ethereum
- **Myne properties:** Myne provides a blockchain-based platform to enable buying and selling of residential real estate from your smartphone or other digital channels. The niche feature of the platform is that it enables anyone to buy and sell high-end homes by the square foot.
  - o **Technology used:** Undisclosed

Education

Education is a core part of the society and economy. Blockchain can disrupt the education market by providing a secure, trusted and verifiable golden source of record globally. The technology can be harnessed to offer the following use cases. There are multiple POCs in progress to offer value-addition services for education. The term used for technology revolution within the education sector is called EDTech.

Use cases

- **Certification of student records and accreditation:** Provide a trusted source of education records globally
- **Reduction in education fraud:** Provide an immutable and trusted record of education history for an individual that can be used as a golden source by employers, universities and others to verify the authenticity of accreditations.

  For instance, Singapore has launched a platform called OpenCerts to enable the issuance and validation of academic certificates that are tamper-resistant.
  - o **Website:** https://www.smartnation.gov.sg/initiatives/digital-government-services/opencerts
    https://www.opencerts.io
  - o **Technology used:** Various

Digital assets

A digital asset is anything that exists in digital format and does have the right to use or have an ownership right. Some examples of digital assets are audible music, movies, audible books, digital books, digital pictures/paintings, digital documents etc.

Blockchain footprint

We have already seen multiple examples of digital assets in Chapter 2 as well as in this section. Some of the examples of digital assets are listed below. Blockchain is being used to enable and establish an ecosystem to make them more transparent, secure and global reachable.

- Cryptocurrencies
- CBDC
- NFTs (Non-fungible tokens)
- Entertainment (movies, music and games)

MARKET VALUE POSITIONING BASED ON BLOCKCHAIN ADOPTION

Blockchain disruption

As discussed in this chapter, there are multiple use cases of blockchain that are either partially live or under a POC to create value for businesses. In the following section, we will go through the industry sectors/sub-sectors and work out the value added by using blockchain.

Before we dive into individual sectors and value add for the businesses beneath these sectors, let's run through the common financial and non-financial benefits of adopting blockchain.

Financial benefits

- Removal of intermediaries that can ultimately provide cost efficiency and financial benefits
- Facilitate upgradation or replacement of legacy IT systems or IT debt through the adoption of blockchain can significantly improve cost efficiencies
- Improvement in security through the use of blockchain can not only minimise hacking attacks that cost brand and monetary losses but also gain market share by attaining customer trust
- Use of blockchain decentralised features, businesses can target global markets quickly and safely

- Reduction in financial fraud through blockchain can significantly reduce costs for businesses
- Blockchain can automate the KYC process that can reduce fraud and in essence improve regulatory trust
- Blockchain can enable cross-border payments and provide a simple, quick, transparent and safe process

Non-financial benefits

- Banking for the unbanked can provide financial inclusion for the people without any bank account or services
- Providing end-to-end transparency of goods origin can improve farmers' and goods producers' lifestyles as well as gain customers' trust towards the brand. This can have a social impact on society and improve the brand of business by being ethical
- Providing transparency to the end customers of goods' carbon footprint can force businesses to be more carbon neutral, saving the planet

Sector-specific benefits

I think it is the right moment to qualify the blockchain benefits specific to the different sectors. The following section will articulate and focus on specific benefits and bind them to the sectors:

Capital Markets

- Enable businesses to have global reach and increase their footprint quickly
- Gain the trust of regulators and customers globally by offering seamless and secure products and solutions
- Reduce fraud by automation of KYC, consortium-based blockchain and sharing the knowledge between stakeholders within the members of the blockchain
- Faster cross-border payments
- Reduce cost by using automation contracts through smart contracts

Trade Finance

- Provide seamless end-to-end trade finance solutions to not only cut the time to complete a transaction, but also reduce the cost by avoiding intermediaries from the life cycle of the trade
- Make the global trade transaction seamless, transparent, secure and automated through the use of blockchain ledger and smart contracts

Insurance

- Reduce insurance fraud by sharing historical claim data and criminal records with other insurance providers who are part of the blockchain consortium
- Automate insurance buying/selling as well as claim filing and payout for a successful claim without waiting for days and weeks
- Prospective reduction in insurance premiums through the use of blockchain that can cut the insurance fake claims and fraud

Supply Chain

- Blockchain can effectively cut down the end-to-end timeframe within the supply chain by reducing intermediaries throughout the ecosystem
- Provide resiliency for the supply chain ecosystem by offering a hybrid blockchain infrastructure that is immune to fraud, hacking and misuse
- Provide end-to-end transparency throughout the supply chain to detect risks and delays and take resolution measures. This whole process can be automated using blockchain technology

Digital Identity

- Blockchain has disrupted the concept of digital identity by further improving the technology through decentralised identity, SSI and many more. As you know, digital identity is one of the core elements of digitalisation and it has been further appreciated within the blockchain world
- Blockchain can reduce identity fraud by providing a secure and transparent system to create and validate the digital identity automatically
- Blockchain can enable decentralisation of the digital identity rather than having to rely on a central organisation or government departments controlling the digital identity. This can avoid various fraud and illegal tactics
- Digital identity is the core element to digitalise traditional services

Agriculture

- Blockchain is already assisting the agriculture industry by providing agriculture insurance to protect the farmers
- Framers can get rewarded directly by the buyers for their product. This will rule out any brokers and farmers getting their product value worth rather than paying too much commission to brokers
- Blockchain is capable of creating a global decentralised marketplace (P2P) whereby farmers can directly interact with buyers and carry out a trade

Telecommunications

- Telecoms are using blockchain to provide solutions to their customers and partners to create simple, transparent and secure trading as well as offerings with a seamless experience

Healthcare

As you have recognised by now, healthcare is one of the most effective sectors for blockchain useability and can benefit substantially through it.

- Decentralised COVID-19 vaccine deployment, vaccine supplies and transparency throughout the global supply chain can be accomplished through blockchain use
- Sharing the scientific knowledge and artefacts securely and safely
- Provide digital health care to patients
- Create an ecosystem to use the confidential patient data based on their consent and also financially reward them to use their data. This can improve the patient's participation in medical trials as well as sharing the health data with medical corporates and researchers
- Create an ecosystem to share scientific ideas with patent protection features

Energy

- Provide end-to-end solutions to make the lifecycle of the oil and gas supply chain secure and transparent
- Provide a functionality to create a marketplace of energy suppliers and buyers to buy and sell utility based on demand and supply with automated pricing and contracts
- Disrupt the green energy market by creating a marketplace of energy suppliers and end customers, to adopt green energy and get rewarded

GovTech

- Enable digitalisation of public services
- Reduce bureaucracy within the legacy system and provide a simple, seamless, transparent and secure platform to citizens, businesses and entrepreneurs
- Digitalise traditional public services like voting, taxation, road tolls/ tax, council tax, national insurance, social benefits, National Health Service, employment benefits etc. through the use of blockchain
- Digitalise identity documents like the driving licence, national security card and passport
- Digitalise the ecosystem of the land registry

Real Estate

- Improve quick time to market in terms of buying and selling real estate through digitalising the whole lifecycle of a real estate transaction
- Enable smart cities through the use of innovative technologies like blockchain, AI and IoT
- Enable a marketplace to buy and sell a fraction of real estate globally through the use of blockchain technology
- Provide a secure, auditable and transparent system to buy and sell real estate with the establishment of ownership security

Education

- Reduce education fraud through a secure and transparent registry to validate the authenticity of the qualification and accreditations of individuals through a decentralised blockchain solution
- Support and provide benefits to universities, schools and colleges by providing a validated and trusted source, to validate the authenticity of the accreditations
- Provide benefits to businesses in hiring appropriate employees and skills by validating their accreditations, employment experience, and references in advance through the global hybrid blockchain solution
- Create a marketplace to match skills with employment requirements with trust, validation, authenticity, and security through blockchain to provide value to employers, universities and individuals

Digital Assets

Blockchain benefits towards digital assets are horizontal across all use cases and industries. In essence, the following are the high-level benefits:

- Enable Crypto currencies marketplace through the use of blockchain
- Enablement of CBDC to enable digitalisation of the whole ecosystem of various use cases and industries globally. CBDC will enable financial disruption and a major enabler would be government
- Enable innovative technology and use cases like DeFi (decentralised finance) and NFTs

BARRIERS TO BLOCKCHAIN ADOPTION

Although there are a hefty number of benefits of blockchain, the adoption is not as quick as expected. There is no doubt that blockchain is an innovative and one-of-its-kind technology that is here to say, but there are some barriers to its adoption.

Obviously, the barriers can be minimised through various solutions; however, it is worth going through them.

The following are some of the barriers to blockchain adoption industry-wide:

- **Flexibility and interoperability:** Retaining flexibility in terms of changing the architecture, technology, people and processes are vital in achieving long-lasting success. There are multiple protocols, products and standards of blockchain technology, and it makes it difficult for an organisation to select one, due to the lack of interoperability with other ledgers and platforms. There is also a lack of common standards.
- **Cultural resistance:** Resistance from society due to various social factors like employment, business losses, culture etc. can also slow down the adoption.
- **Government support:** Government support is crucial for Blockchain adoption including regulatory support. Lack of regulatory approvals can slow down Blockchain adoption.
- **Skills:** Insufficient skills and knowledge for firms to develop, operate and support blockchain solutions effectively is essential for blockchain adoption. Lack of skills and knowledge can drastically slow down the adoption.
- **Inappropriate use cases:** Blockchain use cases are being wrongly adopted and a lot of money is wasted due to businesses not understanding the appropriate real-life benefits and fit for use case scenarios. This can be a potential trigger for wasteful investment. Investment is being wasted by using blockchain for unsuitable use cases.

BLOCKCHAIN ADOPTION TO SOLVE CRITICAL AND COMPLEX BUSINESS PROBLEMS

As discussed in the previous chapter, blockchain evolution is disrupting all industries. Most of the traditional business use cases are trying to save cost, gain market share, reduce fraud and ultimately improve customer services through automation, transparency and security. As you might have guessed, blockchain plays a vital role in reshaping businesses around the globe.

In this section, we go through a couple of real-world business problems and then articulate how blockchain is disrupting the status quo and is creating value add for businesses and society.

Business problems

Although there are thousands of use cases that are either being used or are going through producing MVP, the following real-world business problems are close to my heart.

Business problem #1

Anti-Money Laundering (AML): Within the financial sector, companies must comply with regional regulations in order to do business. There can be severe penalties and also cancellation of the banking licence if the financial company does not adhere to and comply with the local regulations.

The regulations have been further tightened due to the 9/11 terrorist attack in New York and the financial crisis in 2007–2008. AML is essential to stop or minimise illegal activities to fund terrorist attacks, drug smuggling, arms smuggling and much more.

In order to comply with local and global regulations, companies have to spend millions of dollars in order to establish processes, upskill employees and set up infrastructure to comply with regulations. This obviously has a negative impact on companies' profits and can lead to cost-cutting. The existing financial AML process is manual and there is a high probability to make a mistake. This can have an impact on the company's brand image, risk of losing the licence and more importantly increase illegal activity including terrorist funding. This also can have a severe social impact and create a danger to society.

There is also a lot of duplication whereby companies spend time and money to carry out similar AML checks multiple times to comply with local and global regulations. There is an opportunity here to simplify the process and sharing of the information across regulators, banks and intermediaries as part of a consortium through blockchain.

Solution #1

Figure 3.3 articulates how blockchain technology can provide value.

A: A customer or a client of Bank A would like to start doing business with the Bank. As per the financial regulations, Bank A must onboard the client. One of the core requirements of the bank is to carry out the KYC of the customer.

B: Once all paperwork for the client has been collected, Bank A will carry out checks for verification of the client. This will go through a consortium-based blockchain whereby other banks do participate. If by any chance other banks have already carried KYC for the same customer, Bank A can use the same data. Multiple banks can provide and approve the client's KYC verification anonymously. It will be based on the proof of authority algorithm. The blockchain setup can offer multiple layers of security and only the information required to verify the client can be shared with other banks, so the client's financial details are not disclosed to other banks for competition and business reasons.

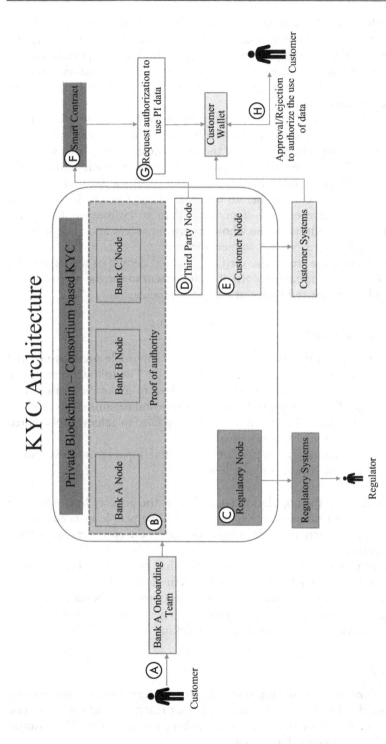

Figure 3.3 KYC use case blockchain architecture.

C: Traditional KYC systems and processes use a hefty amount of administration and resources and consume too much time. Once regulators are part of the private blockchain, the whole reporting can be automated and on-demand. In this architecture, regulators can get a report as a self-service and in real-time. This will save time and cost and reduce fraud.

D, F, G, H: Third-party nodes within a private Blockchain are for marketers, researchers and financial solution providers who would like to use the personal information of the Bank's customers to offer solutions or sell solutions. In the Blockchain model, customers can monetise the use of their personal information. Obviously, third parties need to get the customer's consent before using the data. The Blockchain-based system can give control of personal data to customers. The smart contract can automate the whole approval process and also share the financial rewards with customers directly.

E: Customer node stores the verified personal details of the customers, KYC record, auditable record of their consent to use the personal data by which party and financial rewards of the customer.

Business problem #2

Social impact: In the modern world there are multiple social issues and unfair disparity amongst part of the world. The following are some of the social issues that need to be resolved to make the world a better place. There are multiple non-governmental organisations (NGOs) and social entrepreneurs that are working hard to achieve UN (United Nations) sustainable development goals.

Blockchain technology can play an exponential impact to address critical social and environmental challenges.

- A high % of the population is still below the poverty line. Although NGOs organisations are trying to assist the people in need, due to corruption, there is no clarity on how much the end users are getting assistance
- There is a lot of administration cost that could have been used to make a real impact with the budget secured for them
- Employees or small businesses in poor countries are being used by big organisations and intermediaries. They get below-average pay with poor working conditions and long working hours

Solution #2

The following blockchain solution can provide transparency and end-to-end immutable record to make sure all grants reach the end user (farmers, NGOs, schools, universities and social workers) to enhance the UN sustainable development goals (Figure 3.4).

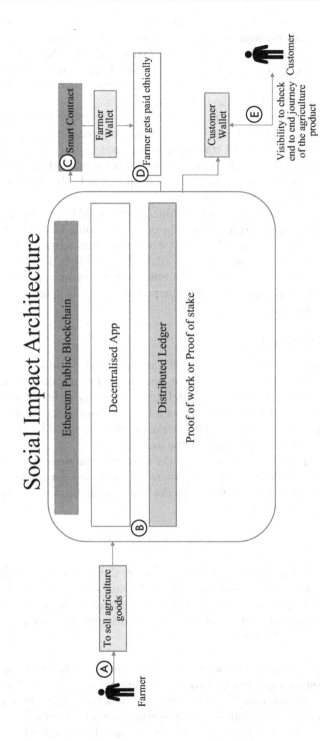

Figure 3.4 Social impact use case blockchain architecture.

A: There are multiple use cases of social impact, but the above architecture goes through an agriculture use case. The main question and problem statement is 'How can a farmer who produces agriculture products is fairly and ethically rewarded for their hard work and time'

The first part of the ecosystem is a farmer who would like to sell his products through the blockchain system.

B: The request from the farmer will come to the public blockchain. The platform allows the farmers to auction or negotiate globally/locally to sell their products. All transactions are securely recorded within the distributed ledger and verified by platform participants globally.

C, D: The whole end-to-end process is automated whereby the farmer gets paid as per the agreed contract.

E: Last but not least is the end customer, who would like to buy the product like a piece of fruit/coffee. The customer would like to know if the product being bought has been produced from sustainable sources and if the farmer was treated ethically and fairly by the business before buying the product. The customer wallet or app can provide an end-to-end supply chain of the product from its origin to the shelf of the supermarket.

Business problem #3

Media and entertainment: With the advancement of digitalisation, the media and entertainment sector has been substantially impacted by piracy and infringements of intellectual property rights. There is also a significant issue of monopoly of a few big brands who basically control the whole industry. This makes it near impossible for an individual artist to get a break in the industry.

The whole industry also works on the influence and who know philosophy. Independent artists have to work harder to get a break in the industry and have to work harder than usual below the minimum wage or sometimes for free.

Solution #3

Decentralised blockchain can solve some of the issues surrounding the media and entertainment industry. The following architecture will explain and provide insights on how blockchain-based solutions will disrupt the media and entertainment industry and provide opportunities for creative and artists personal (Figure 3.5).

A: Blockchain-based ecosystems have really disrupted the media and entertainment market. It has provided a platform for individual artists to launch their own products and buy/sell products through a marketplace. One of the latest examples of the distributed network for the media and entertainment marketplace is NFT as discussed in Chapter 1.

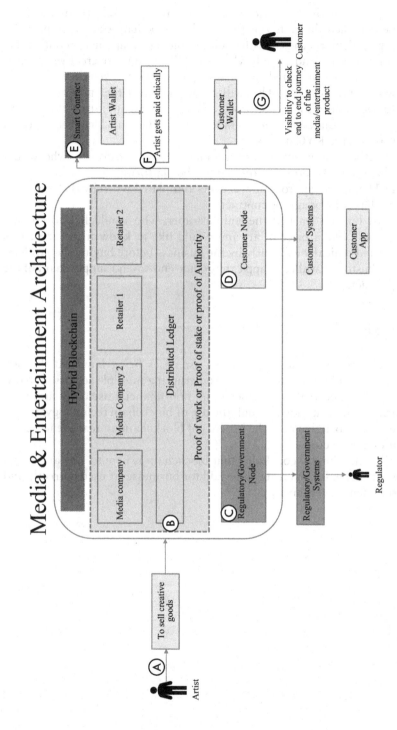

Figure 3.5 Media and entertainment blockchain architecture.

B: Once the artist has an offering and is ready to sell, the request can be launched through a platform. The blockchain ecosystem provides a global marketplace with multiple media companies, retailers, art collectors and individuals who would like to buy the creative product.

C: Local regulators can demand to be part of the blockchain with a node within the network. This will allow them to either take part in the verification of the transactions or carry out an audit to make sure all artists, media companies, retailers and individuals have been verified through the KYC process.

D: Another important part of the blockchain is customers who would like to buy the products offered on the platform.

E, F: The whole end-to-end process is automated whereby the artist gets paid as per the agreed contract.

G: Last but not least, if the end customer, who would like to buy the product like a piece of art and would like to know if the artist was treated ethically and fairly by the business before buying the product, the customer wallet or app can provide end-to-end supply chain of the product.

SUMMARY

In this chapter, we discussed various use cases being launched through blockchain and how the technology is disrupting multiple sectors globally. We also discussed real-life financial and non-financial use cases and their technical implementation through the use of blockchain technology. In this chapter, we also articulated the benefits of blockchain on real-life use cases within various sectors.

Finally, this chapter concluded that blockchain is here to stay and by no means it is hype. It can create value add for businesses if used correctly and with sufficient governance.

Chapter 4

Blockchain: Is it a hoax?

The blockchain revolution started with the release of a whitepaper, authored by a pseudonym developer called Satoshi Nakamoto, to establish the model for the blockchain. It was primarily to explain the cryptocurrency called Bitcoin, which has been the first and the best use case of blockchain so far.

Since the successful launch of Bitcoin in 2009, there has been a storm of thousands of cryptocurrencies in the market. However, the dream of becoming a millionaire through the cryptocurrency channel comes with high risks and scams as well.

In this chapter, we will discuss the value of blockchain, if any, and critically analyse it to establish a point 'Is blockchain a hoax?' The sections will walk through crypto success and failure, initial crypto offering (ICO) success and fraud, failed use cases of blockchain and much more.

The following statistics highlight the launch of cryptocurrencies globally. As of the date of writing (18 September 2021), there were about 16,000 cryptocurrencies created; however, not all of them exist now. As of September 2021 (Figure 4.1):

- There are roughly 9,336 cryptocurrencies (as tracked by coingecko. com)
- There are ~5,728 active ICOs (as tracked by icobench.com)

You might be surprised to know that ~87% of the ICO were launched on the Ethereum platform. We will go through the total number of ICOs launched, failed and in progress and also the successful ones in this chapter.

INSIGHTS ON CRYPTOCURRENCIES

As per coinmarketcap.com (https://coinmarketcap.com/all/views/all/), there were about 6,000 currencies listed in 2020 on CoinMarketCap. As of 7 August 2021, there were about 11,145 currencies listed on the same site. The tokens or cryptocurrencies get launched with a project or use case behind them.

DOI: 10.1201/9781003225607-4

Roughly 16,000 Cryptocurrencies Were Created Between 2014 and 2021

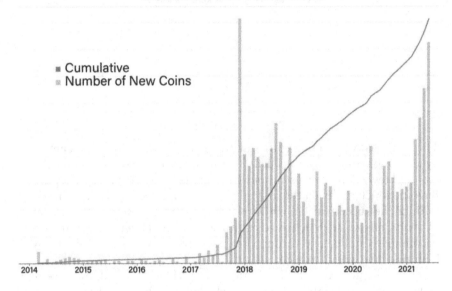

Figure 4.1 Cryptocurrencies between 2014 and 2021.

As per an *Economist* online article published on 7 August 2021, the combined market capitalisation has exploded from $330bm to $1.6trn as of 7 August 2021. It is roughly equivalent to the nominal GDP of Canada.

The holders of the coins have also become more sophisticated and deep-pocketed as well now as it is not only the retail investors that are trading in Bitcoin but also financial institutions. Financial institutions account for about 63% of trading cryptocurrencies (*Economist* – https://www.economist.com/finance-and-economics/2021/08/02/what-if-bitcoin-went-to-zero).

As per SkyBridge Capital, a Hedge fund, run by Anthony Scaramucci, the following is an illustration of their portfolio:

- Within the diversified $3.5bn fund, they began investing in crypto in November 2020. They launched a $500m Bitcoin fund in January 2021. Bitcoin now accounts for 9% of the value of its main vehicle. The Bitcoin fund was already up by 5% and the dedicated fund is worth $700m.

As more and more financial institutions are widely showing interest in cryptocurrencies, a big question gets raised: *What would be the impact if Bitcoin collapsed? How will it impact the financial systems and more importantly the GDP and society?*

Bitcoin sank from $64k in April to $30k in May 2021. Today, Bitcoin is hovering around $18k (as of 18 December 2022). Financial investors take advantage of the heavy volatility to make huge gains. Hedge funds are using algorithm trading to buy Bitcoin when it falls by applying a certain threshold through automatic 'buy' orders. As cryptocurrency is now integrated into the financial mainstream markets, imagine that the price of Bitcoin crashes all the way to zero. Can you feel the fear of a market crash?

There is also a direct link between Bitcoin and alternative currencies with regard to the rise and fall. When the Bitcoin price falls, most of the cryptocurrency market falls. An impact on Bitcoin could be triggered either by the shocks originating within the crypto ecosystem like a technical failure of the blockchain network or hacking on the Bitcoin exchange. There can be more shocks to the Bitcoin market through outside factors like clampdown by regulators or impact throughout the markets including crypto or capital markets in response to the central bank raising interest rates etc.

The following will be the expected outcomes and domino effect if Bitcoin crashes to zero:

- Bitcoin miners get rewarded with a new % of Bitcoin as an incentive for validating the transactions. Miners will have less incentive to carry on, hence they will slow down or stop investing their money to facilitate transaction verification through mining. It will in essence halt the supply of Bitcoin. This will also have a reactive impact whereby investors will most probably dump other alternative cryptocurrencies.
- The worse impact would be on the ones who purchased Bitcoin around the average price of about $37k. This will include most of the institutional investors exposed to cryptocurrencies including Hedge funds, university endowments, mutual funds and other financial investors.
- Bitcoin crash would also wipe out private investors in crypto firms such as crypto exchanges, and listed crypto firms on mainstream markets like the Nasdaq exchange.
- Other Payments companies like PayPal, Revolut and VISA would also lose a substantial growing business.
- Companies like Nvidia, a microchip and GPU maker, would also lose substantial business and take a hit on their balance sheet.

The contagious impact could also spread through several channels to other assets including crypto as well as mainstream markets. The following is a list:

Leverage

- 90% of the money invested in Bitcoin is spent on derivatives like 'perpetual swaps – bets on future price fluctuations that never expire'. As most of these transactions are traded on unregulated exchanges (such as FIX and Binance), customers could also borrow more to make bets even bigger. Exchanges would take a hit and swallow big losses on defaulted debt.
- The investors would try to liquidate conventional assets to meet the margin calls in cryptocurrency. They might also give up trying to meet the calls and it will trigger liquidations.
- Regulated exchanges and banks have a lot of faults as they lent dollars to investors who then bought Bitcoin. Some even lent dollars against crypto collateral. In both cases, borrowers will default and might seek to liquidate other conventional assets.

Stablecoins

- It is a cumbersome process to change dollars for Bitcoin. For this reason, cryptocurrency traders use stablecoin, which is pegged to the dollar or euro, to realise gains and reinvest proceeds. Some of the stablecoins are Tether and USDC coins. Investors issues back their stablecoins with piles of assets in money market funds. For instance, Tether has 50% of its assets that were held in commercial paper, 12% in secured loans and 10% in corporate bonds and precious metals at the end of March 2021. They are worth more than $100bn. A cryptocurrency crash could lead to a run on stablecoins, which will force issuers to dump their assets to make redemptions.

Market sentiment

- Cryptocurrency collapse could affect the broader sentiment of the market including crypto as well as mainstream. Low interest rates have led investors to take more risks by investing in stocks and cryptos. A crypto collapse could cause them to cool on other exotic assets.
- Recently, conventional banks have started offering crypto exchange-traded funds and also debit cards that pay customer rewards in Bitcoin. Crypto collapse will also have the potential to cause wider market disruption.
- In summary, leverage, stablecoins and market sentiment are the main channels through which any crypto downturn can happen which in effect causes a market-wide impact.

Crypto fraud

There have been multiple frauds within the cryptocurrency market, but the following is one of the biggest ones to date from a monetary as well as ethical perspective.

It is a real story about a person known as Ruja Ignatova, who is called the Cryptoqueen. She marketed that she had invented a cryptocurrency to rival Bitcoin and persuaded investors to invest billions. The cryptocurrency was called OneCoin. She disappeared one day, and no one knows where she's hiding (as of the time of writing on 16 October 2021).

> *In early June 2016, a 36-year-old businesswoman called Dr Ruja Ignatova walked on stage at Wembley Arena in front of thousands of adoring fans. She was dressed, as usual, in an expensive ballgown, wearing long diamond earrings and bright red lipstick.*
>
> *She told the cheering crowd that OneCoin was on course to become the world's biggest cryptocurrency 'for everyone to make payments everywhere'.* [emphasis added] – BBC News (https://www.bbc.co.uk/news/stories-50435014)

People all over the world were already investing their savings into OneCoin as they were hoping to be part of the revolution and become mega rich.

The conclusion from cryptocurrency enthusiasts was that there was no blockchain behind OneCoin but a mere standard SQL server database and a website as a front end. The rising number on the OneCoin website were meaningless as they were numbers typed into a computer by a OneCoin employee.

Investors were growing more and more concerned by the delaying of the long-promised exchange that would allow OneCoin to be turned into cash. All these worries and concerns were supposed to be clarified at a large gathering of European OneCoin promoters in Lisbon, Portugal in October 2017.

Dr Ignatova did not turn up to the gathering. As per the FBI, she had gone underground 2 weeks after her Lisbon no-show. She boarded a Ryanair flight from Sofia to Athens on 25 October 2017. That was the last time anyone saw or heard from Dr Ignatova.

Figure 4.2 shows the picture of Dr Ignatova.

In summary, Dr Ignatova identified several weak spots in society and especially the digital revolution, whereby enough people are either desperate or greedy enough to take bets on OneCoin to become rich quickly. The most important point was that she took advantage of the timing and contradictory information online about cryptocurrency. She knew by the time lawmakers, police, media and people realise that it was a fraud, she would be gone, along with the money.

As per the BBC News (https://www.bbc.co.uk/news/stories-50435014), apart from the above-mentioned highly visible cryptocurrency fraud, there have

RUJA IGNATOVA

Conspiracy to Commit Wire Fraud; Wire Fraud; Conspiracy to Commit Money Laundering; Conspiracy to Commit Securities Fraud; Securities Fraud

Figure 4.2 Picture of Dr Ignatova. Courtesy of the FBI (https://www.fbi.gov/wanted/topten/ruja-ignatova).

been multiple scams that have ruined people's life by taking all their retirement savings. It is highly unlikely that credit card companies or banks will refund any of the losses as banks have been issuing warnings about fraudulent cryptocurrency trading that is not even regulated by regulators, for instance, in the UK.

There have been multiple incidents around cryptocurrency exchanges in the past. One of them is related to an exchange called Bitconnect. The platform would enable investors to convert their Bitcoin investment into Bitconnect coins that would then be lent out with proposed returns of as much as 120%. There were many accusations surrounding Bitconnect and its involvement in the Ponzi scheme. United States authorities forced the exchange to shut down abruptly making investors lose as much as 96% value of their investment in Bitconnect coin.

There have been other cryptocurrency exchanges that have been hacked costing traders and investors tens of millions of dollars. Some of the incidents are listed below:

- FTX was founded by Sam Bankman-Fried when he was only 28 years old. FTX cryptocurrency exchange was one of the top five Crypto exchanges in the market. It collapsed by early November, 2022 and filed for Chapter 11 bankruptcy protection in the United States on 11 November, 2022 due to liquidity crisis and with unsuccessful attempt to search for bailout funds from rival exchange Binance. FTX valuation of $32 billion wiped out to nothing after the crisis. FTX collapse shook the whole crypto market loosing its trust and confidence.

- Terra blockchain, which includes TerraUSD (UST) and Luna crashed on 9 May 2022. On 7 May, an algorithm stablecoin called TerraUSD (UST), which is supposed to maintain a USD 1 peg, started to go down in value and fell to 35 cents on 9 May. Terra blockchain companion token called Luna also fell from $80 to few cents by 12 May 2022. This has been one of the biggest disasters in the crypto world so far. About $45 billion were wiped out in just a matter of days.
- Mt Gox attack of 2014 is the most infamous cryptocurrency exchange incident. Hackers stole 850,000 Bitcoins which were never recovered.
- Binance crypto exchange has been hacked multiple times and again costing traders and investors tens of millions of dollars.
- In March 2014, the Flexicon crypto exchange was hacked and hackers took away 896 Bitcoins.
- Poloniex exchange was shut down after losing 12% of its total Bitcoin to hackers.
- In February 2020, an Italian cryptocurrency exchange called Altsbit was hacked. They announced that almost all funds were stolen – 6,920 BTC, 23,210 ETH and other cryptocurrencies.
- In November 2019, a South Korean exchange Upbit suffered a massive breach when hackers stole 342,000 ETH (worth $51 million at the time of the hack).
- In November 2019, Vietnam-based cryptocurrency exchange called VinDAX was hacked, and $500,000 worth of cryptocurrency was stolen.
- In July 2019, a Japanese exchange Bitpoint was hacked due to a security breach. Hackers made off with over $30 million worth of cryptocurrency at the time of the hack. 1,225 BTC, 169 ETH, 1,985 BCH, 5,108 LTC, and 28 million XRP were stolen. Bitpoint was able to recover about $2.3 million of the stolen crypto from overseas exchanges.
- In June 2019, a Singapore-based cryptocurrency exchange Bitrue experienced a major hack to its hot wallet. Cryptocurrency worth $5 million was stolen from about 90 Bitrue users.
- In June 2019, a UK and Slovenia-based cryptocurrency exchange called GateHuB suffered from a large hack where hackers made off with $10 million worth of Ripple (23,200,000 XRP). It appears hackers managed to access encrypted secret keys; however, it is still unclear as to how exactly the hackers gained access to users' funds.
- In May 2019, hackers managed to use a phishing scam and malware to hack into Binance and ran off with $40 million worth of Bitcoin (about 7,000 BTC).
- In March 2019, a Singapore-based crypto exchange DragonEx suffered an attack in which hackers made off with $7 million worth of cryptocurrency. The North Korean hacking group Lazarus was responsible. It appears that hackers created a legitimate-looking fake company and convinced DragonEx employees to download malware onto their computers through Telegram and LinkedIn messages.

- In March 2019, a South Korean cryptocurrency exchange was the victim of a suspected insider job. 3 million EOS and 20 million XRP were stolen.
- In February 2019, the Coinbin cryptocurrency exchange (formerly known as Youbit and later rebranded as Coinbin) was hacked. It appears this hack was an insider job. The employee allegedly had access to private keys and was able to transfer funds from multiple accounts. Coinbin filed for bankruptcy and shut down whilst still owing users about $30 million.
- In February 2019, cryptocurrency exchange Coinmama users' data were leaked and shared on the dark web. It was a less conventional hack as rather than stealing money, hackers stole users' personal data (450,000 user emails and passwords) from the exchange. Coinmama informed the users rapidly once they learned that users' data are being leaked on the dark web.
- In January 2019, New Zealand-based crypto exchange called Cryptopia was hacked and hackers stole 1,674 ETH. This was the second hack 15 days after the first one. They are now going through the liquidation process.
- In January 2019, a New Zealand-based crypto exchange called Cryptopia had a security breach. The exact amount stolen in the hack is still unknown.
- In December 2018, the Canadian largest cryptocurrency exchange called QuadrigaCX, owned by Gerald Cotton had a disastrous incident losing 26,350 BTC. Gerald Cotton was the only person who knew the cold wallets belonging to the exchange. In December 2018 Gerald Cotton died whilst on his honeymoon in India. During the investigation, six cold wallets were identified but five of them had emptied around April 2018. No one is really sure or knows what happened and how to track the money; however, investigations are ongoing.
- In October 2018, a small Canadian cryptocurrency exchange called MapleChange was in a debatable hacking incident (whether it was a hack or another scam). All funds worth $5.7 million (or 913 BTC) were withdrawn. As a result, MapleChange announced that it was closing its doors for good (the website was removed, and social media accounts, discord and telegram channels were removed).
- In September 2018, a Japanese exchange called Zaif was hacked with 5,966 BTC. It is unclear as to how hackers stole the funds; however, Zaif did file a criminal case with their local authorities. They lost about $60 million worth of cryptocurrency at that time valuation of BTC.
- In June 2018, a small cryptocurrency exchange called Coinrail was hacked. Hackers stoke 1,927 ETH, 2.6 billion NPXS, 93 million ATX, 831 million dent coins and a large amount of six other tokens. In total, the exchange lost an estimated $40 million.

- In June 2018, a cryptocurrency exchange called Bithumb was hacked. Hackers stole $31 million worth of XRP coins. The North Korean hacking group known as the Lazarus group claimed the hacking. It appears Bithumb exchange promised to pay back its users for any stolen funds.
- In May 2018, Bitcoin Gold cryptocurrency was stolen. This is one of the strange hacks whereby exchanges holding the Bitcoin Gold currency (hard fork of Bitcoin) became victims of a 51% attack, where hackers managed to gain control of more than 50% of the network's computing power. Once they managed to do that, hackers were able to prevent confirmations allowing them to stop payments between users and make changes to the network's blockchain ledger. Once in control of the Bitcoin Gold ledger, hackers put their Bitcoin Gold onto exchanges, traded them for other cryptocurrencies and withdrew the amount after selling the cryptocurrencies.
- In May 2018, a cryptocurrency trading app known as Taylor was hacked. Taylor went through a successful ICO valued at 1.5 million. Hackers managed to gain access to the company device and took control of the password file. Hackers stole all of the Ethereum (about 2,578 ETH) raised in the ICO.
- In April 2018, an Indian cryptocurrency exchange called CoinSecure was hacked. Hackers stole 438 BTC worth $3.5 million. It appeared that this incident was an inside job as the suspect was CoinSecure former Chief Information Officer who was later arrested.
- In February 2018, an Italian cryptocurrency exchange called Bitgrail was hacked. Hackers stole 17 million NANO coins worth $170 million. This incident looked suspicious as people are sceptical as to whether it was a real hack or a scam.
- In January 2018, a leading Japanese cryptocurrency exchange called Coincheck was hacked because of an insecure platform. The hackers managed to spread a virus through email that allowed them to steal private keys. Coincheck did not use smart contracts or multisignatures and also all coins were stored in the same wallet. Hackers stole 523 million NEM coins worth $533 million at the time of the hack. The hack was believed to be carried out by North Korean hackers, and the malware originated from Russian hacking groups. Strangely and luckily, the exchange is still in business and began to offer full services again in November 2018.
- In December 2017, the NiceHash cryptocurrency mining marketplace, which allows miners to rent out their hash rate to others, the payment system was compromised. Hackers stole the contents of users' Bitcoin wallets. About 4,736 BTC were stolen worth about $62 million at the time of the hack. NiceHash managed to return 60% of the stolen funds to its users.

- In December 2017, a small South Korean cryptocurrency exchange called Youbit (formerly known as Yapizon) was hacked. This was another hacking attempt for Youbit. Hackers stole 17% of the exchange's holdings which led to them filing for bankruptcy on the same day.
- In December 2017, the Bithumb cryptocurrency exchange has another hacking incident. Hackers managed to gain access to an employee's personal computer and stole the details of over 30,000 Bithumb users. Bithub users started noticing their account balance being drained post this incident.
- In April 2017, a cryptocurrency exchange known as Yapizon (before they changed its name to Youbit) was hacked. Hackers managed to steal $5 million worth of Bitcoin.
- In August 2016, a Hong Kong-based cryptocurrency exchange Bitfinex was hacked. Hackers made off with about 120,000 BTC.
- In May 2016, the first regulated cryptocurrency GateCoin was hacked. Hackers managed to gain access to user wallets and stole cryptocurrencies (250 BTC and 185,000 ETH) valued at $2 million at the time of the hack. The exchange never recovered.
- In April 2016, cryptocurrency exchange ShapeShift was hacked three times over the course of 1 month. According to ShapeLift CEO Erik Voorhees, a former employee was responsible for all three hacks. ShapeShift was one of the few exchanges that managed to rebuild themselves successfully and is still in action.
- In February 2015, China-based exchange BTER had its cold wallet hacked, leading to a loss of over $1.5 million worth of BTC (7,170 BTC).
- In February 2015, a cryptocurrency exchange called KipCoin was hacked with a loss of 3,000 BTC. The exchange became a victim of the hosting provider. A hosting server providing hosting to a few cryptocurrency exchanges was hacked and hackers managed to gain control of the entire platform by changing passwords internally. It took the exchange 1 month to regain control of the exchange, but hackers still had some presence within the platform.
- In January 2015, the first regulated cryptocurrency exchange in Europe called Bitstamp was compromised and lost 19,000 BTC. Hackers sent a malicious email to Bitstamp employees, and it took only one employee to follow the link leading to compromising the whole exchange. The attack cost the exchange about $5.1 million as per the valuation of BTC at the time of the hack.
- In January 2015, a small incident happened to a cryptocurrency exchange called LocalBitcoins. The attack only cost the exchange 17 BTC, but it was a lesson for the exchange to spend more money on their cyber security. Hackers used the LocalBitcoins live chat to distribute malware.

- In January 2015, a Chinese cryptocurrency exchange known as 796 was hacked by comprising an infrastructure server. Hackers tampered with withdrawal addresses to trick their users. A major shareholder of the exchange had to absorb the loss due to the hacking of 1,000 BTC. Users of the exchange did not have to take an impact.
- In October 2014, a cryptocurrency exchange called MintPal was hacked with a loss of 3,700 BTC. It was a second hack after the hack on July 2014. After the first hack in July 2014, MintPal was purchased by a company called Moolah Ltd. owned by Ryan Kennedy. After a failed relaunch of MintPal, Moolah Ltd. announced that it was closing its doors; however, users would be able to still use MintPal. Users' accounts were locked, and users were able to track funds being removed from their wallets and sold on another platform. Ryan Kennedy was the only one with access to customers' funds and ran away. He was arrested in 2016 for fraud charges and is now in jail. He also faced charges from the UK police for his involvement in the MintPal hack.
- In July 2014, a cryptocurrency exchange called Cryptsy was hacked by hackers stealing 13,000 BTC and 300,000 LTC. A hacker known as Lucky7Coin inserted a Trojan virus into the code of Cryptsy. Paul Vernon, the owner of the exchange, was accused of destroying evidence and stealing Bitcoin himself. The exchange filed for insolvency. Paul Vernon was successfully sued for $8.2 million in a class-action lawsuit.
- In July 2014, a cryptocurrency exchange called MintPal was hacked with a loss of 8 million VRC (Vericoin). The hacker found a vulnerability in the withdrawal system on the exchange and managed to authorise a withdrawal from the Vericoin wallet. The hack resulted in the loss of 30% of all Vericoin coins.
- In March 2014, Mt.Gox came still into the limelight. It appears that when Mt.Gox was originally hacked in 2011, some private keys were also stolen by malicious actors. The hackers gained access to a substantial number of Bitcoin wallets and started emptying them. Due to the flaw in the Mt.Gox systems, the exchange was interpreting these withdrawals as deposits for nearly 2 years. It cost users $45 million and also cost exchange to close. Mt.Gox filed for bankruptcy within a month. The former CEO of Mt.Gox was arrested in 2015 for fraud as it was discovered he had $2 million worth of Bitcoin that had allegedly been stolen in the hack. In November 2017, a Russian national by the name of Alexander Vinnik was arrested by the US authorities for playing a key role in laundering the Bitcoin that has been stolen in the hack.
- In March 2014, a US-based cryptocurrency exchange called Poloniex was hacked, losing 97 BTC. Hackers managed to take advantage of an

incorrect withdrawal code of the exchange. There is still some speculation on the amount of the hack and whether it was a hack or an inside job.

- In November 2013, a Czech Republic-based crypto exchange called BitCash was hacked losing 484 BTC. The hackers gained access to email servers and sent out phishing scam emails, pretending to be BitCash to obtain customer information, which they used to steal funds worth 484 BTC.

- In May 2013, a cryptocurrency exchange called Vicurex was hacked losing about 1,454 BTC (the exchange has not confirmed the amount). Vicurex claimed bankruptcy and froze all withdrawals, leading several former customers to sue the company for withholding their money.

- In September 2012, a US-based cryptocurrency exchange called BitFloor was hacked for 24,000 BTC. The hackers managed to gain access to the exchange servers and found unencrypted backup wallet keys. Once hackers had access to private keys, they simply withdrew the funds worth $250,000 at the time of the hack.

- In May 2012, a cryptocurrency exchange called Bitcoinica was hacked whereby hackers took away 18,457 BTC. Bitcoinica was unlucky as it was a second hacking incident for them after the initial attack 2 months earlier. It appears the original security issues highlighted by the first attack (from the Linode attack) were never effectively dealt with. The exchange site was immediately shut down and the exchange was ultimately closed for good.

- In March 2012, Bitcoinica and Slush cryptocurrency exchange was hacked. They were the victim of security flaws with their hosting provider called Linode. Linode was a web hosting provider and hosted the cryptocurrency exchanges Bitcoinica and Slush. Hackers compromised hosting provider Linode infrastructure and stole 43,000 BTC from Bitcoinica and 3,000 BTC from Slush.

- In June 2011, the MT.Gox cryptocurrency exchange was hacked. It appears to be the beginning of problems for MT.Gox. In this incident, hackers were able to gain access to a computer belonging to an auditor at the cryptocurrency exchange. Hackers were able to change the price of Bitcoin to $0.01, managed to purchase the BTC at the artificially low price and made off a fortune with 2,643 BTC.

- In October 2011, a cryptocurrency exchange called Bitcoin7 was hacked whereby hackers nearly stole 11,000 BTC from the exchange. Hackers from Russia and eastern Europe managed to gain access to Bitcoin7's servers. This gave them access to the exchange's main BTC depository and two backup wallets. Bitcoin7 still exists with an obvious spammy website, so please be aware and stay miles away from them.

To summarise and conclude on cryptocurrency fraud and scams, the following points are worth highlighting:

- Most of the cryptocurrency exchanges were hacked due to inside jobs (employee's fraudulent behaviours)
- The infrastructure hosting the exchanges were lacking appropriate cyber security controls
- The exchange software code had security vulnerabilities
- There were no software and infrastructure audit requirements or the audit policies adherence/compliance were lacking
- Cryptocurrency exchange employees were not appropriately trained for cyber security policies and controls
- The owners of the exchanges were involved in fraudulent activities and scamming customers for their own greed
- There was a lack of regular requirements to assess the physical, infrastructure and application software code security requirements as per the standards
- The end users were not educated enough and wanted to become rich by blindly betting on their money. They were trusting the upcoming coins and exchanges supporting them
- Finally, most of the incidents happened during the years whereby a majority of the exchanges were not regulated by governing financial regulators.

INSIGHTS ON ICOs

ICO stands for initial coin offering. It is like crowdfunding whereby start-ups try to raise funds for developing projects and launch new companies, by the means of 'token sales'. Participants of the ICO receive digital tokens in exchange for invested funds (fiat currencies like USD, GBP etc.). The tokens are provided in the form of a cryptocurrency. It can be already established currencies like Bitcoin, Ether or the ICO will launch its own tokens and distribute them to the ICO participants. ICO is the cheapest and quick channel to raise funds for a project as it is not regulated like IPOs and can avoid huge costs surrounding financial regulators and comply with local laws. ICO is also the best and most popular channel to raise funds for a project from the public and investors directly. The funds raised are utilised to support the development of a project as mentioned in the ICO documentation. The tokens (or coins) are promoted as functional units of currency, once ICO's funding goal is met as defined in the ICO roadmap.

Most ICOs are unregulated and hence can be part of a scam or fraud. However, some of the ICOs like Ethereum have been very successful, so it all depends on the project team and their vision along with their project roadmap. We will go through some insights and pointers that will help you to assess if the ICO is a scam or a real project with a high potential for success.

As the ICOs are unregulated, customers are not protected by the financial regulators in case of fraud. The lack of protection offered to investors of ICO is a cause for concern; hence, regulators are reviewing the ICO rules, and it is a matter of time before they come up with regulations to tighten the rules surrounding ICOs like initial public offering (IPO).

The very first ICO was held by Mastercoin in July 2013. As mentioned within this chapter, Ethereum raised money with a token sale in 2014, raising 3,700 BTC in its first 12 hours. The funds raised for Ethereum were equal to approximately $2.3 million at the time of ICO.

Successful ICOs

In this section, we will walk through the most successful ICOs of all time and then also run through unsuccessful ones whereby investors lost money or the ICO was closed due to it not meeting the minimum token sell.

- **Ethereum (https://ethereum.org/en/):** Ethereum ICO was one of the early pioneers in 2014. The token was listed at around USD 0.31 and it raised about $18m in just 42 days. The current price of Ethereum at the time of writing was 4,681 USD. Ethereum was the only platform that has an inbuilt digital currency called ETH, providing a development platform for decentralised applications and NFTs and also came up with smart contracts.
- **IOTA (https://www.iota.org):** IOTA's ICO was launched in late 2015 and sold about a billion IOTA tokens raising over USD 400k. The initial token price during ICO was $0.63. At the time of writing, the IOTA price was $1.30. IOTA provides a unique offering that provides combined elements of the internet of things (IoT) and blockchain technology to conduct transactions.
- **NEO (https://neo.org):** NEO is a Chinese open-source blockchain project that went through the ICO in October 2015 raising about $550k. NEO went through a second ICO in late 2016 raising $4.5m. At the time of writing, NEO was trading at about $47.50. Neo ICO token was only $0.032. NEO has provided exceptional return on investment (ROI) to many early investors and is therefore considered a successful ICO.
- **Stratis (https://www.stratisplatform.com):** Stratis ICO happened in 2016. Stratis ICO raised around 1,000 Bitcoins valued at around $675k at the time of the ICO. Stratis's initial token (STRAX) price was set to $0.007 and at the time of writing was trading at $2.0. The Stratis platform enables businesses to create, test and deploy customers' blockchain applications without having to set up or maintain their own infrastructure. It is also compatible with multiple programming languages.

- EOS (https://eos.io): EOS ICO happened in 2017. EOS cryptocurrency tokens were sold by a blockchain architecture start-up called Block.one. ICO raised about $185m in just 5 days. The initial token price was $0.925 and climbed to $5 within a few days after release. Over the years since the ICO launch, EOS has gone as high as $22.89.

  EOS claims to be a competitor to the Ethereum network by providing application developers with a comprehensive ecosystem comprising of databases, account permissions, scheduling, authentication and internet application communication tools.

- NXT (https://nxt-token.com/en/accueil-next-token-nxt-english): NXT went through ICO in 2013 at an initial token price of $0.0000168. It was one of the earliest ICO and NXT was one of the most successful ICOs with one token selling for just $0.0000168 and raising about $16,800 worth of Bitcoins at that time. The project used the funds to develop a digital currency platform and also designed its proprietary open-source consensus mechanism. NXT was trading at as high as USD 2.16 around late 2017.

- ARK (https://ark.io): ARK ICO happened in 2016 with an initial token price of $0.04. Ark's goal was to create a decentralised digital currency platform that allows for the quick integration of other cryptocurrencies into its own blockchain. ARK ICO was successful and returned over 35,000% ROI to investors when its token price climbed to about $11.00 in late 2017.

- LISK (https://lisk.com): Lisk ICO happened in mid-2016 with an initial token price of $0.076 and raised about 14,000 Bitcoins worth about $6m at the time. Lisk hit a long-time high of $39.15 providing an ROI of over 19,000% to investors, who purchased tokens at the time of its ICO. Lisk was the first modular blockchain platform enabling developers to create blockchain apps with Javascript and operate these apps on side chains.

- Particl (https://particl.io): Particl ICO was launched in March 2017 with an initial token price of $1.50. It created a ROI of about 3,495%. Particl token went as high as $52.40 around 2018; however, it is trading at $1.65 now. Particl was designed to offer total privacy to its users. It offers cryptocurrency and a decentralised marketplace cantered on anonymous transactions to offer its users total anonymity.

Unsuccessful ICOs including scams and fraud

Although there has been a flux of successful ICOs that has made a difference in the financial and non-financial world, there are also multiple ICOs that have failed to cause distress to society. We will walk through some of the past ICOs as well as coins in this section.

Dead coins

As the name suggests, dead coins are the coins that have been abandoned, used as a scam by fraudsters, the project website is down or has various technical issues such as

- wallet issues
- no social media updates
- no real project development as developers ran out of funding or walked away from the project
- low volume of coins

There are various types of dead coins. Many websites track the dead coins through community assistance. One of the websites is https://www.coinopsy.com/dead-coins/

- **ICO dead coins:** ICO dead coins are the ones raised through ICO. They are high-risk and reward types of coins, whereby you can earn a substantial amount of money if the ICO is successful, as well as if the project behind it, goes live. However, as per the statistics from coinspy (https://www.coinopsy.com/dead-coins/), over 60% of the ICO end up as dead coins, before they are listed on the exchange to enable trading of their coins.
- **Joke dead coins:** Joke coins are types of coins launched as a joke. About 90%–95% of joke coins end up dead so you need to be careful and do your research before investing in joke coins.
- **Scam dead coins:** There are lots of ICO that launched the coins to raise money as a scam. They do not have a real project behind them, and they usually end up as dead coins. You as an investor need to be really careful before investing in these types of ICO.
- **Abandoned dead coins:** Abandoned coins are the ones where the project has halted without any communication or social media update, and the project website is dead. This classification is a default bucket to capture any coins or tokens that do not belong to the other three categories listed above (Figure 4.3).

The following is a list of some of the dead coins listed as a scam. The full list can be searched at https://www.coinopsy.com/dead-coins/

Avoid ICO fraud and investment

As discussed in the above sections, a large portion of the ICOs are either scams or fail due to multiple reasons including failure to raise the minimum amount of investments through coins. We will go through types of past

LIST OF DEAD CRYPTO COINS	search..			S
Name	Summary	Project Start Date	Project End Date	Founder
Bamboo	Abandoned or No Volume	2020	2011	Adam Carlton
Neblio	Scam or Other Issues	2017	2011	Dives Evgenii
bidao	ICO Fail or Short Lived	2011	2011	Unknown
Epifania Owens	Scam or Other Issues	2012	2018	Unknown
Rustyzen	Scam or Other Issues	2011	2014	Unknown
umq	Joke or No Purpose	2011	2011	Unknown
lawyer turkish citizenship by investment	Scam or Other Issues	2011	2011	Unknown
vhl	Scam or Other Issues	2011	2011	Unknown
rocket league car hitboxes	Joke or No Purpose	2011	2011	Unknown
FX Profitude Forex Course Free	Abandoned or No Volume	2011	2011	Unknown

Figure 4.3 List of some dead crypto coins.

scam coins and also recommendations to assist you to avoid falling victim to scams and fraud.

Disappearing with the investors' money

This is one of the classic scam/fraud tricks. As the ICOs are not regulated, you as investors are not protected either by local financial regulators. The ICO developers will wait till the coin offering is at a set market cap and then walk away with the money. In some cases, they get arrested; however, sometimes they are hard to track and even if they are arrested, recovering money becomes very hard.

- **Recommendation:** Always read the whitepaper of the ICO and research the team and the project. The roadmap and project delivery timelines should have some confidence level of success. Always avoid any ICO investment if the team looks shabby, the project roadmap is not clear and there is no transparency on how the money raised will be invested in project delivery.

Pump and Dump the Coin

You must have heard the term *Pump and Dump* in relation to cryptocurrencies. This is the approach of buying a hefty sum of cryptocurrencies by a group of investors at the same time to increase the price and then sell a hefty sum of crypto to decrease the price. This process gets repeated multiple times in a year to fluctuate the price.

In relation to ICO scams, developers of the cryptocurrency influence the prices of the coin by highlighting the issues with the platform or codebase like security flaws/lost coins etc. to push those prices right down and buy in when the prices are rock bottom. They then communicate to social media that the security flaw has been fixed again by inflating the price. They then do a massive sell-off to earn a massive margin. Developers use some of the profit to move on to the next project.

- **Recommendation:** Do not react blindly to fake news or social media messages from the developers of the project. Always do your research before reacting to patriciate into a massive sell-off of the coins, impacting the price to go rock bottom.

Massive Premine

Premining is an act of mining or creation of coins/tokens as part of the ICO to reward the founders, developers and early investors.

Usually, in a standard and normal ICO, the ratio between investors and developers is 80%–20%. For instance, 80%–90% of the tokens are shared with early investors to raise initial money for the project. The founders or developers of the project keep 10%–20% of the tokens/coins. There have been some scam ICOs whereby 80%–90% of the coins are used to push the price of the coin due to limited supply in the market. When the prices reach very high, developers can sell the whole supply of the coin making the coin worthless and ICO fail.

- **Recommendations:** Avoid coins or tokens where development teams have a substantially large portion of the coins.

Scammers/Tricky People

This category is interesting. Developers of the project tend to launch a new version (2.0) of the coin by forking it into two currencies. This can involve moving all the money raised onto an online platform that might not be safe or into the developer's account.

Sometimes, an exchange whereby you are holding the coins can delist the coins from their exchange platform after making an announcement. You need to transfer it to another exchange or into your private wallet else you can lose your coins altogether.

- **Recommendation:**
  - Trade your coin holdings into a different coin till after the new version (2.0) is out and stable, if possible. Always pay attention to the announcements from the project.
  - Always pay attention to the exchange announcement for delisting of the coins and take timely action to avoid losing your crypto, token and coins.

Fake Platform

This is a well-planned scam. The fraudsters make a platform to provide the functionality to deposit and trade your cryptocurrency. They make sure it looks established and legit. One of the best examples of a fake platform is Bitconnect. They were well-established and seemed legit. Bitconnect was put under pressure from regulators to show its trading system and it turned out that they were a Ponzi scheme. Many people ended up losing all the money, and some of them were as high as $100k+ investments.

- **Recommendations:** Always carry out your research before depositing your cryptocurrencies on an online exchange platform. Preferably always make sure that you store your cryptocurrencies on your own local wallet and do not share your private keys with anyone.

Holding User's Private Keys

Many exchanges hold your cryptocurrencies in their wallet. This means your investments are under full control of the exchange as they own the private keys. There have been multiple incidents whereby the exchange gets hacked losing all the cryptocurrencies including yours.

- **Recommendations:** Avoid transferring your crypto assets into an online platform. Always store your crypto offline inside your own wallet, or if you want to use an online wallet, then make sure that it is protected by your private keys and you own the private keys without disclosing them to anyone.

EDUCATIONAL AND CAPABILITY GAP IN BLOCKCHAIN TECHNOLOGY

Although the footprint of blockchain-based projects, ICOs and cryptocurrencies have significantly increased over the last decade, the skill uplift has not been matched to the growth. There is a significant gap in the market for blockchain resources and essentially leaving a gap in appropriately matching skills to support the use cases.

A lot of private training companies and universities have some shape or form of blockchain modules; however, in my opinion, the quality of education (majorly) is not practical enough to suit the businesses. Due to the lack of skills, any company that would like to launch a use case using blockchain, need to spend a lot of money on consulting with blockchain specialists. It can be an expensive business.

Education gap

Blockchain is one of the emerging technologies that has started to disrupt the industry because of its unique decentralisation, transparency, immutability and prospective cost saving benefits. There are other emerging technologies that can be used together to compliment businesses even further. Other technologies are listed below:

- **Artificial intelligence (AI):** 'Artificial intelligence leverages computers and machines to mimic the problem-solving and decision-making capabilities of the human mind'. (https://www.ibm.com/cloud/learn/what-is-artificial-intelligence)
- **Internet of things (IoT):** 'The IoT is the concept of connecting any device (so long as it has an on/off switch) to the Internet and to other connected devices'. (https://www.ibm.com/blogs/internet-of-things/what-is-the-iot/)
- **Serverless computing:** Serverless computing has become possible with the launch of the cloud. It enables developers to build and run applications without worrying about infrastructure (servers, storage etc.) and capacity.
- **Quantum computing:** 'Quantum computing harnesses the phenomena of quantum mechanics to deliver a huge leap forward in computation to solve certain problems'. (https://www.ibm.com/quantum-computing/what-is-quantum-computing/)
- **Biometrics:** 'Biometrics are unique physical characteristics, such as fingerprints, face and eyes, that can be used for automated recognition'. (https://www.dhs.gov/biometrics)
- **Augmented/Virtual reality:** 'Virtual reality is the term used to describe a three-dimensional, computer-generated environment which can be explored and interacted with by a person'. (https://www.vrs.org.uk/virtual-reality/what-is-virtual-reality.html)
- **Robotics:** 'Robotics is the study of robots. Robots are machines that can be used to do jobs. Some robots can do work by themselves. Other robots must always have a person telling them what to do'. (https://www.nasa.gov/audience/forstudents/k-4/stories/nasa-knows/what_is_robotics_k4.html)

Some universities are much ahead of others in terms of providing top-notch education as well as establishing research centres to derive real-life blockchain solutions in collaboration with businesses. There has been a flux of private and university-based courses on blockchain, however, there still needs to be more focus on practical project-based blockchain modules in collaboration with employers. As the demand for blockchain programmers is peaking, the skill market is creating a domino effect of demand and supply for blockchain skills.

Multiple IT companies are now training their employees, with good programming skills, on blockchain privately to create a centre of excellence (CoE) within their organisation.

University courses on blockchain

As blockchain is getting massive popularity, most universities around the globe would like to launch blockchain courses. Usually, the blockchain module becomes part of the bachelor's or master's degree course. Some universities are even launching a dedicated course on blockchain.

The following are some of the reasons behind launching blockchain courses/modules by universities:

- Attract national and international students.
- Make the existing degree courses more attractive by including blockchain modules.
- Assist the industry by producing skilled resources on the blockchain.
- Build innovative culture within the university.
- Produce entrepreneurs.
- Improve the university brand name by attaining patents in blockchain technology.
- Assisting Governments by improving practical and innovative education. This in effect improves employment opportunities for students.
- Collaborate with businesses in producing skilled students with upcoming disruptive technologies like blockchain.

In September 2022, CoinDesk (www.coindesk.com) released a report on top universities for Blockchain courses (Figure 4.4): (https://www.coindesk.com/layer2/2022/09/26/best-universities-for-blockchain-2022/)

- **Sample size:** CoinDesk rated 240 schools internationally.

Training courses from private institutes

There has been an explosion of private training courses, free as well as paid ones, on the blockchain. I will list some of the best free as well as paid courses in this section. In my opinion, the best way to learn blockchain from a technical perspective is to learn, practise and create a proof of concept (POC) or proof of value (POV).

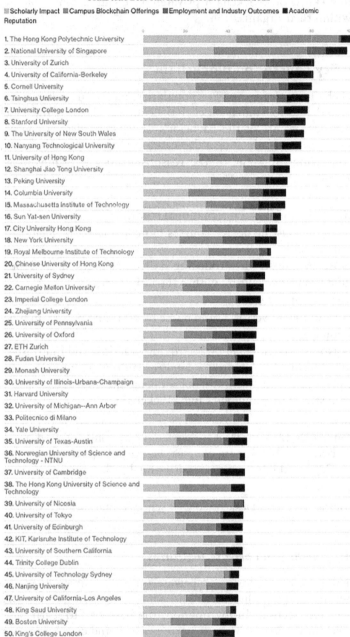

CoinDesk's Best Universities for Blockchain 2022

Scholarly Impact ▪ Campus Blockchain Offerings ▪ Employment and Industry Outcomes ▪ Academic Reputation

1. The Hong Kong Polytechnic University
2. National University of Singapore
3. University of Zurich
4. University of California-Berkeley
5. Cornell University
6. Tsinghua University
7. University College London
8. Stanford University
9. The University of New South Wales
10. Nanyang Technological University
11. University of Hong Kong
12. Shanghai Jiao Tong University
13. Peking University
14. Columbia University
15. Massachusetts Institute of Technology
16. Sun Yat-sen University
17. City University Hong Kong
18. New York University
19. Royal Melbourne Institute of Technology
20. Chinese University of Hong Kong
21. University of Sydney
22. Carnegie Mellon University
23. Imperial College London
24. Zhejiang University
25. University of Pennsylvania
26. University of Oxford
27. ETH Zurich
28. Fudan University
29. Monash University
30. University of Illinois-Urbana-Champaign
31. Harvard University
32. University of Michigan--Ann Arbor
33. Politecnico di Milano
34. Yale University
35. University of Texas-Austin
36. Norwegian University of Science and Technology - NTNU
37. University of Cambridge
38. The Hong Kong University of Science and Technology
39. University of Nicosia
40. University of Tokyo
41. University of Edinburgh
42. KIT, Karlsruhe Institute of Technology
43. University of Southern California
44. Trinity College Dublin
45. University of Technology Sydney
46. Nanjing University
47. University of California-Los Angeles
48. King Saud University
49. Boston University
50. King's College London

CoinDesk   Chart: Daniel Ferraz / CoinDesk

Figure 4.4 Blockchain university rankings from CoinDesk (www.coindesk.com). Reprinted from CoinDesk with permission.

Online and offline resources by universities

There are plenty of free as well as paid online courses from private as well as public companies including universities. Paid courses are individual courses as well as part of the university's main degree syllabus. The following is a list of free and paid blockchain courses provided by educational institutions:

Massachusetts Institute of Technology (MIT)

The MIT is one of the top and most recognised universities in the world. The MIT is highly recognised for research and strong academic programmes and has released multiple numbers of blockchain publications. The following are some of the programmes and courses offered by MIT on the blockchain.

Website: https://dci.mit.edu/courses#mitstudentcourses

Paid courses:

- Blockchain Lab
- Blockchain Ethics: The Impact and Ethics of Cryptocurrency and Blockchain Technology
- Blockchain and Money
- B Digital Frontier: Emerging Blockchain Havens
- Crypto Finance
- Shared Public Ledgers: Cryptocurrencies, Blockchains, and Other Marvels
- Cryptocurrency
- FinTech: Shaping the Financial World

Free courses:

- **Blockchain and money:** This course is for students wishing to explore Blockchain technology's potential – by entrepreneurs and incumbents – to change the world of money and finance. The course begins with a review of Bitcoin and an understanding of the commercial, technical and public policy fundamentals of blockchain technology, distributed ledgers, and smart contracts. The class then continues to current and potential blockchain applications in the financial sector.

   Website: https://ocw.mit.edu/courses/sloan-school-of-management/15-s12-blockchain-and-money-fall-2018/
- **Cryptocurrency engineering and design:** Bitcoin and other cryptographic currencies have gained attention over the years as the systems continue to evolve. This course looks at the design of Bitcoin and other cryptocurrencies and how they function in practice, focusing on cryptography, game theory and network architecture.

   Website: https://ocw.mit.edu/courses/media-arts-and-sciences/mass-s62-cryptocurrency-engineering-and-design-spring-2018/

Cornell University

Cornell University is an Ivy League University known for its high academic standards and the strength of its research. Cornell has plenty of blockchain courses in its portfolio. Cornell University was recognised as the top university in the world for crypto education in 2019.

Paid courses:

- Blockchain Essentials
- Cryptocurrencies and Ledgers
- Cryptography Essentials
- Blockchain Fundamentals
- Applications of Blockchain Technology

Website: https://ecornell.cornell.edu/certificates/technology/

Harvard University

Harvard University is one of the world's most prestigious universities and the oldest higher learning institution in the United States

Paid courses:

- Introduction to Blockchain and Bitcoin

Website: https://pll.harvard.edu/course/introduction-blockchain-and-bitcoin?delta=0

Free courses:

- Blockchain Specialisation (free online course)
- Blockchain: Foundations and Use Cases (free online course)
- Blockchain Foundations for Developers (free online course)
- Blockchain Essentials (free online course)
- Blockchain Fundamentals (free online course)
- Bitcoin and Cryptocurrency Technologies (free online course)

Website: http://tech.seas.harvard.edu/free-blockchain

University of California-Berkley

UC Berkeley is one of the most sought and famous public universities in the world. It also has a high reputation in the blockchain industry and offers multiple educational courses on blockchain technology. UC Berkeley provides many free courses through edX as well.

Free courses:

- Bitcoin and Cryptocurrencies edX
- Blockchain Technology edX
- Blockchain Fundamentals Decal
- Blockchain Developers Decal

Website: https://blockchain.berkeley.edu/courses/

University of Oxford

The University of Oxford is one of the world's leading universities and the oldest among all higher education institutions in the English-speaking world.

Paid courses:

- **Oxford Blockchain Strategy Program:** https://www.sbs.ox.ac.uk/programmes/executive-education/online-programmes/oxford-blockchain-strategy-programme
- **Blockchain for Managers:** https://www.conted.ox.ac.uk/courses/blockchain-for-managers-online
- **Blockchain Software Engineering:** https://www.conted.ox.ac.uk/courses/blockchain-software-engineering

National University of Singapore (NUS)

The NUS is one of the best high-level education universities in Asia, known for its research, diverse areas of study and academic excellence.

Paid courses:

- *Blockchain, Digital Currencies, and Distributed Ledgers Starts from Here*:
  Website: https://ace.nus.edu.sg/event/blockchain-digital-currencies-and-distributed-ledgers-starts-from-here/

University College London (UCL)

UCL is London's leading multidisciplinary university with global reach. UCL has a dedicated Centre for Blockchain Technologies (CBT).

Paid courses:

- UCL Blockchain Rules Online Programme
  Website: http://blockchain.cs.ucl.ac.uk/blockchain-rules-online-programme/

Free courses:

- Introduction to Blockchain and Distributed Ledger Technology (DLT)
  Website: https://www.futurelearn.com/courses/demystifying-blockchain

Royal Melbourne Institute of Technology (RMIT)

The RMIT is a public research university in Melbourne, Australia. The RMIT offers various courses on blockchain technology.

Paid courses:

- **Designing Blockchain Solutions:** https://online.rmit.edu.au/course/sc-designing-blockchain-solutions-blc201
- **Developing Blockchain Strategy:** https://online.rmit.edu.au/course/sc-developing-blockchain-strategy-blc101
- **Graduate Certification in Blockchain Enabled Business:** https://online.rmit.edu.au/course/pg-graduate-certificate-blockchain-enabled-business-gc180

University of Zürich (UZH)

The University of Zürich is a public research university located in the city of Zürich, Switzerland. It is the largest university in Switzerland.

Paid course:

- **Certificate of Advanced Studies (CAS) in Blockchain:** It offers high-quality education tailored for industry leaders: https://www.ifi.uzh.ch/en/studies/cas/Blockchain.html

ETH Zürich

ETH Zürich is a public research university in the city of Zürich, Switzerland.

Paid courses:

- ETH offer Blockchain modules as part of degree courses

Nanyang Technological University

It is a national research university based in Singapore.

Paid courses:

- **Embrace the Era of Blockchain:** https://www.ntu.edu.sg/ntc/programmes/professional-development/skillsfuture-series/blockchain-innovation-strategy-programme
- **Blockchain and Hashgraph:** Technology Development and Business Applications for Industry 4.0
  Website: https://www.ntu.edu.sg/pace/programmes/detail/blockchain-and-hashgraph-technology-development-and-business-applications-for-industry-4.0

Stanford University

It is a private research university in Stanford, California. Stanford is ranked among the most prestigious universities in the world.

Paid courses:

- **Blockchain and Cryptocurrency:** What You Need to Know: https://online.stanford.edu/courses/soe-xcs0001-blockchain-and-cryptocurrency-what-you-need-know
- **Cryptocurrencies and Blockchain Technologies:** https://online.stanford.edu/courses/cs251-cryptocurrencies-and-blockchain-technologies

edX

edX was launched in 2012 by the MIT and Harvard University. In February 2012 Professor Agarwal's launched MIT Circuits and Electronics course on edX.org. The main focus of launching the edX.org education portal was to increase access to high-quality education for everyone, everywhere in the world without the barriers of cost or location. The vision statement of edX was 'As a mission-driven organization, we're relentlessly pursuing our vision of a world where every learner can access education to unlock their potential, without the barriers of cost or location'.

In 2013 edX platform was released as open-source software whereby universities or private training companies can launch their courses on its open platform. Since then, edX has partnered with some of the world's best universities and private teaching institutes.

The following is a list of blockchain courses available on edX.org:

Paid courses with certification:

Website: https://www.edx.org/search?q=blockchain&tab=program

List of certifications:

- **Professional Certificate in Blockchain Fundamentals from UC Berkeley:** https://www.edx.org/professional-certificate/uc-berkeleyx-blockchain-fundamentals?index=product&queryID=65850fc730e82ebba77a7f6fdcc7bcc1&position=1
- **Professional Certificate in Developing Blockchain-Based Identity Applications from The Linux Foundation:** https://www.edx.org/professional-certificate/linuxfoundationx-developing-blockchain-based-identity-applications?index=product&queryID=faed173cd85cf485aeb7451d7dfa455c&position=2
- Professional Certificate in Blockchain for Business from Linux Foundation:
  https://www.edx.org/professional-certificate/linuxfoundationx-blockchain-for-business?index=product&queryID=284164c93c1de6d37a59deda54eece28&position=3

Free courses:

Website: https://www.edx.org/search?q=blockchain&tab=course

List of courses:

- Blockchain Technology from UC Berkeley
- Bitcoin and Cryptocurrencies from UC Berkeley:
- Blockchain: Understanding its Uses and Implications from LinuxFoundationX
- Blockchain and FinTech: Basics, Applications and Limitations from HKUx
- Fintech: Blockchain for Business and Finance from UTAustinX
- Introduction to Hyperledger Blockchain Technologies from LinuxFoundationX
- Hyperledger Besu Essentials: Creating a Private Blockchain Network from LinuxFoundationX
- Becoming a Hyperledger Aries Developer from LinuxFoundationX
- Introduction to Hyperledger Sovereign Identity Blockchain Solution: Indy, Aries & Ursa from LinuxFoundationX
- Hyperledger Sawtooth for Application Developers from LinuxFoundationX

Other free Blockchain courses:

- Blockchain Specialisation from Coursera: https://www.coursera.org/specializations/blockchain
- Introduction to Blockchain Technologies from INSEAD via Coursera: https://www.coursera.org/learn/introduction-blockchain-technologies
- Blockchain Revolution Specialisation from INSEAD via Coursera: https://www.coursera.org/specializations/blockchain-revolution-enterprise
- Blockchain Revolution in Financial Services Specialisation from INSEAD via Coursera: https://www.coursera.org/specializations/blockchain-financial-services
- Transacting on the Blockchain from INSEAD via Coursera: https://www.coursera.org/learn/transacting-blockchain
- Blockchain and Business: Applications and Implications from INSEAD via Coursera: https://www.coursera.org/learn/blockchain-business
- Blockchain Essentials from Cognitive Class: https://cognitiveclass.ai/courses/blockchain-course
- Enterprise Blockchain Fundamentals from 101 Blockchains: https://101blockchains.com/free-blockchain-course/
- Cryptocurrency and Blockchain: *An introduction to Digital Currencies from Wharton* (University of Pennsylvania) via Coursera: https://www.coursera.org/learn/wharton-cryptocurrency-blockchain-introduction-digital-currency
- Blockchain and Cryptocurrency Explained from the University of Michigan via Coursera: https://www.coursera.org/learn/crypto-finance
- The Blockchain from the University of California via Coursera: https://www.coursera.org/learn/uciblockchain
- The Blockchain System from the University of California via Coursera: https://www.coursera.org/learn/blockchain-system
- Blockchain Scalability and its Foundations in Distributed Systems from the University of Sydney via Coursera: https://www.coursera.org/learn/blockchain-scalability
- Smart Contracts from the University of Buffalo via Coursera: https://www.coursera.org/learn/smarter-contracts
- Decentralised Applications (Dapps) from the University of Buffalo via Coursera: https://www.coursera.org/learn/decentralized-apps-on-blockchain

Government support

It is essential to have government support to improve education as well as innovation in the country. There are various ways that the government can engage to grow innovation and education and ultimately support local businesses and society. The following are some of the ways the government can influence education, innovation and skill growth.

- Provide innovation funds to universities to improve research and development facilities
- Create a digital ecosystem so that new upcoming technologies can flourish
- Establish regulatory frameworks to support blockchain technology adoption
- Create a simpler and transparent ecosystem to attract international skilled students and skilled resources
- Establish partnerships with other countries to support disruptive technologies
- Establish partnerships with technology companies and start-ups to further support innovation
- Support entrepreneurship culture by providing funding support for start-ups
- Provide internship funds to small-to-medium-size companies to support university students to get practical experience through internships

Capability gap in business

Throughout this book, we have emphasised the power of blockchain to disrupt the whole business ecosystem. As the blockchain footprint is rapidly increasing in solving and improving business pain points, the demand for blockchain skills is also rapidly shooting high. Businesses are finding it difficult to find interns and professionals with blockchain technology experience.

Businesses have difficulties in multiple dimensions of skillsets; however, there are multiple strategies they can apply to improve the capability of the workforce to support blockchain transformation. The following are some of the measures businesses can use to tackle the ongoing skills and capability issues.

Partnership with universities to influence the syllabus

Businesses can have a collaborative partnership with universities to provide feedback on their existing degree courses and influence making changes to the syllabus. This would be beneficial for universities as their students will have higher chances of getting employment as an intern or through graduation intake. It would also help businesses as they will get focusing educated students with skills in demand.

Businesses can also have partnerships with universities to carry out research on the business problem at hand. In summary, education institutes and business partnership is a win–win situation for universities, businesses and also society.

Employee training programme

Apart from university partnerships to get a pipeline of skilled students, businesses can establish employee training programmes for existing as well as new graduates. This will make sure employees adapt to the culture as well as get trained on upcoming technologies. This is the utmost approach for capability uplift and also to retain the employees. This is also the best approach to win the loyalty of the employees and increase their productivity.

Employee experience

Businesses are finding it difficult to employ experienced employees with practical experience due to the demand and supply scenario. There is a high demand for blockchain skilled resources but the supply of these resources with experience is also lacking.

The solution to this problem is to train existing employees through training programmes. The use of hackathons, internal specialised engineering programmes, sponsored external training, degree programmes and executive education can certainly help as well.

Resource capacity to support

Most businesses still treat information technology (IT) as an expense. In an event of revenue challenges, the tendency is to cut the IT resources and projects as a first opportunity. It causes a domino effect whereby the remaining resources post the cost-cutting still have to support the same business process, application and customers. This creates an extensive workload on the employees with the following impact:

- Long hours of work
- High % of human mistakes
- Impact on work–life balance
- Mental health impact
- Lack of self-learning on upcoming technologies
- Lack of productivity
- Higher turnover of staff
- Lack of innovation
- Higher customer impact through application downtime and complaints

Process gaps

The majority of incumbent businesses are facing challenges from upcoming start-ups. In order to compete with them, they need to go through a massive transformation throughout the whole ecosystem of the business.

The majority of the issues faced by incumbent businesses can be classified under the following categories:

- Legacy manual processes that are complex
- Legacy IT infrastructure supporting the business
- Lack of funding for innovation to exist in parallel to running legacy processes and business models
- Lack of innovative culture
- High reliance on low-cost unskilled resources rather than employing high-cost skilled resources
- Lack of transformation to digitalise the business applications
- Lack of transformation to change the culture to be innovative, transparent and agile
- Lack of funding to support employees to go through training and practical experiences on upcoming technologies

Prospective transformational steps for the incumbent businesses to be competitive can be classified as follows:

- Establish a capability uplift programme to improve the knowledge and skills of all employees.
- Support training programme for all employees across all levels.
- Establish innovation funding to start building new products in parallel to running the existing legacy ones.
- Establish partnership with start-ups and use their technologies or acquire them if it fits the business model.
- Simplicity is the king. Establish a transformation stream to simplify the business and IT processes throughout the organisation.
- Establish HR policies to make sure employees have work–life balance.

Business knowledge gap

In my career of 25 years in consulting, software houses and banks, I have noticed a huge gap between IT and business knowledge and skills. This gap is shrinking in technology companies and start-ups like Google, Instagram and Challenger Banks; however, it is a huge gap and a problem in large companies. In large companies, employees working within a department have no or lack knowledge about the company's vision and mission. This creates a huge gap and can impact the overall strategy of the company to meet its vision and mission.

The following are some of the measures and steps that can be taken to flourish the culture of 'Always for the customer' across the whole organisation:

- Continuous road shows and town halls from senior management to publicise the vision and mission statement.
- Transparency and road show from senior management on company's strategy.
- Mandatory training to make sure each employee understands the company strategy to achieve its mission and vision.
- Business training for all employees with an achievement target under their yearly objectives.
- Setting up key performance target (KPI) objectives for employees to make a positive impact on customers.

Use of blockchain for wrong business problems

Over years, blockchain has become a buzzword to attract CIO-level attention. Sometimes even the inclusion of blockchain within the company's strategy can increase the stock price. This perception of blockchain as a means to solve all business problems can lead to product failures and cost a significant amount of budget.

In this section, we will go through some of the key issues that have led to unsuccessful blockchain use cases.

Key issues surrounding blockchain project failures

Although blockchain brings multiple benefits, if it is used for inappropriate use cases, it can have significant negative impacts like wastage of money, resource time and also competitive disadvantages. The following are some of the high-level issues and challenges that can lead to project failures. *Chapter 5 will go through a framework to assess if the blockchain use case is a good fit for the business problem.*

- Blockchain projects can deliver value when multiple entities are part of the ecosystem to share a single version of the truth without any single entity in control. Blockchain projects fail when there is a single entity in the ecosystem and also they do not deliver any value.
- Blockchain projects also often die due to ecosystem management issues and lack of funding.
- Blockchain projects can thrive value if they can create a consortium with organisations with similar use cases and business interests. Lack of collaboration within the industry can lead to project failure. It is

also essential to start your own ecosystem with trusted parties as members or join an existing consortium after due diligence.

- Blockchain projects or POC fail in the middle of the project due to the appearance of unknowns that were not thought of before starting the project. Some of the surprises are listed below:
  o Incorrect choice of blockchain technology components
  o Incorrect selection of blockchain product
  o Incomplete non-functional requirements like performance, scalability, security requirements etc.
  o Lack of architecture design for the blockchain use case to incorporate data security, data governance and regional compliance requirements
- It is highly recommended to create a detailed project plan with a detailed business and technical design before kicking off the project.
- Blockchain projects can turn out to be very expensive from a finance cost perspective. It can also have high environmental costs like electricity usage due to mining activities. All these factors can have a potential for regulatory, social and political retaliation against the project or a business.
  o Cryptocurrencies' electric consumption is getting noticed by environmental and government agencies now.
  o Cambridge university has created a webpage to calculate Bitcoin Electricity Consumption Index. It gets refreshed every 24 hours (https://ccaf.io/cbeci/index).
  o Bitcoin is the biggest contributor to electricity consumption as it uses a consensus algorithm called 'Proof of Work' and each block takes about 10 minutes to be added to the blockchain by miners, due to the complexity of the puzzle (Figure 4.5).
- There is still a lack of regulatory oversight and standards for blockchain technology including cryptocurrencies. Blockchain projects are subject to high risk due to a lack of regulations and governance from governments. Although regulators are continuously working on setting up legal standards to govern and control blockchain technology use, we are still not at the end of the tunnel yet.
- Blockchain technology usage is still getting mature. There is a lack of practical experience and skills in the market to initiate, design and deliver an end-to-end project for production use. This gap in skills can lead to project failure prematurely.
- There can be a misconception about blockchain technology as a means to an end. For any enterprise-level application or ecosystem to work in a production environment, there are multiple components involved. Blockchain is one of the components to provide an immutable and transparent record within a distributed ledger. This lack of knowledge to produce an end-to-end application using blockchain can lead to a potential delay or failure of the project.

Figure 4.5 Bitcoin electricity consumption index. (The Cambridge Bitcoin Electricity Index from the Cambridge Centre for Alternative Finance. Dated: 19 Nov 2022.) Reprinted from the Cambridge Centre for Alternative Finance with permission.

- Blockchain projects can also fail drastically due to the skill gap in the technical team. Launching a blockchain product without going through a thorough review of the software code (website, exchange, smart contract, mobile app, token, coin, etc.) can lead to a major hack that can demolish the brand, lose money and court cases against the company.
- Companies need to continuously review the external factors that can influence their projects like legal and regulatory frameworks and their implications. Companies also need to assess the future viability of blockchain ecosystems they have selected to participate in. Projects can have a drastic negative impact in the future if external factors are ignored.

SUMMARY

Although there has been a lot of publicity for blockchain footprint and use cases, the POC fails quite frequently due to the various reasons highlighted in this chapter. Businesses and customers need to be extra vigilant before putting their time, resources and money on the blockchain.

There have been multiple cryptocurrencies and ICO scams/failure in the past decade, but there have also been many successful ICOs that has led to some of the major successful ecosystems of blockchain projects like Ethereum. Blockchain projects have been filed due to education and regulatory gaps in society. There have been multiple ICO and crypto scams due to people's greed to become rich overnight and putting their money on the ICO or cryptocurrencies without carrying out due diligence.

As discussed in this chapter, the majority of the crypto exchange hacking was due to a lack of cyber security measures, lack of internal employees' knowledge, infrastructure/application vulnerability and more importantly fraud by project owners or employees.

In this chapter, we have concluded that blockchain is not a hoax. Blockchain is a disrupting form of technology and can assist businesses to have competitive advantages if used appropriately and with due diligence.

In Chapter 5, we will go through a framework to assist in the feasibility of blockchain use cases.

Chapter 5

Blockchain framework

A model to assess the Blockchain for Business use case

As the use of blockchain adoption, within mainstream business use cases, increases, there is a need for a framework to assist the decision makers to select the use of blockchain to solve the real business problems. In this section, we will define a framework with business problems in mind.

BUSINESS PROBLEMS

The first rule of the blockchain journey within our organisation is to find a real business problem statement or pain points impacting the customers. Every CEO and senior management of the company needs to assess the end-to-end business journeys and look out for quantitative and qualitative benefits that can improve customer experience and business models.

The following are some of the current business problems faced by businesses globally.

- **Pandemic concerns:** Who could have imagined a global pandemic like coronavirus disease 2019 (COVID- 19), which has shattered all businesses? Most of the businesses either have closed or have to ask for Government help to survive. Apart from all negative impacts, there have been some good lessons and changes in way of working globally for all businesses. Some of the lessons learnt will be highlighted in this section; however, the following are the key concerns face by businesses due to the unexpected pandemic:
  - **Impact on Brick-and-Mortar businesses:** Businesses that were relying on physical shopping experience suffered a lot. Businesses with online only or hybrid (physical and online) presence flourished during the pandemic.
  - **Supply chain:** Supply chain reliance on one country or supplier had a significant impact. This will also be discussed in resiliency and concentration risks sections.
  - **Way of working:** The pandemic has taught us to trust the employees to deliver. The companies who have assisted employees from working from home or any remote location have reduced the impact of the pandemic on the business. Obviously, there are some businesses

that need employees to be physically present to carry out the work, but they can also change their model to have online presence or make the backoffice processes online to reduce the impact.

- **Demographic change:** There has been changes in the demographics within our society. There have been changes in the society with regards to older population, retired population, growth of women in working class and also the younger generation called millenniums. There are also population changes happening with regards to rich, middle class and poor. A lot of developing counties like India are growing with lot of educated middle class population. All these changes are forcing businesses to change their business models to attract a variety of people towards their products and services.

- **Challenges from FinTech and other start-ups:** Over the few years, there has been a significant growth in upcoming entrepreneurs. This has changed the footprint of incumbent and non-incumbent players within a variety of sectors such as financial, healthcare, supply chain, research, education and technology. Incumbents' players are forced to change their business model or face severe business impact including financial distress and insolvency.

- **Digitalisation:** Digital has become a de facto term within every single business around the globe. Businesses are unable to survive without some sort of digital presence either for customer facing websites/mobile applications or for their back and middle office process digitalisation. The external competitive forces have created a domino effect whereby businesses without digital presence must change their business model to have online presence or have severe financial and brand impact. Many businesses without online presence have either gone out of business or are in financial loss. Some of the examples of external threats from competitors can be easily described from a company like Amazon.

- **Innovation:** Innovation needs to be built into every business operating and nervous systems. There have been multiple examples of incumbents who were mega successful but ignored the external forces of competition. They went out of business. Some of the examples are as follows:
    o Nokia lost most of the business to smart phone introduced by Apple.
    o Kodak lost its business due to digital cameras.
    o Blackberry lost its business to Apple and Samsung innovative smart phones.

Each successful incumbent needs to start adopting innovation ideas in parallel to the existing business model. This will make sure that they are ready to compete when a competitor becomes a threat.

- **Globalisation:** Globalisation has also impacted multiple businesses and is still forcing businesses to change their business model to compete. Businesses in developed countries had to adopt to globalisation due to cheaper labour, cheaper manufactured products and also raw materials available globally. Most of the companies now outsource the skilled labour globally and also make their products globally to reduce the cost to compete. We will go through the multiple business models in Chapter 6.

- **Resiliency:** Resiliency has become an important term in every CEO's priority now. There have been multiple economic, pandemic and financial disasters to awaken the business senior management to think seriously about resiliency of their business models. Resiliency can be defined as how resilient our business is against unexpected incidents like climate change, supply chain issues, resource constraints, natural disasters, technology issues (like data breach, hack, downtime), regulatory changes and political policies, which can impact our global businesses.

- **Concentration risks:** Concentration risk has become a limelight of regulators, controlling financial and non-financial markets in the recent competitive environment. Concentration risk can be described as when our all eggs are in one basket. This kind of risk can have a significant impact on our business and have huge regulatory, financial and non-financial impacts. One of the examples is that we migrate all our applications to one cloud provider. If that cloud provider increases the cost of the services or went out of business, we will have significant financial and brand impacts and can also have possible regulatory fines. That can possibly close down our business.

- **Cost:** Cost factor has been influencing the businesses for decades; however, it has become a more concerned factor in recent years. Fintech, globalisation, digital economy and severe competition are some of the factors that have impacted businesses whereby they have to cut down on the cost to survive. Businesses also have to look at the business processes and model to save cost on unnecessary wastage and use the money on innovation to become more sustainable to competition.

- **Skills:** As the innovation is taking over each legacy process and social interaction, there is a tsunami of skill shortage. Technologies like blockchain, cloud, artificial intelligence (AI), robotics and quantum computing require specialised skills. Although there is a supply of these resources, suitable and experienced resources being available to the industry are lacking. This shortage of resources is uplifting the cost of human resources and increasing the competition due to demand and supply. Skilled resources nowadays look for the company culture, innovation power, senior management capability, brand name and probability of where the company will stand in future (Figure 5.1).

Blockchain technology is still on a journey to become mainstream technology that can replace or improve existing business processes that can ultimately create a value add. However, the following are some of the business concerns on blockchain adoption:

- **Regulatory rules uncertainty:** Obviously, there are firm regulatory standards, policies, rules and governance for existing business processes on data sharing/movement, privacy, competition and taxation to name

Business Problem	Description
Pandemic	Business impact due to Pandemic or An act of God
Demographic Change	Population growth, ratio of young and old population, culture shift, ratio of rich and poor
Fintech and new startups	Competition from new startups and fintechs
Digitalisation	Challenges from digitalization on way of working and shift in customers purchasing habits
Innovation	Challenges from disruptive innovation in technology
Globalisation	Impact from globalisation whereby world is within close reach
Resiliency	Business models need to be changed to incorporate resiliency in each process
Concentration risks	Business process need to have less reliance on single entity. Don't put all your eggs in the same basket
Cost	More pressure on businesses to reduce run cost to carry out BAU (Business as Usual) activities and divert more budget toward change budget for innovation
Skills	Challenges on hiring appropriate skilled workforce

Figure 5.1 Business problems.

a few. However, blockchain regulations globally are still being developed. Due to the sudden growth of blockchain technologies such as blockchain products, Crypto currencies, tokenisation, NFTs (non-fungible token), DeFi (decentralised finance), DAO (decentralised autonomous organisation) and CBDC (Central Bank Digital Currency), a lot of existing financial and non-financial regulations needs to be changed to incorporate the similar governance for new technologies and a new way of doing business. This is causing a lot of regulatory uncertainty and concerns for businesses to adopt blockchain. Businesses need to carefully monitor the evolution of regulatory laws as regulators try to learn and encompass the existing laws for blockchain.

- **Audit/Compliance concerns:** Audit and compliance are also a big concern for businesses when it comes to allocating their budget towards blockchain. Any blockchain project needs to comply with local regularity laws before going live. As the regulatory environment matures, businesses need to adopt and make sure to comply with local and global laws. For instance, blockchain projects need to comply with data protection, Cyber, Anti-money laundering (AML) and know your customer (KYC) laws as per the local and global jurisdiction of the company offices as well as customers.
- **Data protection regulation concerns:** Several data protection laws have been established in the past few years. Some of the big ones are GDPR (General Data Protection Regulation) and CCPA (California Consumer Privacy Act). These laws were put in place to protect customers' PII (Personally Identifiable Information) data.

Blockchain projects need to make sure to comply with these laws as well; however, there are no firm laws which are directly related to blockchain. Businesses need to make sure to comply with these laws even if the blockchain data protection regulation is not clear.

- **Difficulty to establish a blockchain eco-system:** As highlighted before, a successful blockchain project should have multiple parties within a consortium. To get a value from the blockchain project, it is essential to establish an eco-system with multiple parties with similar interests and goals. Businesses often find it difficult to get buy-in from different parties to create a blockchain eco-system with several parties.

- **Trust issues amongst parties:** There are often trust issues between parties due to various reasons like competition and uncertainty on regulations. In the existing financial system, there are strict regulations, rules and standards. All parties within the existing financial system need to comply with the local and global regulations. However, the regulations, standards and rules are still not clear when it comes to blockchain. This is the main reason why companies are reluctant to trust each other within the consortium. This point is also closely related to the above point of 'Difficulty to establish a Blockchain eco-system'. The other aspect of trust issue is amongst end users. End users of the blockchain are still reluctant to trust the technology fully. Some of the main factors of lack of trust can potentially be regulations and blockchain education.

- **Difficulty in establishing a consortium:** Establishing a consortium with parties with similar business interests is essential to establish a successful permissioned blockchain. Although there has been substantial progress on a variety of consortiums in financial and supply chain sectors, there are a very few of them that have gone to mainstream production use case. Companies are finding it difficult to convince other parties to join their consortium. There can be a variety of reasons, but the key ones are intellectual property (IP) concerns, trust issues, financial gain distribution conflicts, and so on.

- **Intellectual property concerns:** IP concerns is a key point that acts as another potential blocker for blockchain adoption. Within a permissioned blockchain, parties within a consortium have concerns surrounding who will own the IP for the innovative project. There is workaround like sharing an IP with all key parties, but lack of trust and percentage of control dither parties to agree on common grounds for IP ownership.

- **Scalability issues:** The key private and hybrid blockchain products still have significant scalability issues against the existing technology used for use cases like payments and data storage. There are many blockchain start-ups in pipelines to solve the scalability issues of blockchain, so we will see multiple solutions in near future.

- **Performance issues:** Blockchain performance issues are also a key point impacting the adoption. The existing use cases in financial and data use cases offer thousands of TPS (transaction per second) performance KPI (key performance indicators); however, blockchain products are still lacking this kind of TPS. Again, there are many start-ups working on blockchain products to solve these problems by using different kinds of consensus mechanisms and also technologies like shading.

- **Blockchain interoperability issues:** There have been multiple products for blockchain recently and continuously growing every day. One common issue amongst all of them is interoperability. For blockchain to be successful, we need common standards and protocols, so any product can talk to each other. One of the great examples of common standards is the Internet, that is, HTTP and HTTPS protocols that enable a browser or API (Application Programming Interface) to talk to each other. There are multiple start-ups that are working on products to provide a middleware layer, so different blockchain products and protocols can understand each other. However, still there is belief that there is a need for a global standard for blockchain for it to talk to any other product seamlessly.

- **Lack of Governance:** Governance is an essential factor for any business. Blockchain projects need a similar robust governance framework for it to accelerate the adoption on mainstream. The governance framework for blockchain should adopt existing risk and control frameworks to make sure that blockchain adoption does not have any hiccups in future from regulators. An established governance framework is also required for permissioned and permissionless blockchain to make sure that all parties within the eco-system are protected and have improved trust from regulators, management and end users. Currently, the lack of formal and effective governance standards is potentially leading to a slow adoption of blockchain.

- **Skill gap:** As discussed in Chapter 4, skill gap is one of the main issues hindering blockchain adoption. There has been inauguration of many emerging technologies over the past few years. Blockchain, AI, robotics, quantum computing and cloud are a few of them. There is a growing demand for experienced blockchain architects, engineers and software developers in the industry to fulfil the growing demand, but the supply is lacking.

- **C-Suite buy-in:** In any business, it is essential to get a buy-in from C-Suite stakeholders in order for any project to get a green light. The board of directors and C-Suite including CIO (Chief Information Officer), CEO (Chief Executive Officer), CTO (Chief Technology Officer), CFO (Chief Finance Officer), CISO (Chief Information Security Officer) and CDO (Chief Data Officer) need to give a go-ahead for our project to start. They control the strategy, finance, governance, regulations, data and so on for the company, and we need to get their buy-in to get funding for the project as well as green light to kick start the project. Currently, it seems to be difficult to get their buy-in due to blockchain education, uncertainty on regulations, uncertainty on how to start the blockchain project and so on. However, as technology and regulations continue to improve, we will see most of the C-Suite showing their interest in blockchain and showcase the value it can create for their businesses (Figure 5.2).

Barriers	Description
Regulatory rules uncertainty	Concerns surrounding Blockchain regulatory laws as they are still maturing
Audit/Compliance concerns	Audit and compliance concerns to comply with local and global jurisdiction for blockchain projects
Data Protection regulations concerns	Concerns on data protection laws compliance for Blockchain projects
Difficulty to establish Blockchain eco-system	Difficulty in getting buy-in from multiple parties to join the common Blockchain eco-system
Trust issues	Trust issues amongst multiple business parties and also end users to adopt Blockchain
Difficulty in establishing consortium	Businesses find it difficult to establish a consortium to create a successful Blockchain eco-system
Intellectual Property concerns	IP ownership is one of the key issues hindering Blockchain adoption
Scalability	Blockchain scalability concerns are acting as one of the Blockchain adoption barrier
Performance	Blockchain performance issues are also one of the concern for Blockchain adoption
Blockchain interoperability	Interoperability amongst different Blockchain is a key issue for Blockchain adoption on mainstream production use
Governance	Lack of governance surrounding Blockchain adoption is slowing Blockchain adoption
Skills gap	Blockchain skills shortage are a concern for Businesses to adoption and support Blockchain
C-Suite buy in	Blockchain adoption is slow due to difficulty in getting senior management buy-in to adopt Blockchain technology

Figure 5.2 Business concerns on blockchain adoption.

QUESTIONNAIRE TO ASSESS MATURITY
OF THE BUSINESS PROCESS

- **What is the nature of our business?** To know a high level of business nature and sector, this question is essential in knowing the industry sector, geography and type of business. For instance, a business can be a hedge fund within the financial sector dealing with capital markets. Another example can be a business providing technology services to the healthcare sector or a start-up developing a healthcare product to automate some of the business processes, required for healthcare records management.
- **Does our business interact with multiple internal and external parties?** Most of the businesses rely on internal departments or child companies and also external vendors to provide the services. For instance, a retail bank under financial industry having a global presence will have multiple subsidiaries. They will also have multiple vendors such as telecom providers, stock exchanges, content delivery service providers, cloud providers, cyber security product vendors and also consulting services, required to provide services to their customers.
- **What percentage of your business uses digital channels?** Due to the ongoing digitalisation journey for a decade, it is important to know what percentage of customer journeys, including front, middle and back offices, has been digitalised or is in the process of digitalisation. This is the key to shape the strategy and recommendation that should be part of the future strategy of the company.
- **What is the ratio of your budget across run and change?** Every company has a set of budgets to run the business-as-usual activities to serve existing customers with seamless experience and good customer service. The run budget is also required to make sure that the business is up and running and secure as required and expected by its customers. This kind of budget is called run budget. Businesses also have a change budget for any transformational activity like moving to cloud, automation of the business processes, adopting innovative technologies and also innovating a product themselves to have an IP rights. This question is essential to know about any gaps within the finance model of the company and provide appropriate recommendations.
- **Do you have a business process map of your 'Important Business Services (IBS)' under the operational resilience framework?** During the past decade, we have experienced multiple frauds, financial disasters and now pandemic. Regulators specially within financial markets

have commenced a process and asked all banks under their jurisdiction to provide a formal documentation to articulate each and every customer's journey for 'Important Business Services'. The specific task is for banks to know the end-to-end business process journey to provide services to end customers. Some of the examples of IBS are 'Access to Cash' or 'Obtain a Mortgage'.

This process was started by UK financial regulators – Bank of England (BOE), Financial Conduct Authority (FCA) and Prudential Regulatory Authority (PRA). It is a matter of time when all other global financial regulators will demand the same from all retail banks under their jurisdictions.

The paper from PRA had the following ask from all the banks in UK under operational resilience of their service offering to the customers:

o *Identify their important business services by considering how disruption to the business services they provide can have impacts beyond their own commercial interests,*

o *Set a tolerance for disruption for each important business service, and*

o *Ensure that they can continue to deliver their important business services and are able to remain within their impact tolerances during severe (or in the case of FMIs, extreme) but plausible scenarios.*

This applies to all other sectors as well due to the fact that all businesses should have the operational resilience strategy in place to minimise the business impact due to severe incidents like cyber-attacks and natural causes like floods, pandemic, earthquakes, tsunamis and so on.

- **Do you have technology components mapping for the 'Important Business Services (IBS)'?** As part of the above operational resilience point, another task of the UK regulator for financial retail banks was to also identity technology components underpinning the IBS. This is to make sure that businesses understand all the technology components required to provide a business service to the customers and what resiliency is in place to avoid or reduce the disruption in case of severe incidents.

  Again, this point also applies to other sectors to make sure that they have a solid operation resiliency strategy.

- **What are the key touchpoints for a single business process?** To shape up the strategy for an organisation, it is essential to know the journey of end-to-end customers from the business process and unpinning technology components, required to fulfil the business journeys.

This question will allow a company to understand how many journeys of end-to-end customers are in existence. It will also provide an opportunity to reduce the number of touchpoints as well as consolidate the reusable journeys and touchpoints across multiple customer journeys, wherever possible.

- **Do you have repetitive processes across multiple business processes?** As part of the questionnaire, the value add would be to recognise the repetitive activities within a single or multiple business processes. This will provide an opportunity for a company to consolidate the processes to reduce the customer journey touchpoints. This will also provide cost savings and improve the customer experience from the services offered.
- **Do you use the standardised process that can be reusable across multiple business processes?** As part of digitalisation journeys, a lot of innovative technologies have been recognised to simplify the product development as well as standardisation of the existing business processes. Technologies and concepts like agile development, microservices and APIs (application programming interfaces) are some of the concepts that can really simplify the products, provide cost savings and benefit from quick to market. In order to flourish the reusability of processes and underpinning information technology (IT) components, the very first steps are to know end-to-end touchpoints of all business processes for a service and then find opportunities to standardise the process to gain advantages of reusable components.
- **Do you have a robust adoption of the risk and control framework?** Many organisations have some sort of risk and control framework or adoption of industry wide standards for risk and controls. This is an essential question to assess the maturity of a company's appetite for risk and what controls are in place to mitigate a variety of risks. Every company under a regulated industry must comply and showcase their risk appetite and what standards/controls are in place to mitigate the risks. One of the industry standards on risk management is as follows:
  - o ISO 31000 Risk Management: https://www.iso.org/iso-31000-risk-management.html
- **Are you regulated by local and global regulators?** Usually most of the businesses are regulated; however, depending on their size and territory, businesses can be under different kinds of regulations. For instance, a small challenger bank like Monzo or Sterling Bank will be regulated by the UK regulator, that is, FCA and PRA. A global bank like HSBC will be regulated by various local regulators due to their presence in various markets around the globe. It is important to know about business footprint globally in order to assess and review their strategy for legal and compliance. It is

also important to check their budget spend on regulatory compliance and reporting to find opportunity for automation and standardisation.

- **Do you have existing projects to automate the business processes?** Every company, regardless of size and location, is undergoing some kind of automation initiative to be more competitive in the market. It is important to assess the level of their journey with automation of business processes and technology. The more mature an organisation is with the automation journey, the more possible competitive opportunity it will have in future.

- **What are the strategic programmes in our organisation to adopt innovative technologies?** Knowledge of strategic programmes and their progress within an organisation is essential to come up with recommendation for improvements. An organisation with a compelling strategy to adopt innovative technologies to improve their customer journeys will have more advantages over their competitors. It is essential not to ignore disrupting technologies like AI, robotics, blockchain, quantum computing and cloud to have a competitive advantage.

- **Does our board and C-Suite stakeholders understand the upcoming innovative technologies like blockchain, artificial intelligence, robotics, IOT (Internet of Things), cloud and quantum computing?** Most of the start-up board of directors and employees of Fintech have a good understanding and even experience of most of the upcoming technologies. The traditional businesses, that is, incumbent players, board of directors and C-Suite stakeholders, are still lacking a basic knowledge with these disrupting technologies. It is essential, without saying, that the board of directors and senior management must have a fair understating of these disrupting technologies to shape up a company's vision and mission.

- **Do we have employees upskills programmes to prepare them for innovative technologies?** It is essential to upskill our employees with upcoming technologies to support our business and be competitive. This is also essential to reduce staff turnover, improve loyalty, improve productivity and also to create an innovative culture within an organisation.

- **What is our strategy towards resiliency and concentration risks?** The strategy of resiliency and concentration risks is one of the most important for an organisation. It has become even more critical in the past few years due to the pandemic, financial disasters, globalisation, cyber-attacks and also political cold wars. Resiliency is a tool to make sure that the company has mitigation plans to avoid or reduce severe incidents and carry on to run the business. Concentration risks means not to put all our eggs in one basket.

For instance, a company must have a resiliency plan to keep the supply chain running by having more than one supplier in different countries for the same product. In the same way, a company must have multiple vendors to provide them services like cloud. They should also make sure to have a defined process to test the end-to-end process and be able to switch to other suppliers when needed in a timely fashion.

- **Who are our direct and indirect competitors?** It is essential for every business to have a clear insight of their direct and indirect competitors. Direct competitors are the ones that offer identical or similar product or services as us. On the other hand, indirect competitors are the ones that offer services or products that are close substitutes as our product/services.
- **What is our strategy towards blockchain adoption?** As one of the disrupting and innovating technologies with a growing footprint across the industry, it is essential to know about the blockchain strategy, if any. This also helps in articulating existing gaps in the strategy and recommend use of blockchain to deliver value addition to the business and customers.
- **What is our data use and storage strategy?** As the digitalisation disrupts all the industries and its footprint is continuously growing, it is essential to know about a company's strategy about data. The company also has to comply with global and local data protection laws, and the problem becomes more complicated as the digitalisation footprint continues to grow.
- **What is our Cyber strategy?** This is in addition to data and storage strategy. Due to the growth of digitalisation, cyber security has become one of the key points even on board and C-suite levels. Regulators have strict laws about cyber security, and especially, financially regulated companies must have a clear and transparent cyber security strategy. It is also essential for the businesses to have significant cyber security capability due to the rise in the global cyber-attacks and data breaches. The role of CDO and CISO has become more important recently due to digitalisation.

All the above questions will provide enough knowledge about a business, the strategy, gaps and pain points to articulate the improvements and shape up a plan to provide a competitive advantage.

ASSESS THE GAPS AND RECOMMENDATIONS

The questionnaire is a vital tool to gather the required primary data from all areas of the company and understand existing pain points. This provides a baseline to formulate the recommendations that can prospectively be part of the strategy of the company. In this section, we will categorise the concerns into appropriate buckets and provide recommendations to overcome the barriers.

Reference: A – Regulations

Regulations surrounding blockchain are one of the main concerns that are slowing its adoption. There are three barriers that are slowing blockchain adoption within the industry.

1. **Regulatory rules uncertainty:**
- **Concerns:** Concerns surrounding blockchain regulatory laws as they are still maturing
- **Recommendations:**
  - As the regulatory laws are changing, businesses need to monitor them carefully
  - A continuous interaction with the appropriate regulators based on our business jurisdictions
  - Contribution and collaboration with regulators on draft regulation papers and making sure to provide appropriate feedback
2. **Audit/Compliance concerns:**
- **Concerns:** Audit and compliance concerns to comply with local and global jurisdiction for blockchain projects
- **Recommendations:**
  - The regulatory domain is still not mature enough for blockchain technology. My recommendation for businesses is to comply with existing audit and compliance laws for the business use cases to be on the safe side.
  - For instance, we must comply with financial, payment and risk regulations if our business case is related to any of the concerned existing regulated use case.
  - By following the above point, businesses will be in a good position when regulators firm up new laws to govern and regulate blockchain use cases.
3. **Data Protection rules concerns:**
- **Concerns:** Concerns on compliance of data protection laws for blockchain projects
- **Recommendations:**
  - Recently due to digitisation, governments around the globe have come up with multiple data protection laws to protect consumer personal data. Some of the notable laws are GDPR and CCPA. These laws were established to make sure that consumers PII are not used improperly and consumers have the right to provide consent before businesses use their personal data.
  - My recommendation for businesses, who are on the journey of adopting blockchain for existing and new use cases, is to follow the data protection laws carefully. Regulators are still learning and in the process of constructing new laws, so it is in businesses interested to adopt the existing data protection laws. Otherwise, it will be a difficult, lengthy and costly process to reverse engineer the production use cases to comply with data protection laws for blockchain use cases.

Reference: B – Collaboration

For a successful blockchain implementation and getting a real value out of its uses cases, it is essential to have multiple parties within the eco-system. The following are some of the businesses concerns related to the collaboration that is indeed essential to gain value.

4. **Difficulty to establish the blockchain eco-system**
- **Concerns:** Difficulty in getting buy-in from multiple parties to join the common blockchain eco-system
- **Recommendations:**
  - One of the requirements to deliver a value for the business to get value from blockchain use cases is to have multiple parties involved.
  - As there are various businesses with different interests involved, there are more chances of tractions with regards to business interests and personalities.
  - Businesses need to collaborate with other parties to reach an agreement on common and agreeable ways of working for blockchain projects.

5. **Trust issues**
- **Concerns:** Trust issues amongst multiple business parties and end users to adopt blockchain
- **Recommendations:**
  - It is always difficult to collaborate with competitors, and with respect to blockchain, it is one of the positive criteria to collaborate with third parties with similar interests to establish an eco-system.
  - It is essential to have a common ground amongst multiple parties and also share the value add for their businesses to make sure that all have common interests in creating a blockchain eco-system.
  - It is also recommended to earn trust amongst parties to have collaborative, transparent and ethical business cases together.

6. **Difficulty in establishing consortium**
- **Concerns:** Businesses find it difficult to establish a consortium to create a successful blockchain eco-system
- **Recommendations:**
  - Blockchain useful business cases require an establishment of consortium with multiple third parties, who agree to common business interests. One of the difficulties business faces is to convince different parties to join the consortium.
  - The recommendation is to collaborate and showcase the shareable benefits for other parties to join the consortium.

- o There are various models that can be implemented to attract the participation in a consortium.
- o **Option 1:**
  - – Either one or multiple parties can start the blockchain eco-system as co-founders and share the cost, risks and rewards.
  - – Founders and/or co-founders define and govern the rules and standards of the blockchain eco-system.
  - – Once the blockchain platform and eco-system is established and in production, they can invite other trusted parties to the consortium and charge the license fees or mutually beneficial cost sharing models.
- o **Option 2:**
  - – An early adopter innovative party can invest a substantial amount of time and money to create a full-blown blockchain as a service (BaaS) platform for a few use cases.
  - – They can then charge the 'pay as you go' fees to interested parties that want to be part of the consortium.
  - – A single entity establishes the rules and standards for the blockchain platform.
  - – A single entity takes a leadership role to invest, own risks and get a full reward including ownership of IPs.

7. **Intellectual property issues**
- **Concerns:** IP ownership is one of the key issues hindering blockchain adoption
- **Recommendations:**
  - o Blockchain is an upcoming innovative technology. As the technology is growing, it brings an unlimited number of opportunities with it.
  - o One of the concerns and difficulties in establishing a consortium with different independent entities is the ownership of IPs.
  - o The party who is the sole founder of the consortium also owns the IP; however, the problem becomes worse when there are a number of co-founders with similar interests in the technology.
  - o Ownership of the IP solely or sharing it with parties who share the risk and rewards needs to be sorted beforehand to have a successful eco-system.

Reference: C – Technology

There are some concerns from businesses towards blockchain technology when it comes to adopting the technology for production use cases. As the blockchain technology is continuing to improve and mature, there are some technological pain points that need to be resolved for a mainstream adoption of the technology.

8. Scalability:
- **Concerns:** Blockchain scalability concerns are acting as one of the blockchain adoption barriers.
- **Recommendations:**
  - One of the concerns for blockchain adoption is for the technology to be scalable like existing use cases such as payments or supply chain.
  - Although there are multiple start-ups working on highly scalable technology and platforms to support scalability, we are not there yet.
  - My recommendation is to monitor the technological trends within blockchain closely.
  - Another recommendation is to start small on existing single customer journeys and be ready to expand whilst the technology is improving.

9. **Performance**
- **Concerns:** Blockchain performance issues are also one of the concerns for blockchain adoption.
- **Recommendations:**
  - As discussed in the previous point about scalability concerns, performance concerns are also key factors that are slowing the blockchain adoption.
  - Again, various start-ups are working on updating the technology to improve the performance.
  - Some of the recommendations and various technological improvements being worked on are listed below:
    - Establish data models to be stored on blockchain DLT (distributed ledger) as well as off-chains or sidechains that can be utilised
    - Use front-end distributed applications, which will be utilising blockchain, as microservices
    - Effective use of messaging queues
    - Use scalable and high-performance storage for blockchain DLT
    - Use scalable and performant infrastructure hosting the blockchain. For instance, use Kubernetes to host microservices that use vertical and horizonal auto-scaling
    - Make use of sharing to store the data

10. **Interoperability**
- **Concerns:** Interoperability amongst different blockchains is a key issue for blockchain adoption on mainstream production use.
- **Recommendations:**
  - There are multiple different blockchains, products and silo companies supporting them.
  - Some of the products are open source or commercial.

o The main problem with the whole footprint of blockchain products is that they cannot talk to each other.

o There are multiple start-ups trying to come up with products to translate the protocols and messages used by different products.

o The recommendation for the community and commercial organisations, who are working on various blockchain products and improvements in the technology, is to set a common standard and a protocol to make the adoption seamless.

o Another recommendation is also to have a common organisation that is community-supported and funded by governments to set up and enforce the standards like ISO (International Organisation for Standardisation), NIST (National Institute of Standards and Technology), IEEE (Institute of Electrical and Electronics Engineers) and W3C (World Wide Web Consortium)

Reference: D – Operating model

To have a successful business model to create value for the business and customers, it is essential to have a correct operating model. Governance is one of the key points within the operating model. We will discuss a full-fledged strategy formulation in Chapter 6, but for this chapter, we will have a deep dive into governance.

11. Governance:
* **Concerns:** Lack of governance surrounding blockchain adoption is slowing blockchain adoption.
* **Recommendations:**
  o With existing use cases for financial and non-financial, there are mature governance frameworks like risks and controls and cyber security frameworks.
  o As blockchain adoption is maturing, we are still lacking a solid and mature governance model. It is also more important than before to have a governance model to continuously monitor the parties within the eco-system and consortium.
  o It is also important to have a mature blockchain governance model to comply with regional regulations.

Reference: E – Education

Human resources and a talented team are the key for a successful business. Every organisation needs to uplift the skill of their resources to adopt innovation and new technologies to thrive the business and to have a competitive advantage over the competitors. There are a couple of pain points and concerns that can slow down the blockchain adoption for businesses.

12. Skill Gap:
   - **Concerns:** Shortage of blockchain skills is a concern for businesses to adopt and support blockchain.
   - **Recommendations:**
     o Blockchain technology is evolving at a fast pace. We are already seeing a huge demand for the blockchain skills like developers, architects, sales, marketing and trainers to fulfil the demand.
     o Some of the recommendations are as follows:
       – Collaborate with the industry and share blockchain developments
       – Collaborate with University to assist in supply of upcoming students as interns
       – Establish blockchain training programmes within the company
       – Establish blockchain experience programmes for existing and new employees
       – Establish Centre of Excellence (CoE) within the company as well as with other third parties with common interests
       – Collaborate with regulators to make sure that there is common leaning across industry to progress on regulations and standardisation
13. C-Suite Buy-in:
   - **Concerns:** Blockchain adoption is slow due to difficulty in getting senior management buy-in to adopt blockchain technology.
   - **Recommendations:**
     o It is essential to get C-Suite buy-in to kick-off any new innovative programmes within a company. Without C-Suite buy-in, projects cannot go ahead.
     o One of the concerns is that C-Suite stakeholders still do not have a high level of confidence with blockchain adoption as compared to other technologies that have been in existence for decades.
     o One recommendation is to educate senior management on the value addition of blockchain in terms of improved security, reduction of risks, lowering operation cost, improved customer experience and improving the brand name of the company to further increase profits (Figure 5.3).

Reference	Category	Barriers	Description
A	Regulations	Regulatory rules uncertainty	Concerns surrounding Blockchain regulatory laws as they are still maturing
		Audit/Compliance concerns	Audit and compliance concerns to comply with local and global jurisdiction for blockchain projects
		Data Protection regulations concerns	Concerns on data protection laws compliance for Blockchain projects
	Collaboration	Difficulty to establish Blockchain eco-system	Difficulty in getting buy-in from multiple parties to join the common Blockchain eco-system
		Trust issues	Trust issues amongst multiple business parties and also end users to adopt Blockchain
B		Difficulty in establishing consortium	Businesses find it difficult to establish a consortium to create a successful Blockchain eco-system
		Intellectual Property concerns	IP ownership is one of the key issues hindering Blockchain adoption
	Technology	Scalability	Blockchain scalability concerns are acting as one of the Blockchain adoption barrier
C		Performance	Blockchain performance issues are also one of the concern for Blockchain adoption
		Blockchain interoperability	Interoperability amongst different Blockchain is a key issue for Blockchain adoption on mainstream production use
D	Operating Model	Governance	Lack of governance surrounding Blockchain adoption is slowing Blockchain adoption
	Education	Skills gap	Blockchain skills shortage are a concern for Businesses to adoption and support Blockchain
E		C-Suite buy in	Blockchain adoption is slow due to difficulty in getting senior management buy-in to adopt Blockchain technology

Figure 5.3 Blockchain adoption barriers and recommendations.

FRAMEWORK TO ASSESS BLOCKCHAIN USE CASE

To have a successful business use case, it is essential to select the right technology to support it. Although blockchain is an innovative and disrupting technology, it is not always beneficial to use it. If blockchain is used for wrong use cases, then an organisation not only will waste resources and money but also can have a negative impact on its brand.

In this section, we will go through a framework and decision tree to assist organisations to determine if blockchain is a good fit for the concerned use case. We will also review and discuss a decision tree to select right type of blockchain and assist in selecting the correct consensus type.

Blockchain technology usage – decision tree

The following framework will assist organisations to ask the right questions and firm up a decision to use blockchain technology for the right purpose. It will provide a clear direction and a decision tree to make a decision on if blockchain is the correct technology to solve complex business problems and fund the use cases effectively.

List of questions

The following are a list of questions to ask business and technology including business and technology product owners, senior management within business and technology, strategists, architects and engineering teams. It is also advisable to establish a partnership with experienced consulting firms, third parties with similar and mutual interests and blockchain product vendors to help in answering the questions accurately.

- **Do we interact with multiple entitles (internal and/or external)?** Blockchain budget can be justified, and business can create value addition if there are multiple entities involved. Blockchain can have a lot of positive impacts if there are multiple third parties involved. Organisations with several internal departments or subsidiaries can also benefit from blockchain use by avoiding manual work and duplication across the workflow.

  Blockchain does not deliver any value if there is only a single entity involved.

- **Do we deal with globally distributed parties?** Blockchain can be useful if our business interacts with globally dispersed parties. It can even be a good use case to implement blockchain if those parties have a lack of trust amongst them.

- **Do we need a consistent data store shared across multiple parties?** One of the functionalities of the blockchain technology is a consistent data store (called distributed ledger=DLT) that can be shared securely across multiple parties. Blockchain technology adoption for similar use cases would bring value addition for the business.

There are other technologies like relational databases that can provide data store functionalities. Business should select other available technologies if the requirement is not to store consistent data and share it with multiple parties.

- **Do we need a tamper-proof log of all transaction to the data store?** Blockchain technology has provided an immutable record of transactions since the initiation of the first record. This makes it easy to review historical records with a confidence that they have not been tampered with. Business should implement blockchain if there is a requirement to have tamper-proof and immutable records of transactions.
- **Do we need to modify or delete the data records?** Blockchain provides a data store with an immutable log of the transactions. Business with requirements to modify or delete the log of the transaction from the data store must not select blockchain as a technology.
- **Do we require transparency and high availability for the shared data across multiple parties?** One of the qualities of blockchain technology is to have multiple copies of the consistent data store (DLT) across multiple parties who are part of the blockchain network. This feature provides in-build functionality to provide transparency as well as high availability of the data store. Businesses should evaluate if they have the similar requirements to provide transparency of the transactions (historical as well as current) and high availability of the data store.
- **Are we within a regulated industry like financial services?** Over the past few years, there have been significant growth on blockchain use cases within financial services. Financial services industry is highly regulated, and businesses spend a huge amount of their budget on legal/compliance and audit activities as per the demand from local/ global regulators. Blockchain can provide significant cost savings and reduction in the risk. Blockchain can also provide real-time audit of transactions for a specific use case.
- **Do we need to carry out an audit for the business transactions?** Any business that is regulated by the regulators needs to provide various types of audit reports to the regulators frequently. Most of the time, businesses hire big consulting and accounting firms who are specialised in the audit activities. The whole process of auditing and compliance takes lot of time, resources and more importantly money. Blockchain can simplify and provide repetitive audit reporting in real time to the regulators. This can be one of the important and cost-effective use cases for any business that needs to comply with regulations and laws.

- Do we have to provide business transactional activity reporting to regulators?

  As part of the regulated companies, especially, financial services need to provide reporting frequently. For instance, investment banks need to provide a daily report to regulators for liquidity and risk. Blockchain can add value by facilitating the reporting in real time and bring substantial cost savings and transparency as well as keep the regulators happy.

- Do we interact with non-trusted third parties?

  Blockchain technology has in-built functionalities to provide transparency, immutable logging of the transactions, historical reporting and more importantly providing all these features with security as the topmost priority.

  Businesses can add value where there are multiple parties within the blockchain eco-system. Blockchain can improve the workflow of the transactions and use cases even if the parties do not trust each other by using the features of consensus algorithms like Proof of Work (PoW), Proof of Stake (PoS) and Proof of Authority (PoA).

- Do we have transactional workflow such as transfer of digital information and/or assets between multiple parties?

  Businesses with a high percentage of digital assets within their business model can benefit from blockchain technology. Blockchain technology offers multiple functionalities to facilitate the completion of digital asset transactions quickly and securely. Blockchain features like tokenisation, coins, NFT, digital identity, audit of all records, immutably and so on are some of the value-addition features.

- Do we have an existing or future strategy for digital transformation?

  There has been a shift in customer choice and taste with respect to online shopping. There has also been a disruption of digitalisation and globalisation. The world has become reachable through the Internet, and online activities have taken a major positive shift. Most of the companies now have an online presence or are shaping up their strategies for digitalisation of their business offerings. The COVID-19 pandemic has also taught all of us the value of Internet. Businesses without any online presence have significantly suffered, and some of them have also gone out of business. Businesses with digital transformation should carry out a feasibility study of blockchain and see if it can create value addition or competitive advantage for them.

- Does our business model involve transferring funds globally?

  Businesses that are involved with transferring the funds globally must bear the commission costs for foreign exchange as well as commission from multiple intermediaries. The whole cross-border payments can also take a substantial amount of time like 2–3 days. Blockchain can provide value addition to the businesses by substantially saving the time for payment transfer as well as cost. For instance, Ripple (XRP) is a start-up that has disrupted cross-border payment market using blockchain. Ripple can transfer money globally with minutes rather than days. There are other blockchain technologies like CBDC that will digitalise fiat currency like GBP and USD soon. One of the other initiatives was the launch of JPM Coin from JP Morgan bank.

- Do we have a requirement to comply with data regulations like GDPR?

  Any business which interacts with and stores customer data needs to comply with various data protection laws regionally as well as globally. One of the data protection laws is GDPR. Anyone who does business in the European Union and stores PII data of European Union citizens needs to comply with the law. There are hefty fines if a business does not comply with GDPR. As per the GDPR, the following is the summary of one of the biggest fines if the business does not comply with the law:

  Under the GDPR, the EU's data protection authorities can impose fines of up to up to €20 million (roughly $20,372,000), or 4% of worldwide turnover for the preceding financial year—whichever is higher.

- Do we have a need to securely share the full transactional history of digital assets with multiple participants?

  Businesses who need to provide transparency and audit of all digital asset's transactions to multiple parties and customers can significantly benefit from blockchain. Blockchain can provide historical transaction records that are trusted, verifiable and immutable to multiple parties in real time. Businesses can substantially provide value addition to customers and multiple third parties in the network by using blockchain.

- Does our strategy require to eliminate or reduce manual efforts for reconciliation and dispute resolution?

  Businesses who deal with multiple third parties and have to frequently deal with reconciliation and dispute resolution activities should review the use of blockchain. Blockchain adoption can assist in reducing manual repetitive efforts with transaction reconciliation and dispute resolution activities.

- Do we store the proof of digital assets ownership and are we accountable for protecting it?

  Any business with substantial footprint on digital assets needs to protect and store the transactional records as well as ownership of the assets. Blockchain can provide value addition by providing secure, transparent, auditable and trusted technology to store the ownership and transactional history of the digital assets (Figures 5.4 and 5.5).

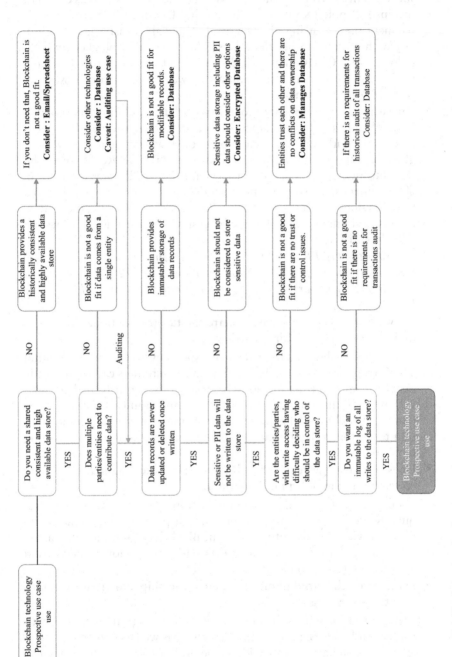

Figure 5.4 Blockchain technology use – decision tree.

Business Problem	Description	Best-fit technology
Shared consistent data store	Business impact due to Pandemic or An act of God	
Immutable records	Population growth, ratio of young and old population, culture shift, ratio of rich and poor	
Multiple	Competition from new startups and fintechs	
Digitalisation	Challenges from digitalization on way of working and shift in customers purchasing habits	
Innovation	Challenges from disruptive innovation in technology	
Globalisation	Impact from globalisation whereby world is within close reach	
Resiliency	Business models need to be changed to incorporate resiliency in each process	
Concentration risks	Business process need to have less reliance on single entity. Don't put all your eggs in the same basket	
Cost	More pressure on businesses to reduce run cost to carry out BAU (Business as Usual) activities and divert more budget toward change budget for innovation	
Skills	Challenges on hiring appropriate skilled workforce	

Figure 5.5 Blockchain technology use – matrix table.

Type of blockchain – selection decision tree

There are various types of blockchain and products available in the market. The whole blockchain product innovation is growing continuously. It is important for businesses to select the right blockchain technology as part of the initialisation of the use cases. In this section, we will go through a set of questions to gather the requirements and provide recommendations as well as a decision tree to assist businesses to select the appropriate Blockchain technology.

List of questions

- **Do we have a business model with multiple globally distributed customers without any trust between them?**

  If our organisation interacts and does business with multiple globally distributed customers who do not trust each other, then blockchain technology could be a good fit.

  A permissionless public blockchain could be a good choice for the use case whereby an organisation business model deals with end customers through the online interface. For instance, Ethereum could be a good blockchain product to be used in this situation due to its footprint on thousands of successful use cases with global distributed use cases like NFT and many more.
- **Does our business model highly rely on digital assets?**

  Businesses with a high proportion of digital assets within their business model should review how blockchain could be used to create business value. Depending on the business model, various types of blockchains could be a good fit.
  - **Distributed end user customers globally:** A public blockchain could be a good technology to establish a use case whereby business needs to provide transparency, security and trusted systems without any central controlling authority.
  - **Group of organisations globally with similar interests and goals:** If a group of organisations interact with each other to conduct business and have a lack of trust between each other, they should establish consortium blockchain or hybrid blockchain.
  - **Organisation with global distributed departments:** An organisation with multiple distributed department or subsidiaries, who do manual and repetitive work for similar interest or use cases must review blockchain technology. A private blockchain (permissioned blockchain) can provide multiple business values for such an organisation by reducing the manual efforts and reuse the common components. It can also provide a consistent data store to be used and shared amongst various departments with transparency and security.

- **Does our business require to store confidential information?**

  Some businesses need to store confidential information of customers. Specially in financial services, the business might be required to store highly critical information like certificate of bonds or investment records and so on. In these scenarios and business models, it would be appropriate to assess the blockchain technology to provide transparency, security and immutable audit of the information as well as digital documents.

  In this scenario, a private or hybrid blockchain (permissioned blockchain) would be the best choice of blockchain technology.

- **Is our business regulated by local and/or global regulators?**

  Any business under regulated industries has multiple requirements to provide various reports and comply with risk, leverage, liquidity and operational resiliency to protect the financial system of the country. Blockchain technology can provide various benefits for these use cases. Companies should assess the use of private blockchain (permissioned) for these kinds of use cases.

- **Do we require to provide audit for transactional activities to regulators?**

  Businesses under regulated industries need to provide various transaction audit reports to regulators locally as well as globally depending on the business. There is a substantial value-addition creation of using blockchain for these frequent and repetitive tasks. A private blockchain with the regulator as one of the entities within the blockchain network can substantially provide transparency and real-time reporting to the regulators. This can also save significant operational cost to the business.

- **Does our business have multiple globally dispersed entities and departments?**

  Multi-national companies have multiple internal entities and inter-departments within each entity. Usually there is a huge amount of duplication and siloed activities within each entity as well as internal departments within each entity. This is a huge burden on the budget and resources, causing a lot of wastage. There are multiple transformational programmes to reduce the wastage of manual activities and automate as much as repetitive tasks as possible.

  Blockchain technology should be reviewed as part of every transformational programme, trying to improve automation and reduce the manual activities.

With these kinds of use cases, a private blockchain could be a good fit.

Type of consensus – consensus type decision tree

Blockchain technology provides various consensus algorithms. This can be useful for various use cases. We have already discussed the types of consensus algorithms in Chapter 1. In this section, we will provide a set of questions and a decision tree to assist the businesses for the selection of appropriate consensus algorithms for their use cases.

List of questions

- **Do our use cases have a significant volume of transactions?**

  There are various use cases that are evaluating blockchain to replace the incumbent workflows. Some of the use cases are dealing with thousands and maybe millions of transactions per minute or even seconds. It is important to select the right consensus algorithm if there is a requirement of a high throughput of transaction validation. For instance, the PoW algorithm usually takes about 10 minutes to add one block to the blockchain. Obviously, the technology is continuously evolving, and the real use cases are driving the evolution. There are other consensuses like PoS and PoA that can speed up the validation of the transactions.

  In essence, businesses need to decide on the appropriate type of consensus before adopting blockchain for mainstream production use cases. Businesses also need to evaluate the blockchain products and what consensus they support as that can be the core factor in selecting a blockchain product for the use case.

- **Does our business use case rely on low latency of the transactions?**

  Latency of the transactions refers to how many transactions can be completed per second. This is one of the important criteria that need to derive the selection of the blockchain consensus as well as blockchain products. Again, the evolution to provide a high level of TPS for blockchain consensus and products is continuously improving. Businesses need to review multiple products and consensuses before deciding to use them for the POC and going live with the use cases.

- **Does our business deal with multiple parties with similar interests and goals?**

  Business which deals with multiple parties and trying to establish an eco-system through blockchain needs to investigate the type of blockchain, product and consensus algorithm. With these types of requirements, PoA and PoS are the most suitable consensus algorithms.

- **Does our business model require a significant number of end users who do not trust each other?**

  Businesses whose business case is to deal with a significant number of end users without any trust beneath them should review the PoW or PoS consensus algorithms.

- **Does our business provide authority over transaction workflow and dispute resolution?**

  In case an organisation has taken a leadership role in founding a blockchain eco-system, they also become accountable for making sure to govern and provide dispute resolution for transactions between multiple entities. This kind of use case requires a thorough analysis and feasibility study of the blockchain product type and consensus they should invest on. Usually in these type of use cases, PoA and PoS consensus algorithms can possibly work well.

Use of smart contract – smart contract decision tree

Smart contract technology is nothing more than an existing set of processes, workflow and rules of the business processes converted into software codes. Ethereum was the first blockchain product that came up with an in-built smart contract technology and its own Crypto currency; however, many more products do offer smart contracts and a way to integrate with an external payment gateway.

List of questions

- Does our business need to involve multiple intermediators to complete a business workflow?

  If our business deals with multiple intermediaries locally or globally as part of a workflow, smart contract might be an appropriate choice. Smart contracts can automate a complex and manual workflow. Businesses can reduce the operational cost by removing intermediators from the workflow. Smart contract can also reduce human errors, improve security, provide transparency and also make the end-to-end workflow quick.
- Does our business involve in a transactional workflow to transfer the assets?

  If our business model mostly deals with online sales that require transferring the digital assets, we might benefit from the use of smart contracts. Smart contract can make the expensive and time-consuming manual process fully automated. We may save a lot of money by automating the business workflow. Smart contracts can also improve security and transparency of digital asset transfer and ownership. Smart contract can reduce the requirements of legal and operational teams, saving a huge amount of operational cost.
- Does our business involve with end-to-end workflow with legal laws of local as well as global regulations?

  Businesses under regulated industries have a huge accountability to provide reporting to regulators. The whole process of regular repetitive reporting takes a lot of time and cost and a huge sum of money. These types of use cases are the best ones for blockchain adoption. Smart contracts can automate the process, reducing any human errors that can even lead to huge fines from regulators. Smart contracts can also provide value addition by making the reporting on-demand to be used by regulators.

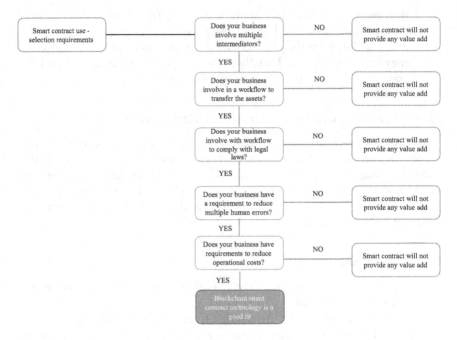

Figure 5.6 Blockchain smart contract use – decision tree.

- **Does our business have a requirement to reduce and/or avoid multiple human errors with digital transactions?**

  As mentioned in the above points, any company with digital business may benefit from the use of smart contracts. If the business needs to deal with a huge volume of digital transactions and the process is manual, there is high probability of human errors. Smart contract can reduce the human errors when appropriately used (Figure 5.6).

CONCLUSION WITH BLOCKCHAIN FIT SCORE

Throughout this chapter, we discussed about blockchain use cases that do not fit the purpose. Organisations can waste their resource time and budget on a wrong use case that could have been successfully implemented using other selections of technologies. Blockchain implementation can be a very expensive exercise. Organisations need to review their business problem and select an appropriate technology to solve it effectively. The framework and decision tree discussed in this chapter can assist organisations in minimising the mistakes, saving them cost and time.

Chapter 6

Blockchain strategies

OVERVIEW

As per the Oxford dictionary, 'Strategy is a plan that is intended to achieve a particular purpose'.

As per the Cambridge dictionary, 'Strategy is a detailed plan for achieving success in situations such as war, politics, business, industry, or sport, or the skill of planning for such situations'.

Every business, regardless of the size, must have some sort of a strategy to achieve its vision and mission. Usually, the strategy execution duration is about 3–5 years. Selecting the right type of strategy can provide competitive advantages to the business and is the key to its success.

LEVELS OF STRATEGIES

There are various levels of strategies. We will go through an overview of them in this section.

The following are the level of strategies:

Corporate strategy

Corporate strategy is the most important and broader level strategy in an organisation. The scope of the corporate strategy is on the whole organisation level. Corporate strategy goals are set on the board level and encompass the following:

- **Establish the vision of the organisation:** Establishing an organisation's vision involves setting up high-level directions for an organisation, its mission to achieve long-term vision and organisation corporate values.
- **Set up long-term objectives to attain competitive advantages for the organisation:** Every organisation needs to compete in the global economy. Corporate strategy needs to set up objectives to attain competitive advantages. Corporate strategy goals usually span across 3–5 years.

DOI: 10.1201/9781003225607-6

- **Allocation of budget:** None of the organisations have an infinite budget to spend on all the priorities. One of the goals of corporate strategy is to allocate budget to attain priorities that have a high confidence level to achieve the vision and mission of the company. This involves allocation of human resources and capital in alignment with aims and objectives of the organisation.
- **Set up priorities for the organisation strategic goals:** One of the goals of the corporate strategy is to set up priorities for the organisation. The priorities should align to the delivery of the strategic goals of the organisation. This involves strategic trade-off of the priorities as part of corporate strategic planning exercise.

Business strategy

Business strategy sets up the strategy for a business unit that is aligned to organisational corporate strategy. Business strategy is aligned to the business unit level to achieve its goals aligned to corporate strategy objectives and ultimately vision of the organisation. Business strategy goals are often set as per their capabilities and market competition with an ultimate goal for them to achieve competitive advantages.

Functional strategy

Functional strategy is the most granular level of strategy as it is aligned to the functional departments of the organisation. Aims and objectives of the functional strategy are derived from business and corporate strategy's vision and mission, with an aim to execute the lower-level plans that can assist in attaining the strategic goals of an organisation. Corporate and business strategy objectives are turned into executable functional targets to attain the vision and mission of the organisation (Figure 6.1).

Types of strategies

In the above section, we have gone through the level of strategies. This section is all about types of strategies.

Michael Porter's generic strategy

Generic strategy

Michael Porter in 1985 in his book *Competitive Advantage: Creating and Sustaining Superior Performance* laid out generic strategies. Michel Porter disrupted the strategy models to create value addition for the organisation through competitive advantages (Figure 6.2).

Features	Level of Strategies		
	Corporate	**Business**	**Functional**
Level	Whole organisation	Business Units	Functional departments
Alignment	Aligned to whole organisation	Aligned to corporate strategy	Aligned to Business and Corporate strategy
Accountability	Board of directors	Business unit heads	Functional unit heads
Deliverables	Organisation vision and mission, cooperate strategic objectives	Business strategic objectives aligned to corporate strategy	Functional strategic objectives aligned to Business and Corporate strategic objectives
Budget allocation	Budget allocation by Board of directors	Budget allocation from corporate strategy budget	Budget allocation from corporate or business strategy budget
Duration for execution	3-5 years	2-5 years	2-5 years

Figure 6.1 Level of strategies.

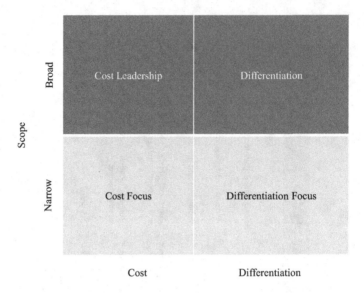

Figure 6.2 Source of competitive advantages.

Porter defined the generic strategies as follows:

1. Cost leadership (no frills)
2. Differentiation (creating uniquely desirable products and services)
3. Focus (offering a specialised service in a niche market)
   o Cost Focus
   o Differentiation Focus

Cost leadership strategy

Porter's cost leadership is all about gaining market share through providing cheaper products to the customers. Within cost leadership strategy, a company can gain market share through the following:

- Reducing the cost of the product whilst charging industry-average prices. The aim is to increase profits by reduction in cost to create a product or service.
- Charging the customer a lower price for a product to increase market share. The aim is to increase market share while still making a reasonable sum of profits.

Recommendation to maintain Cost leadership:

- Continuously review your business model and find new ways to reduce the cost to stay ahead of the competition
- Have access to capital investment to invest in technology to automate workflows
- Review and update your end-to-end supply chain to deliver cost savings
- Find ways to lower cost base through cheap labour, raw materials and facilities (physical building space)

Differentiation strategy

Unlike cost leadership, differentiation strategy involves making products and services different from products offered by your competitors. Under differentiation strategy, a company tries to differentiate their products through unique features, functionality, quality, support, services and establishing a brand image. Companies with a successful differentiation strategy can be rewarded for its unquestioned uniqueness with a premium price.

Recommendations to achieve Differentiation strategy:

- Continuously invest in research and devolvement to innovate
- Invest in high-quality human resources with an innovative mindset
- Effective sales and marketing resources to continuously work on improving the brand name
- Innovate simple and effective but different products and services
- Deliver high-quality products and customer services
- Provide seamless, transparent and effective end-to-end workflow to provide a product or services to the customer.

Focus strategy

Focus strategy is selected when companies have a narrow competitive scope with an industry. These companies have targeted and niche markets where competition is low. They tailor their strategy to stay competitive within a niche market segment. The success of the focus strategy highly depends on the correct selection of the market segments or a group of market segments where the targeted segment buyers have unusual needs, or the production and delivery systems are different from other industry segments.

The focus strategy has two types:

1. **Cost focus:** In this type, a company tries to seek a cost advantage within its target segment of the market.
2. **Differentiation focus:** In this type, a company tries to seek differentiation of its products and services within its target market segment.

Recommendation to achieve Focus strategy:

- First and foremost, an advice is to spend a substantial amount of time before selecting focus strategy. This also depends on the analysis of niche market segments in the industry, where our company can deliver value compared to its competitors.
- Once the market segment has been selected, the company needs to apply similar rules of broader cost versus differentiation strategy, but on a narrow market segment.
- Continue to expand the market segments by analysing the capability against the customer needs in new market segments.

Selection of the strategy

Although there are multiple strategies available, we will select Michael Porter's competitive advantage strategy and apply the various models discussed within his book to assess and apply them on blockchain strategy. We will then formulate an appropriate strategy for a business trying to get into blockchain business or would like to expand on the existing business model.

Strategic models

There are various models to assist in formulating a strategy of the company. We will go through some of the most appropriate ones in this section and try to apply them on blockchain adoption.

Michael Porter's five forces strategy model

Michael Porter's five forces framework was first published in the *Harvard Business Review* in 1979. This model has become de facto to analyse competitiveness in any industry which determines the overall profitability/attractiveness of a firm within that industry. This model looks at the firm in question from the macro-environment (industry-specific) (Figure 6.3).

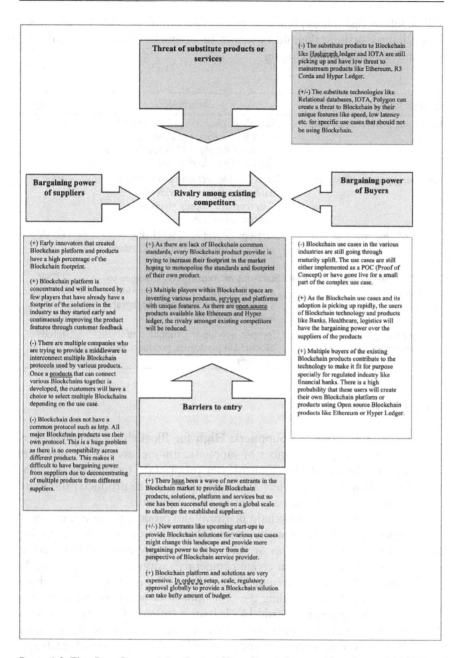

Figure 6.3 The Five Competitive Forces That Shape Strategy [product# R0801E] by Michael Porter published in the January 2008 edition of Harvard Business Review. © 2008. Republished by permission.

The following table explains the stakeholders of this model. We will apply blockchain-specific stakeholders within this model to assist in formulating the strategy later in this chapter

Strategic force	Stakeholders	Rating
Bargaining power of suppliers	Blockchain platform providers and early innovators, e.g. Ethereum, Cardano, Ripple, IBM Blockchain, R3 Corda, Hyper Ledger, etc.	HIGH
Bargaining power of buyers	Buyers of blockchain technology, e.g. banks, healthcare providers, Government, supply chain and logistics providers	HIGH
Threat of new entrants	Start-ups providing blockchain products and services, e.g. Cardano, Polkadot and Chainlink	LOW
Threat of substitute products or services	Start-ups or existing technologies to provide similar or better solutions, e.g. centralised databases, hashgraph ledger and IOTA	LOW
Rivalry among existing competitors	Competition among suppliers of blockchain platforms, products and services	HIGH

Porter's five forces

- **Bargaining power of Suppliers: High for Blockchain Suppliers:** It is determined by the number of suppliers, uniqueness of their products and the degree of their control over proprietary technology or capability. Fewer the suppliers and uniqueness of the products, the more powerful the bargaining power of each supplier is.

  With respect to blockchain platform and product providers, the most important use case is within financial and healthcare sectors. Having said that, there are other sectors such as supply chain, entertainment and so on that can also create competitive advantages by using blockchain. Enterprise Ethereum, Hyperledger, R3 Corda, IBM Blockchain and ConsenSys are leading the development of products and platforms to provide enterprise ready blockchain solutions. The supplier side is concentrated to a few players as they have invested a huge amount over the years on infrastructure and standards and have universal reach and a global client base. It is very difficult for any new entrant to enter or replicate this infrastructure on a global scale. There are new start-ups emerging for blockchain solutions, but it is still difficult to replicate the universal reach, support and/or client base of companies like Hyperledger Fabric, Ethereum, R3 Corda, Consensys and IBM. There is also high power of suppliers as all the cloud providers and software companies that had a massive customer base and establishment have also started to provide Blockchain as a Service (BaaS) solutions. The bargaining power will soon change due to the lack of common standards as every block-chain product is using a different protocol. This makes it impossible for products to communicate with each other. The blockchain industry is eagerly waiting for a solution, which can provide a common protocol or a layer that can translate messages/transactions between different prod-ucts. Start-ups like Polkadot and Blocknet have already come up with a product to provide interoperability between various blockchain protocols and products. This will reduce the bargaining power of suppliers going forward once these products become the mainstream.

- **Bargaining power of buyers: HIGH for Blockchain Buyers:** It is deter-mined by the number of buyers and the importance or size of the buyers to the industry and how easy it is to switch to a competing supplier. The fewer the buyers, the more control they have over suppliers, which ultimately drives prices and profits down for suppliers.

  Blockchain products and platforms are still maturing. There has not been a mainstream blockchain implementation to replace a complex business use case. Most of the implementation so far has been either a POC (proof of concept) or a small part of the complex business use case. As the most of the mature blockchain products are open-source, that is, Ethereum, Hyper Ledger and so on. Buyers have an option to take the source code and create a product themselves, which can fit their purpose. JPMorgan Chase took the Ethereum source code and created a product called Quorum to make it work for financial indus-try. IBM is sponsoring the Hyper Ledger project and using it heavily to provide solutions as IBM Blockchain.

  Buyers also have a high bargaining power as they have a choice to move to another supplier or create their own product depending on how far they have been on the blockchain journey and how much bud-get they can allocate for their own product development.

- **Threat of new entrants: LOW for Blockchain products:** How easy it is for a new entrant to enter the market and provide services?

  There has been a wave of new entrants in the blockchain market to provide blockchain products, platforms and services, but no one has been successful enough on a global scale to challenge the suppliers yet. New entrants like Cardona, Polygon, Polkadot and IOTA might change this landscape and provide more bargaining power to the buyer from the perspective of blockchain product or service provider.

- **Threat of substitutes: Low for Blockchain products:** How easy it is for buyers or suppliers to switch to a similar substitute, which is cheaper and of similar quality?

  There have been multiple blockchain products, but the problem is that they use different protocols. Once buyers select a product and go through adoption for their business use cases, it will not be easy for them to switch to another product. Blockchain implementation is also very expensive, so it would be waste of a lot of money and resource time to switch the solution to another product/platform.

Successful products like Ethereum, Hyper ledger, R3 Corda, Consensys Quorum and IBM Blockchain have established themselves on a global scale, so it would be difficult for new entrants to significantly challenge them. However, there are many start-ups providing a product and platform utilising the open-source products like Ethereum and Hyper ledger. These entrants in the future might create a challenge to the established blockchain solution providers due to their unique features, simplicity, low cost and so on.

Also, once a common protocol and framework to provide interoperability between different blockchain products has been adopted in production/mainstream use cases, it would be easy for companies to use multiple products as per their use cases. This would make it easier for buyers to switch to a similar substitute easily.

- **Rivalry among existing competitors: High for Blockchain products:** How many competitors are in the market with similar capabilities? Too many competitors with similar products can provide bargaining power and switching capabilities to the buyers and suppliers. The opposite is true if there is a player with unique capability that is difficult to replicate. An industry is attractive and profitable if there are few strong suppliers and less substitutes and it is difficult or expensive for new players to enter the market.

As there is a lack of blockchain common standards, every blockchain product provider is trying to increase the footprint in the market hoping to monopolise the standards and footprint of their own product. For instance, R3 Corda is increasing the footprint in financial and other markets to establish themselves. IBM Blockchain and ConsenSys are also increasing their customer base to win more business. In summary, there is heavy competition and rivalry between a small number of large-scale blockchain products and solution providers. Blockchain is still going through a maturity journey for mainstream use cases. As the blockchain interoperability improves through common protocols, frameworks and standards, there will be more choices to the buyers and suppliers. This will reduce the rivalry amongst existing competitors.

Multiple new entrants are inventing products and services based on open-source products. They are differentiating themselves through unique features, simplicity and interoperability. This will significantly reduce the rivalry between existing competitors as there will be a variety of products for niche use cases.

Summary

As mentioned before, there has not been a single successful player yet, who can convince customers to adopt their blockchain product. There are high numbers of competitors fighting for a share of consumers. This rivalry will go on for another few years until a few players convince the customers to adopt to their products by producing common standards and simple and seamless blockchain product deployment with unique functionalities with a value proposition.

Multinational global consulting firms like IBM, tech companies, banks and new start-ups are coming up with products, and the market is fragmented with a variety of solutions with their own standards, framework and protocols. Blockchain industry is demanding for common standards, framework and interoperability between different products, but until we have someone coming up with a product that acts as middleware to translate the transactions between different products, we have long way to go on the mainstream adoption of blockchain.

I believe that someone like the Government and/or ISO organisation needs to come up with a common standard to be used for blockchain in the same way as HTTP protocol for Internet. The market is fragmented with various solutions with their own standards, frameworks and protocols. In order for blockchain to become interoperable and increase its footprint across different real life use cases, it is a high time that a global standard gets published and adopted by all countries.

PEST: political, economic, social and technological analysis

Overview

PEST stands for political, economic, social and technological analysis. PEST is yet another strategic model to assess and analyse the external factors that influence the company operations to be more competitive in the market. There is another variation of PEST called PESTLE to include legal and environmental factors within this model as well.

PEST model is usually used in conjunction with another famous model called SWOT (strengths, weaknesses, opportunities and threats).

By using these two strategic models, a company can assess the external factors as well as internal factors to be more competitive in the market and be profitable.

What are the areas assessed by PEST model?

There are four areas that can be assessed using PEST model. We will go through each of them in detail in this section. The comprehensive assessment of all these external factors can complement an effective strategic planning and formulation. Strategic planning is a must to formulate a strategy that can position an organisation ahead of its competitors by preparing it to proactively take appropriate actions to compete in the market.

- **Political:** The political area of the PEST focuses on regional and international government policies, regulations, laws, taxation and also employment policies. Political and regulatory complexity can significantly influence the organisation's strategy.

The political policies can impact the whole organisation's business sectors or part of them. This is one of the important areas to focus on as it can impact the organisation's survival, sustainability and also profitability.

- **Economic:** As the name suggests, the economic area of the PEST focuses on the economical factors like interest rates of the central banks (like Bank of England or Federal Reserve), exchange rate of the currency against others (e.g. GBP to USD), economic growth (GDP), inflation and recession.
- **Social:** The social factors within PEST model analysis can include anything within social areas. It may include demographic and age distribution (Asian with 18–25 years of age etc.), cultural attitudes (religious, vegetarian, behaviours, etc.), workplace (work from home or work from office) and lifestyle trends (healthy or unhealthy lifestyle). This is also one of the most important factors as not understanding social factors can kill the strategy of the organisation.
- **Technological:** The technological components of the PEST model focus on the impact of technological development, disruptions, innovations (artificial intelligence, robotics, Cloud, Internet, blockchain, digital channels) and also government adoption of the technology within multiple sectors. It includes the Government's and organisations' adoption of upcoming disrupting technologies locally and globally. Government spending on the technology research and support to universities is also an influential perspective under technological factors.

What are the additional areas assessed by PESTLE model?

In the above section, we discussed everything about PEST model. The PEST model has various variants, and one of them is called PESTLE. Apart from all the factors covered under PEST model, there are additional two to form PESTLE model. We will discuss the other two factors in this section.

- **Legal:** The legal factors of PESTLE model relate closely to political factors as well. Legal factors include laws related to consumer, trade and copyright. These are tightly related to political decisions made by local and global governments.
- **Environmental:** The environmental factors of the PESTLE model include everything related to environment. This factor has become more significant than ever due to global focus towards global warming and commitment from all countries to contribute towards reduction in global warming. Some of the environmental factors that impact organisations are climate change, pollution, renewable energy, supply of natural resources and more importantly government policies towards net-zero, that is, use of renewable energy, cutting down on pollution and use of recyclable products to ultimately save the planet earth.

Application of PESTLE model to assess Blockchain use case

PESTLE is a powerful model to analyse the organisation internal and external challenges, including how it can achieve competitive advantage. PESTLE model used along with SWOT can be like ice on the cake as it can further provide insights on current and future challenges and also what actions can be taken to overcome the challenges before it is too late.

PESTLE model can be applied to analyse the organisation's internal as well as external strengths and weaknesses and provide insights on how an organisation can improve to capitalise on the market opportunities.

In this section, we will apply PESTLE model on the blockchain use case to assess the organisation capability to compete in the market through internal as well as external capabilities.

- **Political:** Blockchain technology is under scrutiny from governments and can have a big impact due to potential new policies and standards enforced by governments. As the technology is maturing for mainstream use, policies are still under progress. There is also uncertainty as any new law or policy can have direct and indirect impacts on blockchain adoption by organisations.
  - o **Recommendations:**
    - − My recommendation for organisations is to watch the policies for country the businesses exist in. Organisations also need to watch the policies globally where they do business or their customers exist. Usually, regulators always send the draft policies to get feedback from the key organisations in the country to make sure that policies do not impact them in a negative way.
    - − Another recommendation for organisations is to make relationships with regulators and politicians to get insights on the policies and also contribute wherever possible to assist in designing the policies or laws for blockchain.
    - − The blockchain strategy for an organisation should be agile enough to make changes to their business model as soon as new policies are enforced.
    - − Finally, organisations need to assess where they stand and the impact of political factors to their business model before finalising the blockchain strategy and establish the business models. This assessment can provide sufficient insights to decide if launching blockchain business in a certain country would be beneficial in short and long terms.
- **Economic:** Every business gets impacted by economic outlook of the country and market like interest rates, taxation, economic growth, inflation or recession. Blockchain use cases are no exception to economic outlook. The organisation strategy should consider these economical changes, and their business model should have enough liquidity to survive in case of drastic changes in the economic factors. The organisation also needs to diversify their business model to face off the short-term negative impacts.

- o **Recommendations:**
  - – Enough liquidity to face off the short-term challenges
  - – Set up a research team to look out for economic outlook
  - – Hire SMEs (subject matter experts) and/or consulting firms to provide expert advice on regional and global economic outlook
  - – The economic factors provide insights for the country that an organisation wants to start business in. Organisations should use these insights before making a decision to establish a business in a specific country.
  - – Economic factor insights can assist in strategy formulation based on high or low risk. My recommendation is to start a business in a country that has mature economical policies, a stable government, fair taxation policies and a mature legal system.
- • **Social:** Organisations need to carry out substantial research before formulating the blockchain strategy and business models. The research needs to be focussed on countries the organisation wants to establish the business in. Social and cultural factors can impact the organisation's blockchain strategy.
  - o **Recommendations:**
    - – There is a saying known as 'Culture kills Strategy'. I really believe in this statement as organisations cannot enforce the common strategy globally in all countries. The global strategy needs to be slightly changed for regional regions and countries based on the social and cultures factors.
    - – Carry out enough research on social factors in regions before formulating the blockchain strategy. For instance, the way of doing business in Germany might not work in Japan. The strategy needs to be formulated as per country and regional culture, demographics, people age, ethnicity and so on to name a few factors.
    - – Have a global blockchain strategy with local variants of it as well to focus on competing in the local markets with global vision.
- • **Technological:** Technology innovation is evolving at a rapid pace. Organisations must change their business model to adopt the new technologies to serve and retain customers. Organisations who do not want to adopt the new technologies and new channels to serve the customers will be left behind and probably will be overtaken by competitors. We will go through some of the recommendations for organisations with blockchain business cases in this section.
  - o **Recommendations:**
    - – Organisations need to do thorough research on the blockchain products, platform, Government policies, available skills and so on before making a decision.
    - – Blockchain technology adoption can be complex. Organisations need to make sure that the skills are widely available for the chosen blockchain product or platform.
    - – It is essential to assess the adoption of the selected blockchain technology by other parties in the network as well as end customers.

- Blockchain product selection should go through vetting and validation of the company or community supporting it. Organisations need to make sure that the product/platform continues to evolve and be supported.
- **Legal:** It is important to review local and international laws related to blockchain. As policies and laws are still evolving and maturing in the blockchain space, organisations need to keep an eye on the existing/ upcoming policies and laws. They also need to make relationship with appropriate Government agencies, who are working on blockchain policies and also contribute as much as possible to shape up the legal system governing the blockchain eco-system.
  - o **Recommendations:**
    - As part of blockchain strategy formulation, organisations need to make sure to assess local and international laws related to taxation and blockchain.
    - Before establishing blockchain consortium, it is essential to clarify in writing about the intellectual property (IP) rights. Legal contract at the start to clarify the ownership of the IP would avoid any conflicts in the future when the platform or product adoption goes mainstream.
    - Legal factor deep dive would also highlight readiness and challenges for an organisation to be more competitive.
- **Environmental:** Environmental factors have become more important than ever due to a wakeup call on global warming. Organisations need to assess their strategy and business models to make sure that they are contributing towards net-zero to reduce the global warming.

  Organisations who can actively support environmental projects to contribute towards reduction in global warming would have more potential to have competitive advantages over the competitors.
  - o **Recommendations:**
    - Assessment on Government's environmental policies needs to be done as part of the blockchain strategy formulation. Organisations need to make sure that they comply with local and international laws applicable to them. For instance, some countries might not allow blockchain/Bitcoin mining due to the heavy consumption of electricity.
    - The blockchain product should be selected based on its low usage of utilities like electricity.
    - Organisations should assess the usage of utilities and increase the adoption of renewable energy and showcase the contribution towards low carbon footprint (Figure 6.4).

In summary, PESTLE is one of the vital models to carry out a deep dive and assessment for organisation external and internal factors, required to achieve competitive advantages. The next section will discuss another model called SWOT.

Factor	Description	Impact on Blockchain use case
Political	Focuses on regional and international government policies, regulations, laws, taxation and also employment policies.	Can have big impact on Blockchain adoption due to potential new policies and standards enforced by governments.
Economic	Focuses on the economical factors like Interest rates of the central banks, Exchange rate of the currency against others, economic growth (GDP), inflation and recession.	Blockchain use case can get impacted by economic outlook of the country and market like interest rates, taxation, economic growth, inflation, or recession.
Social	Include demographic and age distribution (Asian with 18-25 years of age etc.), Cultural attitudes (religious, vegetarian, behaviours etc.), workplace (work from home or work from office) and lifestyle trends (healthy or unhealthy lifestyle).	Social and cultural factors can impact the organisation's Blockchain strategy.
Technological	Focuses on impact of technological development, disruptions, innovations (Artificial Intelligence, Robotics, Cloud, Internet, Blockchain, Digital channels) and also government adoption of the technology within multiple sectors.	Organisations must change their Blockchain business model to adopt the new technologies to serve and retain customers.
Legal	Relate closely to Political factors as well. Legal factors include laws related to consumer, trade and copyright.	Organisations need to keep an eye on the existing/upcoming policies and laws. They need to adopt the new legislation within Blockchain use case to comply with local/global laws.
Environmental	Includes everything related to environment like climate change, pollution, renewable energy, supply of natural resource	Organisations need to assess their Blockchain strategy and business models to make sure they are contributing toward Net-zero to reduce the global warming. They need to select a suitable Blockchain technology to adhere to environmental laws of the country.

Figure 6.4 PESTLE model on blockchain use cases.

SWOT: strengths, weaknesses, opportunities and threats

Overview

SWOT is a strategic model to assess and analyse a company's strengths, weaknesses, opportunities and threats. Every organisation needs to assess its capabilities to formulate a strategy to be competitive in the market. Using fact- and data-based analysis through SWOT can provide insights to the organisation, including what sectors, business or entity could succeed on what kind of products or services and in what kind of global markets. SWOT analysis involves collection of facts, data and insights from internal employees, investors, external consulting firms and even competitors.

This section will go through the SWOT model.

Areas assessed by SWOT

- **Strengths:** Assessment of an organisation's strengths is an important factor as it highlights its capabilities, uniqueness and niche to differentiate itself from competitors using internal and external data. Some of the examples of the strengths can be a strong brand, loyal customers, a unique product/platform, a strong balance sheet and so on.
- **Weaknesses:** Weaknesses are the factors that can lead to stop or slow down an organisation to perform at its optimum level. It is essential for an organisation to know its weaknesses in the areas, so business can focus on improvement plans to overcome them to remain competitive. Some of the examples of weaknesses can be a weak brand, high turnover of the staff and customers, a weak balance sheet with a high level of debt, high overheads, an inadequate supply chain, lack of resiliency, lack of capital allocation for innovation spend and so on.
- **Opportunities:** Opportunities refer to external factors that can be favourable to the organisation to have competitive advantages. Some of the examples of external opportunities for an organisation are government policy to cut value-added tax, approval of export of products to new markets, cut in corporate tax, launch of major transformation programmes by Government that can use the organisation's products or services and so on.
- **Threats:** Threats refer to external factors that have potential to harm an organisation or have a negative impact. Some of the examples of threats are natural disaster events (drought, flood, earthquake etc.), an increase of corporation taxes, an increase in cost of raw material, a rise in minimum wage for employees, lack of labour supply, issues with supply chain and so on.

Application of SWOT on a company's blockchain use case

Now that we understand the power and importance of SWOT analysis, we will apply the SWOT model on blockchain use cases to assist in formulating the blockchain strategy.

- **Strengths:** It is vital for an organisation to assess their strengths as part of strategy formulation. The strengths factors of an organisation can determine what areas or sectors of the blockchain the business should invest in, based on the uniqueness, products, skills and specialities.
  - o **Recommendations:**
    - An organisation must do an assessment of their strengths. The assessment needs to focus on blockchain skills within the organisation, blockchain products or platforms, uniqueness of the product or platform, any blockchain IP, supply chains, balance sheets, overheads, existing footprint in countries/regions and so on.
    - The assessment of all strengths can provide enough insights to the board and senior management to focus on specific markets, countries, regions and sectors.
    - The assessment can also assist organisations to rule out any initiatives that cannot be implemented or executed properly due to lack of strengths.
    - For example, an organisation with an existing business model to buy/sell art (paintings/modern art). It should be confirmed that they have substantial liquidity in the balance sheet and have the existing client base and skilled people on Ethereum blockchain; they can decide on developing a non-fungible token (NFT) exchange on top of the existing business model to automate the buying/selling of art.
- **Weaknesses:** It is a universal rule to know our weaknesses. This can apply to individuals as well as to organisations. Once the organisation maps out their weaknesses, they can initiate transformational programmes to improve them. The senior management can also make strategic decisions to stop/hold investment on business programmes that might not sustain or have low probability to succeed on and focus on improvement plans to be more competitive in future.
  - o **Recommendations:**
    - Hiring blockchain skilled resources is still difficult as compared to other technologies. If one of the weaknesses is skill shortage within the team for blockchain, then the organisation must create an educational programmes to upskill internal resources on blockchain to support existing customers or prepare to launch a new product/platform/services in a new market.
    - Organisations can hire SMEs externally or use consulting firms to train their internal resources.
    - If the organisation is struggling with investment budget on product development or innovation, they should review their existing processes and supply chain to reduce the overheads through automation and improved productivity.
    - Organisations with a lack of reputation and brand name will struggle to convince the existing and/or new customers to adopt to blockchain-based products/services. They need to work hard to

listen to customers, take their feedback and improve the internal processes, staff and so on to regain the loyalty of the existing customers and improve their brand name.

- **Opportunities:** Organisations need to continuously assess the external factors to look out for opportunities. The assessment of opportunities can help in formulating the strategy to focus on markets and countries for new business. The following are some of the recommendations to use the opportunities as factors to initiate or grow a blockchain-based business model.
  - o **Recommendations:**
    - Launch the blockchain business in the country, which is favourable to blockchain technology from the perspective of Government policies.
    - Organisations should review the taxation laws, central bank governance and acceptance of various blockchain-based products/platforms as part of their blockchain strategy formulation.
    - Some countries are favourable to innovative and disrupting technologies including blockchain. Organisations should use these grants from Government and tax breaks to launch the blockchain products in those countries first.
    - Countries like Singapore, Dubai, UK, USA, Switzerland, Estonia and so on have established legal and central bank systems. These countries are also launching multiple programmes to use blockchain to simplify the transactions and digital journeys across various industries. Organisations in blockchain business should capture these opportunities before it is too late.
- **Threats:** Threats are related to external factors that have potential to impact the organisation business. Threat analysis is crucial for the strategy formulation as it can impact the new/existing business models and can have a negative impact on the organisation's business, brand and profitability.
  - o **Recommendations:**
    - As part of strategy formulation, organisations need to do analysis on external threats including an assessment of targeted country for new business.
    - Assessment of taxation policies and stability would be beneficial in the long term. A weak and volatile political climate can impact the long-term strategy of the organisation.
    - The organisation should target the countries with established and mature legal systems for longevity and stability.
    - Before deciding on the new blockchain business in a specific country, it would be a good practice to analyse the maturity of core infrastructure (electricity, public transportation, internet, etc.), availability of skilled human resources and employment laws as it can have an impact on the business model.
    - The organisation should invest on blockchain use cases in the country which is favourable for new innovative companies and have existing or upcoming policies to grow blockchain adoption (Figure 6.5).

Factor	Description	Impact on Blockchain use case
Strengths	Highlights its capabilities, uniqueness and niche to differentiate itself from competitors, using internal and external data.	The strengths factors of an organisation can determine what areas or sectors of the Blockchain the business should invest in, based on the uniqueness, products, skills and specialities.
Weaknesses	Weaknesses are the factors that can lead to stop or slow down an organisation to perform at its optimum level.	It is important for an organisation to map out their weaknesses as it provides them insight and focus to initiate transformational programmes to improve them. The senior management can also make strategic decisions to stop/hold investment on Blockchain programmes that might not sustain or have low probability to succeed on and focus on improvement plans to be more competitive in future.
Opportunities	Opportunities refers to external factors that can be favourable to the organisation to have competitive advantage.	Organisations need to continuously assess the external factors to look out for opportunities. The assessment of opportunities can help in formulating the Blockchain strategy to focus on markets and countries for new business.
Threats	Threats refers to external factors that have potential to harm an organisation or have a negative impact.	Threats analysis is crucial for the strategy formulation as it can impact the new/existing Blockchain business models and can have negative impact on organisation's business, brand, and profitability.

Figure 6.5 SWOT on blockchain use cases.

Blockchain strategy formulation

Strategy formulation is an art and involves a lot of deep dives and research on various factors as highlighted in this chapter. Once multiple strategic models have been applied to assist in assessing organisation internal and external factors and its position within the market, the next step is to formulate the strategy. In this section, we will define a framework to formulate the strategy for an organisation.

Set up vision and mission

It is essential to set up an organisation's vision and mission as part of strategy formulation. It is also as important to communicate it internally and externally. They define the organisation values, purpose and where it wants to become in future. Without vision/mission and the organisation's strategy, its existence is incomplete and has potential to fail.

Vision

Vision describes the future desired position of an organisation. Vision defines an organisation's purpose, goals and values. For instance, an organisation with a blockchain business model might define its vision as 'To accelerate Blockchain adoption in the world'. The vision of the organisation often does not change as it defines where the organisation would like to reach in the future. The vision statement defines the *why?* for an organisation.

Mission

Mission describes an organisation's business, objectives and approach to reach those goals. Mission defines the actionable objectives and approach to reach them. The mission of the organisation is set up to achieve organisation vision. The mission statement defines *what?* and *how?* for an organisation. For instance, an organisation with a blockchain business model might define its mission as 'Create the sustainable, energy efficient, transparent and secure Blockchain technology products in the world'.

Understand the external environment and our position

As per the insights gathered from multiple strategic models discussed in the above sections of this chapter, we are aware of the importance of the external factors and their impact on the organisation strategy. All the insights collected through Porter's five forces, PESTLE and SWOT models can be used to formulate various strategic objectives and goals. This analysis can also rule out the objectives that might not be successful, without going through some form of transformation to improve the weaknesses of the organisation and improve its competitive advantage. Knowledge of an organisation's external environment and where it stands against the competition prepares an organisation to take actions proactively to be enable it to be more effective and competitive in the market.

To put all these factors on blockchain technology organisation, the following are some of the factors that would be useful whilst formulating the strategy:

- What is the regulatory and legal framework maturity in the targeted country for blockchain technology?
- What are the political policies to support blockchain in the targeted country?
- What is the political stability in the targeted country?
- Are there any favourable policies, laws or countries that should be considered before launching the blockchain business?

Understand the internal environment and our position

As per the SWOT model analysis, an organisation can gain enough insights into their strengths and weaknesses. This enables them to set correct strategies towards improvement plans to improve their weaknesses that can enable them in the long run. The analysis of the internal environment and organisation position against the competitors can also guide them to set the winning strategies, ruling out the strategies that would be make them less competitive.

Articulate long-term objectives and goals

After considering all internal and external factors, an organisation is in a good position to articulate long-term strategic objectives and goals. These become strategic objectives to assist in achieving the mission of the organisation. These strategic objectives get communicated through the top level down across the organisation and turn into actionable short-term programmes and projects to attain the long-term strategic goals.

Strategy execution

Once the strategy has been formulated, the next big task is to go through strategy planning exercise.

Strategy planning

Strategy planning involves getting buy-in from senior stakeholders of the company and agreeing on the strategic objectives and goals. The following are some of the steps that need to be ironed out before turning the strategic objectives and goals into execution modes:

- Present and circulate the strategy to all senior stakeholders and decision makers. This is an important step to make sure that they agree and sponsor the strategic plan as laid out in the strategy.

- Some of the senior stakeholders and decision makers can be
  - C-suite executives, that is, CEO, CIO, COO, CFO, CISO and the Board of Directors
  - Shareholders with a high percentage of the stocks of the company
  - A venture capitalist or Angel investors if they have a stake in the company
- Get sponsorship and approval for the strategic plan to execute the strategy
- Get budget approval to execute the strategy

Communication of the objectives and goals

Once the strategy has been formulated, the strategic plan is signed off and strategic objectives and goals are defined, the next step is to communicate the strategy to all employees spread across departments in multiple regions. Communication of the organisation strategy is critical to make sure that all employees buy into the organisation strategy and become part of the journey to achieve common goals.

The following are high-level steps to establish a successful communication plan for a strategy:

- Set up a marketing plan to communicate the organisation's strategy internally and externally. External communication needs to be concise and on a need-to-know basis (not to disclose everything) to make sure that competitors do not get to know all the details about the organisation's plans.
- Create a digital version of the strategy to make it simple and easy for all employees to understand the vision, mission, objectives and goals of the organisation.
- Set up multiple townhalls and interactive sessions to go through the strategy with all employees globally.
- Create mandatory training for all employees to go through the strategy.
- Make sure to train all senior management about the strategic goals of the organisation.
- Make sure that all objectives of employees are contributing to the strategic goals.

Create strategic and transformational programmes aligned to the strategic plan

To execute the strategy, an organisation needs to set up multiple strategic and transformational programmes. The key factor of all these programmes needs to be alignment with the strategic plan. The following are some of the considerations whilst setting up these major strategic programmes:

- Each programme needs to have a clear outcome that is aligned to the strategic objective
- The budget allocation for the programme should be based on the outcomes and value addition
- A business case for each programme needs to be created and signed off
- The outcome of the programme must have timelines and quantitative objectives that can be captured
- The roles and responsibilities must be clearly defined for the programmes
- The programme will create multiple projects. All these sub-projects aligned to the programme must share the same strategic objective
- The goals and objectives of each programme and project must be understood by all team members and also they should feel part of it
- The feedback channel must be set up to get transparency and quick issue resolution without any bureaucracy

Define the operating model

Once the organisation's strategy has been formulated and signed off by key stakeholders with communication across the organisation, the next step is to establish an operating model. The operating model defines how an organisation creates value for the customers through various interconnected departments/units and processes. The main aim of an effective operating model is to deliver value to the customers by efficiently using the resources. The following are some of the guidelines to design an effective operating model for an organisation in the blockchain business:

- Operating models are aligned to the strategy. It is created by translating the strategy into an execution plan.
- Operating models are designed to run the organisation effectively to achieve strategic objectives as set out in the strategy.
- The operating model is the current state of how the business is run. It is also called the 'AS-IS' state of the organisation operations.
- Once the strategy is fully in the execution mode and various transformational programmes are executed, the goal of changing the organisation to create a future state of the organisation can be met. The future state of the organisation and how it will be run is called 'Target Operating Model' (TOM). TOM is achieved through completion of the strategic objectives. TOM is 'To-Be-State' of the organisation.

Program and milestone governance

Effective programme management must have key deliverables and quantitative and qualitative measurements to make sure that the programme is on track to be delivered as per the target timelines and regular reporting to all stakeholders are provided.

The following are some of the guidelines to execute a successful programme delivering value addition to the business:

- The programme must have an outcome to deliver value. These outcomes must be aligned to the strategy.
- Projects supporting key deliverables of the programme must have a timeline to complete the deliverables, as set out during initiation of the project.
- All deliverables must have a quantitative measure. Usually, all programmes and underlying projects have baseline and deliverable targets. The deliverables are measured through key performance indicators (KPIs).
- All programmes and projects must have completion timelines to deliver an outcome.
- Risks and issues need to be recorded for programmes and projects.
- All risks and issues need to be communicated to appropriate stakeholders.
- The programme and projects beneath it need to be marked with RAG status. RAG is a high-level status of the programme or projects to show the current status as per the highlighted risks and issues, for example, Red, Amber and Green.

Realignment of human resources to strategic programmes

During the strategy execution process, there are multiple transformational programmes, aligned to strategic objectives, that need to be planned and executed. Mostly all these transformational programmes touch human capital directly or indirectly. For an organisation to meet its strategic objectives, it is essential to align human resources to appropriate job roles. Depending on the level of transformation, the existing job roles might change all together, making the resources incapable or unproductive to carry out the new job roles. Some of these resources might be loyal to the company, know culture and also know the people within the organisation. Organisations should try their best to launch training programmes to uplift the skills of these internal resources.

On the other hand, the resources might have right skills, but they might be in the wrong job role. It is best for the management to align the resources to the right job roles as per their skills, interests and their career inspirations.

There might be situations where the job role will not exist due to the change in the business model or process. In this case, the existing resources either need to be assessed to find an appropriate job role as per their skills and capabilities or make the resources redundant.

In this section, we will do a deep dive of steps to realign the internal human resource to the right job roles and also to hire external resources as per the job role requirements (Figure 6.6).

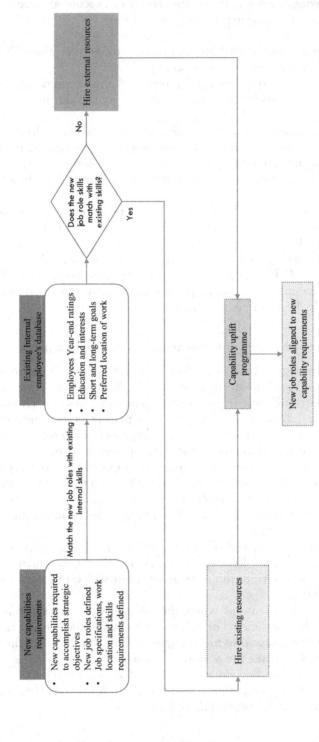

Figure 6.6 Resource alignment (flow diagram to match a job role with the right resource).

Steps to align human resources to the job roles

1. Transformation and target operating model new capability requirements:
   a. Create a database of all new capabilities required to accomplish strategic objectives
   b. Create job roles to deliver the outcomes required by programmes and assign the details for the job roles
   c. Create job specifications; clarify the location of the job role, capability and skills required
2. Existing baseline of job roles and capabilities available:
   a. Create a database of all existing job roles within departments of the organisation globally
   b. Map the job role capability and skill requirements
   c. Acquire employee end year ratings and feedback from the managers
   d. Add employees' education and interests
   e. Add employee short- and long-term career goals
   f. Add employees' preferred location to work from
3. Match the new job roles to existing internally available skills:
   a. Match the internal human resources with newly created job roles based on location preference, skills, resource past performance and career goals
   b. Interview the internal resources again depending on the job roles and department
   c. Create an HR platform for the employees to apply for any newly available job roles and their preference
   d. Establish capability uplift initiatives to uplift the employee's skills which have been selected for new job roles
   e. Capability uplift and Centre of Excellence (CoE) programmes are much wider than resource realignment as part of transformation. These programmes and initiatives are required to continuously uplift the employees to be productive with the adoption of innovative and disrupting technologies.

In the next section, we will go through requirements and benefits of establishing capability uplift and CoE initiatives in the organisation as part of the strategy execution and related transformation programmes.

Capability uplift

As the name stands, capability uplift is a process to improve the capability of an employee to be more productive and fit for the job role. It also improves productivity and retainment of the employee. There are multiple benefits of this initiative for employees and the employer.

Requirements for Capability Uplift

As the whole market is becoming more competitive due to multiple internal and external competitive forces, it is essential for an organisation to train their employees and provide them enough support. The talented and loyal resources can differentiate the organisation to compete in the market.

Steps to establish a successful Capability Uplift initiative

One tool or solution does not fit all. In order to establish a successful capability uplift programme in the organisation, resources need to be motivated to participate and appreciate it. The following are the steps to set up a successful capability uplift initiative.

- Based on the assessment of resources and their existing skills, a job role versus skills/talent matrix needs to be created as a baseline.
- Once the baseline has been established, a skills improvement programme needs to be created for individuals. The skills improvement programme should be personalised to individual employees based on their existing skills and targeted job role requiring new skills.
- In-house and external training programmes need to be set up to provide bespoke training to the employees.
- Set up an internship programme for employees post the theoretical training, so they get practical experience focussed specifically on the new job role requirements.
- KPI (key performance matrix) should be set up to measure the success of the capability uplift initiative and success factors for the individual resources.
- Once the training and internship programme have been completed, the resource could be placed under the new job role.

Benefits of the Capability Uplift initiative:

There are multiple benefits of training the employees through the capability uplift programme. The following are some of the benefits that can differentiate the organisation:

- By evaluating and appreciating the loyal internal employees and providing them opportunities to grow and be productive, an organisation can create a talented human capital.
- A capability uplift programme can also be beneficial to train newly hired employees and prepare them to carry out the job activity effectively and productively.
- The organisation can attain a competitive advantage by having the best trained and skilled people working on disruptive technologies.

- The operating cost can be reduced by increasing productivity of the employees.
- The budget can be allocated for innovation rather than BAU activities to run the existing business.
- The capability uplift programme can contribute towards a successful execution of the strategy for the organisation.

Establish Centre of Excellence

CoE is a shared facility with a group of best-in-class resources with skills specific to the transformation initiative. CoE provides leadership skills, best practices, setup standards, support, mentorship, research and training to other employees for a common strategic objective of the organisation. Usually, there can be multiple CoE initiatives regionally with the common goal of achieving strategic objectives. CoE is usually a shared establishment for a focussed area of the organisation to share ideas and innovation best practices to achieve common technical and business outcomes.

Requirements for CoE

Like the capability uplift initiative, CoE also is an essential and effective tool to create business outcomes and value for an organisation. The following are some of the requirements for CoE:

- The best talents are dispersed within a large global organisation. CoE creates a platform and channel to coordinate the best talent across an organisation.
- The organisation faces challenges to create a virtual team or working group to provide best-in-class internal competency on specific topics or areas. Collaboration and cooperation are essential between highly skilled talents to achieve strategic objectives.
- The department or projects which are stalled or showing a slow progress can benefit from CoE.
- The organisation moving to a new innovative technology and requiring an internal consulting arm with specialised knowledge on that specific technology.
- The organisation changing its business model to compete in different markets or regions.
- Strategic business objectives to reduce the operational cost and shift the budget towards innovation.
- Recent acquisition of a company requiring major training and talent development plans.

Steps to establish CoE

Setting up a successful CoE requires a lot of patience, leadership, influence and people skills. The following are steps to set up a successful CoE:

- Assess the gaps in the organisation as a whole and with departments. This will assist in creating requirements and the need for a CoE.
- The assessment will highlight the potential gaps in resource skills, operational efficiency, resiliency, controls, standards and leadership. It will also highlight deficiency in the operating model, high resource turnover, politics, bureaucracy, lack of productivity, high operating cost, loss of market share and lack of innovation and competitiveness.
- Create a list of all deficiencies and uplift required across the organisation.
- Prioritise the themes requiring CoE.
- Create a business case for the themes to derive efficiencies and assist in achieving business and strategic outcomes.
- Get a sign-off on the CoE budget.
- Coordinate with the leadership of the department requiring efficiencies and CoE setup.
- Create a list of internal and external skills specific to areas highlighted as part of requirement gathering.
- Get a sign-off and sponsorship from leadership of the departments requiring uplift and CoE setup.
- Interview the team that should be part of the CoE for selected uplift initiatives.
- Communicate the CoE membership to selected employees.
- Establish business and technology outcomes for the CoE.
- Establish the agenda for the CoE. It must be aligned to strategic objectives and CoE requirements.
- Depending on the location of the CoE membership, set up workshops and recursive virtual and physical sessions. There can be multiple sessions to accommodate the different time zones.
- Assign a project manager to run the session and communicate the minutes of the meeting with discussion points, actions, timelines for deliverables, risks, issues, blockers, ask from management and any escalations.
- Establish a communication and feedback channel.
- Establish KPIs to measure the delivery of the initiatives that are part of CoE.
- Send communication to the senior leadership and sponsors of the CoE on a regular basis.

Benefits of CoE

CoE can provide multiple benefits to an organisation and can act as a Swiss knife to solve complex integrated issues. The following are some of the benefits of establishing a successful CoE:

- It can enhance the way of working for an organisation to flourish innovation
- Improve staff productivity
- Reduction in operation cost
- Re-energise stalled projects or products
- Improve innovation culture in the organisation
- Decrease turnover of the staff
- Support staff and improve their knowledge of innovative technologies
- Accelerate transformational initiatives and remove any blockers
- Prepare the newly hired and existing staff on transformational programme deliveries
- Transform the organisation to compete in the market to support the business outcomes aligned to the strategy

Evaluation of strategy execution

A successful strategy execution involves evaluation of all programmes supporting on a regular basis. Strategy execution and adoption cannot be successful without a 360° feedback loop and continuous improvement. Evaluation of the strategy execution is one of the most important steps in the whole lifecycle of successful strategy execution and delivering outcomes.

Requirements for Strategy Execution Evaluation

Evaluation of strategy execution is a continuous process. Without an evaluation of the strategy execution, there is high probability for it to fail. There are multiple programmes that get initiated as part of the strategic objectives. It is essential to establish continuous feedback and a communication channel to evaluate the progress and success factors for them.

The following are the requirements:

- Senior management and sponsors of the strategy need to know about the progress
- Release of the allocated budget for strategic objectives and underlying programmes require communication of the deliverables and progress

- Blockers can be resolved by timely communication
- The prioritisation of the programmes can be changed in a timely manner before it is too late and turns out to be very expensive
- There are multiple complex interdependencies between programmes and projects. Having a timely evaluation and transparency can save the whole strategic programmes from a failure
- Timely evaluation of the strategy can assist the organisation to change the priority of the business outcomes on time, saving cost, brand image and competitiveness

Steps for strategy execution evaluation

The following are the steps required to set up a framework for strategy evaluation:

- Establish and flourish transparent culture in the organisation. Employees should not be scared to highlight the issues, blockers and gaps
- Reduce hierarchy and bureaucracy within the departments and whole organisation
- Set up anonymous feedback channels to report hidden and political issues
- Set up governance for all strategic programmes to communicate to all stakeholders regularly
- Enable, influence and support employees to raise risk and issues promptly without a fear of consequences
- Run the programmes in an agile way. Enable the programme and project managers to be transparent and be able to change the goals and timelines of the outcomes in a timely fashion
- Establish various working groups to provide feedback, achievements and risks
- Set up RACI (responsible, accountable, informed and communicate) matrix for the stakeholders of the programme to make sure that right communication goes out and decision makers are involved for a quick decision and priority changes
- Close the programme with a final executive summary of
  - o % of strategic business outcomes delivered
  - o Lessons learnt
  - o Quantitative and qualitative benefits delivered
  - o Communication to all stakeholders
  - o Next steps to accomplish initiatives that could not be delivered as part of existing strategic programmes

Benefits of Strategy Execution Evaluation

There are multiple benefits of evaluation of the strategy execution. The following are some of the benefits:

- Deliver a cost-effective and successful strategy
- Reduce the risk of derailment of strategic programmes risking the failure of the strategy
- Reprioritise the strategic objective and outcome on time without impacting the whole strategy execution
- Deliver the strategy within allocated budget
- Deliver the strategy on time making the organisation gaining competitive advantages over competitors
- Achieving organisation vision and mission
- Insights on why certain objectives are not being delivered as per the set milestones or goals
- Take corrective measures on time to set new goals or reprioritise existing goals

Assess the Blockchain strategy
Use of the strategic model to assess the blockchain business value

This chapter has provided us enough knowledge and tools to evaluate and assess the strategy of an organisation. Now is the good time to apply all knowledge and models to assess the blockchain strategy.

The following are the steps to assess the blockchain strategy:

- **Delivery of the programmes underpinning strategic objectives:** The main objective of any strategy is the accomplishment of the strategic objectives successfully. In order to evaluate it, the success of the programmes underpinning the strategic objectives need to be evaluated and an assessment needs to be done on the % of the programme outcomes achieved. For instance, in the case of the blockchain strategy, the main questions should be
  - o Has the blockchain platform or a product been developed or adopted by the business department within an organisation?
  - o Has % of transformation completion been aligned to strategic objectives?
- **Contribution to Strategic objectives:** As part of strategy execution, there are multiple local and global programmes that were created to support the achievement of outcomes. The blockchain strategy assessment need to articulate how much contribution was achieved as part of those programmes.
- **Contribution to vision and mission:** The main reason for a new strategy execution is to create a competitive advantage for an organisation. The strategy also needs to be in alignment with vision and mission of an organisation. Assessment is essential to evaluate what contribution was attained to support vision and mission.
- **Quantitative benefits:** What are the quantitative benefits achieved through the blockchain strategy execution? This question is de facto

one to ask as business always looks out for the quantitative benefits and a value for money. Some of the quantitative benefits of blockchain strategy execution could be

- o % of market share created by onboarding new customers to use blockchain products or platforms
- o Growth in the sales revenue
- o Reduction in the operational cost by transforming the business processes
- o Amount of automation achieved within business processes
- o Reduction in human errors
- o Reduction in the incidents impacting the customers
- o Improvement in the availability of the blockchain platform
- o Reduction in a single point of failures (platform, human, etc.) by improving operational resiliency
- o Improvement in the resiliency of the number of blockchain products or platforms
- o Reduction in the concentration risks by not putting all our eggs in the same basket

- **Qualitative benefits:** Blockchain strategy execution also delivers qualitative benefits that are hard to quantify; however, they have a major impact on achievement of the strategic business outcomes. The following are some of the qualitative benefits that could be achieved through a successful execution of the blockchain strategy:
  - o % of employees who attained blockchain training and certification
  - o Successful setup of CoE for blockchain
  - o Successful onboarding of internal/external parties to create a consortium for blockchain platform
  - o % of employee productivity improvement
  - o % of reduction in staff turnover
  - o Improvement in customer retention
  - o Acquisition of new customers
  - o Positive customer feedback
  - o Improvement of the brand image of the organisation

- **Competitive advantage**

  The main aim of any strategy is to create competitive advantages for the organisation. The following are some of the criteria to assess competitive advantages:
  - o Unique features and functionalities blockchain products/platforms are providing to the customers
  - o Number of high-profile clients that have adopted our blockchain solution
  - o Regional and global market share for the blockchain solution
  - o Regulatory approval for the blockchain solution in existing and new markets

o Number of quality standards achieved by the blockchain product/platform for cyber security, customer services and service management

o Success and % of completion of TOM (Target Operating Model)

Blockchain sandbox

In recent years, as the blockchain products and solution are maturing, many solution providers have launched test beds to test and try the solution before they become mainstream. It is highly recommended to try the solution on sandboxes offered by the vendors before adopting the blockchain products and platforms.

In this section, we will go through the benefits of a blockchain sandbox and also walk through some of the famous sandboxes.

- **What is a blockchain sandbox:** A blockchain sandbox is a testing instance, with similar features provided by the production instances, of the blockchain products. It provides a facility to the customers to try the blockchain use cases without real funds and hefty budget, required by production grade products and platforms.

    Blockchain sandboxes are also known as testnets. There has been good progress globally in launching sandboxes and testnets to support customers with their use cases.

- **Benefits of a blockchain sandbox?**

    There are multiple benefits of blockchain sandboxes and testnets. Some of them are highlighted below:

    o Organisations can try the use cases and produce a business case to get budget approved

    o A detailed feasibility study can be carried out before selecting a product or platform to solve a business problem

    o Organisations can assess advantages and limitations of the blockchain adoption for a use case

    o Use of a sandbox can provide practical details of implementing a blockchain solution. It can assist in articulating the timelines, features required, resource/skill requirements and budget requirements

    o It can highlight the high- and low-level changes required by adopting blockchain for a business process

    o A POC or MVP (minimum viable product) can be created on a sandbox/testnet to prove the adoption of a blockchain solution. It can also be showcased to regulators and other third parties to gain confidence of the targeted or ToBe solution.

- **List of blockchain sandboxes:** There has been a stream of sandboxes in the past few years. Sandboxes have been established by regulators, banks, software companies and consulting firms. The following is a list of sandboxes that are active and their adoption is growing:

o **FCA (Financial Conduct Authority):** FCA launched a regulatory sandbox in 2016. Since its inception, multiple firms have joined the sandbox to test their use cases. It allows businesses to test innovative propositions and use cases in the market with real customers. Link: https://www.fca.org.uk/firms/regulatory-sandbox/regulatory-sandbox-cohort-7

o **Global Financial Innovation Network (GFIN):** GFIN was launched in January 2019. The stakeholders were an international group of financial regulators and related organisations. FCA, a UK financial regulator, took a lead in establishing a global sandbox to test innovative ideas requiring real scenarios involving customers. FCA now leads and chairs the network involving multiple global regulators. As it stands now, GFIN is a network of more than 60 regulators and organisations committed to supporting financial innovation with a common interest of supporting customers. Link: https://www.fca.org.uk/firms/innovation/global-financial-innovation-network; https://www.thegfin.com

o **IBM Sandbox:** IBM established a sandbox to offer its clients an opportunity to demonstrate their blockchain solutions to clients and evaluate use cases. Another benefit of IBM sandbox is to offer clients an opportunity to grow their knowledge through a hands-on live blockchain environment. Another advantage of using IBM sandbox is to accelerate POC completion without any delays in setting up the environment from scratch. Currently, IBM sandbox includes IBM Blockchain Platform, IBM Cloud Private and IBM License Metric Tool (ILMT). Link: https://www.ibm.com/partnerworld/program/benefits/value-package-sandbox

o **R3 Sandbox:** R3 is the parent company who launched a blockchain product called Corda. R3 launched a sandbox called R3 Sandbox for Digital Currencies. It is a learning and development platform for CBDC (Central Bank Digital Currency) experimentation. The sandbox is used by global financial institutions and regulatory bodies. Link: https://www.r3.com/digital-currency-sandbox/

o **Consensys Sandbox:** Consensus is a blockchain software and platform provider with multiple products under its basket. Consensys launched a sandbox for its clients called 'Codefi'. The sandbox was created to facilitate its customers to try their use cases on digital assets, financial instruments and so on using the sandbox platform and showcase the real value before investing the budget on blockchain solutions. Link: https://consensys.net/codefi/assets/sandbox/

o **Singapore financial regulator sandbox – MAS (Monitory Authority of Singapore):** MAS is a regulator in Singapore who has been ahead of the game with innovation and blockchain. MAS established a sandbox to try the use cases for blockchain and digital technologies to assist the organisations to test their use cases. Link: https://www.mas.gov.sg/development/fintech/sandbox

o **Ethereum Testnet:** Ethereum is one of the blockchains that have disrupted the whole blockchain market. There is a growing industry using Ethereum platform to launch NFT, DiFi (decentralised finance) and DAO (decentralised autonomous organisation). Ethereum has also provided a unique feature for blockchain development called smart contracts. Multiple financial and non-financial use cases in the industry are using Ethereum technology to automate the business processes and adopt blockchain technology. Ethereum also launched a Testnet network, so organisations can test their blockchain use cases without incurring cost. Link: https://ethereum.org/en/developers/docs/networks/

CONCLUSION

In this chapter, we have gone through strategies, strategic models and more importantly how to attain competitive advantages over our competitors. We also discussed how to shape up the blockchain strategy, execute it and finally evaluate it. We also discussed about continuous work happening in the industry to launch sandboxes and testnets to assist the organisations to try out their use cases and work out if blockchain is a correct investment to gain value for the business.

Chapter 7

Blockchain business cases

A framework to produce a business case for blockchain

Every organisation needs to create a business case regardless of whether it being incumbent or a start-up. A business case is an articulation and justification of a new idea, a project, a programme, or anything that requires budget, resources, and time to create a value addition for an organisation. A good business case is always aligned to the strategy and strategic outcomes. A business case must have a sponsor, who will support the business case with financial and non-financial sponsorship. In this section, we will get into deep dive of blockchain business cases and a few frameworks to assist in development of a successful business case.

FEATURES AND ELEMENTS OF A GOOD BLOCKCHAIN BUSINESS CASE

A business case is the most important document like Swiss army knife to define a problem statement related to a business problem and to articulate how the problem will be solved as part of the organisation strategy. The main aim of the business case is to articulate the existing problem and how it will be solved, along with investment requirements and what would be the return on investment (ROI). In this section, we will discuss the important components of a good business case that can lead to successful accomplishment of the strategic outcomes. This section will be focussed on blockchain business cases and their components that can lead to their success.

Problem statement

A business case starts with finding an existing problem. Without being specific to an existing business problem or gaps, a business case cannot be justified for an investment. A problem statement is a crucial step to articulate

DOI: 10.1201/9781003225607-7

the business problem and showcase the existing processes and how it has or can become a major issue for an organisation going forward. To put it within a perspective of blockchain, one of the problem statements can be the lack of interoperability between various existing products and platforms. For instance, without an interoperable solution, blockchain solutions cannot sustain globally where there is a need to create a consortium with many third parties, which might be using different blockchain products and platforms already.

Stakeholders

A business case must include appropriate stakeholders who are accountable or responsible or would like to have information and communication. RACI is one of the best ways to formally define all parties who will be part of the upcoming strategic solution to solve a business problem. The best way to decide on all stakeholders making sure that none is left out is to define an RACI matrix.

RACI refers to

- **Responsible:** Those individuals who do the work to complete a task or activities that are part of the project or programme. There must be at least one role as responsible; however, other participants can be delegated to assist in the work required.
- **Accountable:** An accountable person is an individual who acts as an approver or final authority to make a decision. This role is ultimately answerable for the completion of the delivery of the solution. An accountable individual is the final authority to sign off the outcomes that are delivered by a responsible role. There must be only one accountable person specified for a deliverable.
- **Consulted:** These are the SMEs (subject matter experts) who provide their expert knowledge and experience. Their opinion and advice are sought continuously throughout the lifecycle of the programme or project. There is usually two-way communication with consulted individuals.
- **Informed:** These individuals are kept up to date on the progress and completion of the deliverables throughout the lifecycle of the programme/project. There is one-way communication with these group of individuals.

In the case of a blockchain business case that is trying to solve the problem for interoperability of various blockchain products and solutions used by third parties to establish a consortium, the following can be an RACI:

- **Responsible:** A project manager, programme manager, vendor or consulting firm who has been assigned to deliver the solution as part of the business case.

RACI Matrix – Applied on Blockchain use case

Responsible	Accountable
(Individuals who does the work to complete a task or activities that are part of the project or programme)	(Accountable person is an individual who act an approver or final authority to make a decision)
Project manager, Programme manager, vendor or consulting firm who has been assigned to deliver the solution as part of the Business case.	A business sponsor of the business case who is accountable to sign-off the delivery of the solution as defined in the business case.
Consulted	**Informed**
(These are the SMEs (Subject Matter Experts) who provides their expert knowledge and experience)	(These individuals are kept up to date on the progress and completion of the deliverables throughout the lifecycle of the programme/project)
Blockchain SMEs (Subject Matter Expert), evangelist, third parties and Blockchain associations, whose opinion and expert advice is crucial for the outcome delivery as defined in the business case.	Blockchain Consortium members, regulators, interested parties in the project/programme deliverables and any other interested parties who might be impacted or benefit from completion of the deliverables.

Figure 7.1 RACI matrix.

- **Accountable:** A business sponsor of the business case who is accountable to sign off the delivery of the solution as defined in the business case.
- **Consulted:** Blockchain SMEs, evangelists, third parties and blockchain associations, whose opinion and expert advice is crucial for the outcome delivery as defined in the business case.
- **Informed:** Blockchain consortium members, regulators, interested parties in the project/programme deliverables and any other interested parties who might be impacted or benefit from completion of the deliverables (Figure 7.1).

Alignment to strategy

All deliverables, as defined in the business case, should be aligned to the organisation strategy. The sponsor and other key stakeholders will be reluctant to sign off the business case if the outcomes are not aligned to strategic objectives of the company. For instance, if a strategic objective of the company is to establish a successful consortium with third parties within a blockchain-based supply chain solution, solving the interoperability of the various products is a key outcome. It should also be aligned to the strategic objective of the company.

Approach

In the context of a business case, the approach defines how the solution will be delivered. It includes the following decision and approaches:

- How will the key resources required to deliver the solution be sourced? Will it be through internal teams or the outsourcing to a vendor?
- How will the team be structured, that is, onshore or offshore?
- A decision on buying a solution from a third party or develop it in-house from scratch
- A decision on hosting the solution inside our own data centre or in a cloud or outsource it to a vendor
- A decision on the method of development or delivery. A choice between waterfall and agile or hybrid methodology is essential to be included in the business case.

Financial acumen

It is critical to have enough budget to deliver the outcome of the business case. Key stakeholders must have the financial acumen to estimate the budget ask and control the release of the budget. It should be based on deliverables and also have spare budget to accommodate for the delays caused due to risks and issues. It is beneficial to spend time in analysing the deliverables, timelines and budget requirement during the creation of the business case. The budget asks for the business case outcome delivery to be as close as possible to the expected spend on the delivery of the outcomes. Failing to estimate the budget appropriately, required for the delivery of the business outcomes, can lead to escalations and in a worse situation, a preliminary closure of the project without delivering the final outcomes. This situation can waste time and money and more importantly impact on gaining a competitive advantage for the organisation.

Business benefits

A business case must have outcomes that provide benefits to the organisation. These benefits should also align to assist in achieving strategic outcomes and align with the overall strategy of the organisation. To put a perspective on the blockchain business case, the benefits can be gaining market share in the supply chain digital solution by increasing adoption by third parties as part of the consortium. This can ultimately lead to growth in the customers using the platform which will lead to revenue growth. The ROI can improve, which can satisfy the investment and lead to a successful implementation as defined in the business case.

Risks

Every major strategic transformation programme has risks. In the case of a business case, it is essential to call out the risks upfront. In the case of a blockchain business case, the following can be high-level risks that can be part of the business case:

- Budget deficiency during the execution phase of the programme;
- Regulatory rules that can impact/change the adoption of certain blockchain technologies or solutions;
- Risks from competitors that can make it difficult to gain market share;
- Risks of a pandemic or war that can slow down the adoption of the blockchain solution;
- Financial and regulator sanctions against a country, individuals or a company can lead to failure of the programme.

Leadership

A successful business case must state the leadership team who will be part of the programme to deliver business outcomes. A weak leadership team can lead to delays or even rejection to get the business case approved. A leadership team should be selected with care as it has an impact not only to get the business case approved but also to execute the programme successfully to deliver the business outcomes on time and with quality.

Options

A good business case should articulate a few options to deliver the outcomes. In the case of a blockchain business case, the options can be articulated as follows:

- A choice between various products that can be used to deliver a blockchain-based supply chain platform
- A choice of vendors to support the platform
- A choice of hosting the platform, that is, on premises or cloud
- A choice of raising money through crowd funding, VCs (venture capitalists) or self-funding
- A choice of developing and supporting the supply chain platform ourselves or having partnership with other third parties to share the cost and benefits
- What is the best option to be selected based on its percentage of business value and ROI for the organisation?

Timelines

A business case must define timelines to deliver the milestones. All deliverables must be defined and measured once the business case has been approved and gone into the execution phase. The success criteria are time-bound and also need to be within budget. A successful business case will have a roadmap with business outcomes along with timelines.

Governance

A good business case must define how the delivery of the outcomes will be governed. A weak governance can have multiple impacts during the planning, development and delivery of the business outcomes. There are various steps that can be set up to have a tight governance to deliver a programme (Figure 7.2):

- Set up a baseline or current state of the business problem
- Articulate the target state of the solution that will deliver a transformation and delivery of business benefits
- Set up KPIs (key performance indicators) to measure the delivery of the outcomes

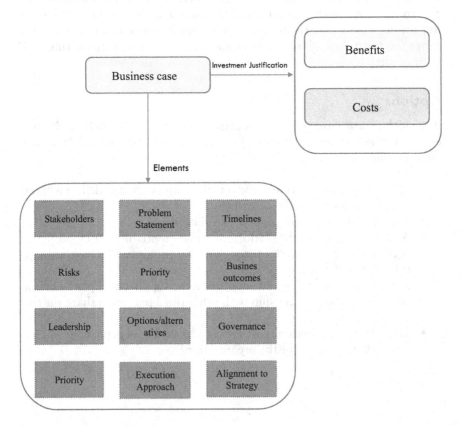

Figure 7.2 Business case elements.

- Set up communication flow to make sure that all stakeholders are communicated on time
- Raise risks and issues on time
- Assess the delivery of the outcomes against timelines, cost and benefits
- Reset the milestones as soon as an issue has occurred or there is a high probability of not delivering the business outcome, by getting sign-off from the sponsor of the programme

FRAMEWORK TO DRAFT A BLOCKCHAIN BUSINESS CASE

Creating a business case is an art and science as it involves creativity to articulate the problem and how the problem can be solved to contribute to strategic outcomes. It is also a science as it requires quantitative data to quantify the business problem. It also justifies the opportunity cost of not improving the existing position and then articulates the future state through transformation that will provide ROI and justify the budget ask through the business case. Although it seems possible in theory, having a framework could assist in creation of the business case based on the best industry practices. A framework can also help to make sure that important aspects are not ignored or forgotten, which could lead to either rejection of the business case approval or potential failure of the execution of the business case.

In this section, we will go through a few templates of the business case framework and also create a blockchain business case for a practical problem (Figures 7.3 and 7.4).

Framework template

Executive summary A high-level summary of the problem statement, remediation initiatives, budget ask, timelines and strategic value gained	**Leadership Team** Name of the leadership team along with their roles and titles, setup to run the strategic programs
Strategic case Includes list of strategic objectives and justification of their value to the vision of the organization	**Deliverables Roadmap** A Roadmap of deliverables with timelines and quantifiabilly measured
Economic case Benefits of the strategic objectives economically e.g. business growth globally or gaining market share	**Benefits** List of qualitative and quantitative benefits that would be delivered as part of strategic programmes execution
Commercial case How the new initiatives will increase revenue, maximise margin or return on investment (ROI)?	**Risks** A list of all risks that could be encountered during the programme lifecycle
Financial case How the investment on new initiatives will grow the company financially e.g improve brand name, increase profits and valuation growth	**Options** A list of options to execute the strategic initiatives. Each option should have cost, benefits, timelines and risks associated against it
Management case Establishment of new senior management including board of directors to drive organisation growth	**Recommendations** A set of recommendations to assist the sponsor of the business case in selecting the most appropriate option

Figure 7.3 Business case framework.

Business case framework 2 – Applied on Blockchain	
Executive summary Transformation of existing Supply chain system with Blockchain based system to improve resiliency, provide real-time visibility, save workflow time, reduce cost and improve security	**Leadership Team** Sponsor: Mr. Kapil Sharma (CEO Scotland region) Programme manager: Mr. John Smith Engineering head: Dr. Nan Lee Product manager: Mr. Sundar Sharma
Problem statement and case: • The current supply chain workflow is manual, complex, time consuming and prone to extensive human errors. • A digital transformation is required urgently to automate the end-to-end workflow to make it simple, transparent, fast, resilient and secure • Blockchain technology is disrupting the whole supply chain space and we must implement the technology for our whisky production department • Blockchain adoption will reduce the time taken by customs processes, acknowledgment of the receipt by the distributors and payment process. • Blockchain can improve the end-to-end time for the 1 business journey by 30% • Blockchain adoption can improve the ROI by 20% • Blockchain adoption can reduce the fraud by 30% by proving authenticity of the whisky	**Deliverables Roadmap** Q1 2023 - Programme initiation, product/platform evaluation, Request for quotation from vendors, start setting up programme teams Q2 2023 – MVP (Minimum Viable Product) of the 3 options, Q3 2023 – Selection of the Blockchain platform/product and a vendor to build it Q4 2023 – Q2 2024 – Platform live and in production
	Benefits Cost reduction, reduce workflow completion time improve security, gain trust from customers, reduce fraud, gain competitive advantage over competitors
	Budget ask: $1m released each quarter as per the deceivable roadmap
	Risks: Delay in regulatory approval or third parties adoption can delay the launch of the platform that can increase the budget ask

Figure 7.4 Business case framework 2.

APPROVAL PROCESS OF THE BLOCKCHAIN BUSINESS CASE

Once the blockchain business case has been created, the next big thing is to get it approved to start the execution phase of the business case. I believe that the approval process of the business case is as important as much as creation of it. This section will go through the process of the business case approval.

The business case approval process within blockchain space is like any other business case approval. The following are the steps involved in the approval process along with suggestions that can assist in getting the approval within a reasonable time.

- Depending on the organisation size and process, the approval process can be simple or complex
- The first step before going through the approval process is to find out a list of all appropriate stakeholders who need to sign off on the approval of the business case. The stakeholders can be as follows:
  - Sponsor of the business case
  - Business key stakeholders
  - Finance department key stakeholders
  - Legal department
  - Cyber security department
  - Vendors or a third party's financial department, if used for the solution delivery
  - Business and IT chief architect for the solution being proposed

    o Regulators, if the solution is involved with anything requiring regulatory approval

    o Any other parties who will be acting as responsible or consulted roles for delivering the business outcomes of the business case

    o Procurement department stakeholders

- Create a PowerPoint deck or a presentation using any method available to summarise the business case for the meeting with the sponsor of the business case. We can use the business case templates discussed in this chapter for it.
- Schedule meetings with the sponsor to get his approval first. Once the sponsor has approved the business case, we need to schedule workshops/meetings with other key stakeholders that are part of the approval process.
- Once we have all approvals from stakeholders, most probably the last step is to get approval from procurement and vendor management teams in our organisation.
- Once the procurement and vendor management has approved the business case, we can take our team for dinner to celebrate the launch of the programme.
- We have now secured approval of our budget for the programme launch.
- The next big steps are to execute the strategic programme, to deliver the business outcomes and to create value for the business.

EXECUTION OF A BLOCKCHAIN BUSINESS CASE

Execution of the blockchain business case is the core of the whole process of creating and getting business case approval. The main purpose of the blockchain business case is to transform the existing baseline that showcased a problem to achieve the business outcomes creating the value for the organisation. The main outcome for a business case is to deliver business outcomes that are aligned to the strategic outcomes, assisting in accomplishing the mission and vision of the organisation.

The following are the steps and recommendations to execute the strategic programmes as part of successful business case delivery.

Steps

- Hire a team that is fit for purpose. It is very important to hire an appropriate team that encompasses skills and positive attitude and that believes in the vision and mission of the organisation.
- Establish a leadership team who will sponsor and be accountable for each strategic outcome of the programmes.

- Execute a programme to improve capability uplift for existing resources and making sure that their skills are aligned to the initiatives in question.
- Establish a programme or a number of programmes aligned to the delivery of the business outcomes within the business case.
- Set up milestones with clear delivery outcomes, budget and timelines.
- Establish clear RACI before the launch of the programme.
- Kick off various projects to deliver the strategic outcomes as part of the business case.
- Make sure to communicate to all stakeholders of the deliverables and strategic outcomes.
- Set up roadshows and workshops to communicate the strategic deliverables, benefits and most importantly how it will benefit the organisation as well as individuals.
- Capture a baseline of the existing state of the organisation, business processes and problems/deficiencies before starting the strategic programme.
- Set up KPIs to measure the progress of the milestones against the strategic outcomes. It is important to measure the milestones through KPI in a timely fashion and raise risks/issues as soon as they are highlighted throughout the lifecycle of the programme.
- Provide an executive report to the senior stakeholders including sponsors of the business case on progress, budget consumption, percentage of deliverables completed and any changes in the scope of timelines, risks and issues. The report must also highlight any ask from the sponsors, when an issue has occurred, or whether support is required from external/internal parties.
- Create POC (proof of concept) and/or MVP (minimum viable product) to determine the suitability of the outcomes and also take quick feedback on the viability of the outcomes.
- Set up an early access programme with all end users and customers to get their feedback on the product features.
- Prioritise the existing or newly highlighted product features. The priority should be based on business value, product improvement, sponsor feedback, competitiveness of the product by including the features, customer feedback, regulator feedback and so on.
- Re-pivot the project plan or deliverables as soon as MVP is ready and feedback highlight that the outcome will not be fit for purpose and it does not provide a business value.
- Once the MVP or POC has been approved, accelerate the delivery of the end product.
- Establish a product launch programme and select customers/regions to launch the product, initially based on multiple factors like regulators' approval, existing customer base, supply chain, financial benefits and competitive advantages by launching the product on certain regions or for a certain customer base.

- Kick off product marketing plans to establish the brand and continuously grow it to gain a competitive advantage.
- Close the programme by providing communication to all stakeholders on success achieved, business value gained, success stories and lessons learnt throughout the execution lifecycle.
- Incorporate all feedback and lessons learnt into the next business case of transformational initiatives.

Recommendations

In my 21+ years of experience within software houses, consulting firms and financial institutions, I have found many strategic programmes being failed over the budget and having the deliverables outcome not fit for purpose. The strategic programmes failed after consuming substantial time and resources of the organisation. Delivering a product that does not deliver any business value as expected has an impact on not only the financial cost but also organisation competitiveness.

The main impact is also through opportunity cost for an organisation as the time and resources could have been used to deliver strategic outcomes required to gain competitive advantages. Failure on the strategic outcomes also impact the company's brand image, losing the existing customers, lack of new market share, wastage of significant budget and staff turnover.

Hence it is important to run the programmes effectively and with care. The following are some of the recommendations to assist in improving the programme success rate of hitting the delivery of the products on time and within the budget.

- Establish a team that has appropriate skills and willingness to deliver the milestones.
- Every team member should understand the end result of the deliverable and how it will contribute to the organisation's strategy. Everyone in the programme team must understand the value she or he will be creating to the organisation's vision and mission by delivering their milestones.
- Hire external consulting company or experts if the internal employees' skills are lacking to deliver the programme.
- Establish a training programme to uplift the skills of employees that will be part of the programme to deliver strategic outcomes.
- Communication is the key. All deliverables and how they will align to the company's strategy must be communicated to all stakeholders, who are or not part of the programme. There will be stakeholders who might just use the outcomes of the programme and some who are actively involved in delivering the outcomes.
- Establish the programme in an agile delivery mode. An agile methodology has multiple benefits. Rather than delivering the whole project as per the waterfall methodology, an agile methodology provides a

benefit of breaking down the deliverable into multiple epics. Each epic consists of mini deliverables.

- Get customer feedback fast to re-pivot the whole deliverables if the initial assessment was not appropriate or the deliverable is not fit for purpose anymore. This can happen because of internal or external factors that might have impacted the business value.
- Depending on the organisation's complexity or way of working, we might have to select a hybrid approach to deliver the programme. A mix of agile and waterfall methodology is fine as long as it provides value addition to the programme in terms of fast delivery of the outcomes.
- Do not be hesitant to close the deliverable or milestone quickly if the customer feedback or MVP outcome highlights that it will not deliver any business value and not anymore align to the strategic objective or outcome.
- Set up multiple workshops or meetings including the Centre of Excellence (CoE) and Community of Practise (CoP) to collaborate ideas, standards, training and knowledge transfer between internal and external SMEs. It is always useful to get a perspective of other SMEs who have already run through similar transformational initiatives or come across similar problems. It is also useful to get opinions from other experts during the execution phase of the transformational programmes.
- It is highly important to oversee the financial spend against the deliverables to make sure that the budget is under control and on target.
- If the deliverable is for regulatory requirements or needs approvals from the regulators in order to go into production (useable by customers), regulators must be kept engaged and communicated throughout with the progress of the programme.
- Risks and issues surrounding the programme deliverables must be raised on time.
- Communication to the sponsors of the programme on the deliverable concerns, risks and issues must be raised and communicated promptly.
- Establish a transparent and simple structure within the programme teams to focus on quick delivery of the outcomes. The focus should be on delivery rather than politics and bureaucracy.
- Establish flat hierarchy to improve communication and feedback from the programme teams.

CONCLUSION

Business case creation and its approval is the heart of any strategic initiative. There can be no programme that can be delivered without sufficient budget. Business cases empower the strategist to sell the transformational initiatives that align to the organisation strategy and get appropriate resources (budget) to deliver the outcomes. In the emerging technologies like blockchain, it is essential to deliver the product on time and get essential help from all parties including internal and external entities. The regulators play an important part within the lifecyle of the outcome delivery as it is very important to engage them and re-pivot the programme as per the guidelines from them as it can have a major impact on the whole strategy.

In this section, we have gained skills on how to create a business case that can have a higher probability to get approval and also how to execute the business case to deliver success to the organisation's strategy, leading to empowering its vision and mission.

Chapter 8

Blockchain case study

Apply concepts on practical use case

The best way to learn any new technology is to apply it on a real-life business problem. The appreciation of the technology is great when the outcomes create a business value. As the blockchain emerging technology goes through a journey of maturity and organisations appreciate the real value of the technology, the time is perfect to incorporate the blockchain technology into business processes and design solutions to improve the organisation's competitiveness.

In this chapter, we will go through a case study that will articulate the business problem and how various technologies including blockchain can be applied to design and implement a solution.

CASE STUDY 1: CREATE A PLATFORM FOR A DIGITAL ART MARKETPLACE

Background

IOSpeed Ltd. is a company registered and based in London, United Kingdom. They have a small business to sell specialised artwork to customers. They have some loyal customers, and most of the business comes from customers visiting the exhibitions onsite in their store. Their existing business model is Business to Customers (B2C). IOSpeed had some senior management changes, and the new CEO would like to transform the business to go global and innovate it through technology transformation to grow. IOSpeed would like to expand in various channels and would like to go through IPO (Initial Public offering) in the near future.

Strategy execution phases

The following are the phases of strategy execution to transform the organisation:

1. Find and articulate the problem statement for business
2. Capture the potential strategic outcomes for the organisation. This is also called To-Be state
3. Organisation analysis to setup a baseline
4. Formulate the strategy
5. Execute the strategy
6. Capture the business value and ROI (return on investment)

DOI: 10.1201/9781003225607-8

Problem statement

IOSpeed CEO, Kapil Sharma, wants to reshape the company through a new strategy and uplift the company's brand image through new strategy. As part of reviewing the existing strategy and business model, there were many problems highlighted. Some of them are listed below:

- The existing business model is not sustainable against competitors. It was highlighted that the company needs to invest in expansion to grow the business and gain market share
- The sales revenue has been declining year on year
- The pandemic [coronavirus disease 2019 (COVID-19)] further declined the revenue and highlighted an urgent need to digitalise the business and expand in multiple countries and markets
- There was a high turnover of staff due to decline in revenue and budget cut on operating cost that included cut in staff as well
- It was highlighted that the cost for physical assets and to maintain them during the pandemic was very high
- There are a lot of competitors in the market, who have already launched digital platforms and attracted new customers and artists. There are many barriers to entry
- There is a need for a new brand image for the company and an innovative strategy to kick-start the new sales channels and attract artists and customers. This needs to be in parallel to existing business as revenue streams need to be active along with retaining existing loyal customers

IOSpeed potential strategic outcomes

Once a high level of organisation gaps and problem statements have been identified, the next steps would be to articulate the target state of the organisation before diving into analysis of the organisation current state and strategic formulation.

The following is the target state the senior management of IOSpeed would like the organisation to be:

1. Improve existing business to sell Art through virtual exhibitions and expand the market from UK to Global. Migrate to new channels such as phone, website, and physical presence.
2. Develop a new online marketplace for customers and artists to buy and sell the ART pieces using NFT (non-fungible token) technology.

Strategic outcomes

- The first strategic outcome of IOSpeed is to sustain the existing business, retaining the revenue stream and customers
- The second strategic outcome is to innovate new planforms to disrupt the business model and enter new markets

Having articulated the strategic business outcomes for IOSpeed, we will now go through the next steps of the process.

Organisation analysis for strategy formulation

The first step for IOSpeed is to carry out a deep dive on the whole organisation before it can start formulating the strategy. We have already gone through various strategic models, strategy formulation, and execution in Chapter 6. In this chapter, we will apply all the knowledge gained throughout this book to analyse the organisation, formulate the strategy, and execute it to make IOSpeed gain a competitive advantage.

Organisation analysis

We will apply two strategic models to carry out the analysis of the organisation and come up with findings needed to start the formulation of the strategy for IOSpeed. We can apply more models as discussed in Chapter 6 to get more insights on the IOSpeed organisation.

Michael Porter's five forces strategic model

Table 8.1 explains the five forces for IOSpeed to launch a blockchain-based art marketplace online.

SWOT: strengths, weaknesses, opportunities, and threats

Overview

SWOT is a strategic model to assess and analyse a company's strengths, weaknesses, opportunities, and threats. We will apply the SWOT model on IOSpeed organisation capability to get insights into strategy formulation for them.

This section will apply the SWOT model on IOSpeed.

Areas assessed by SWOT on IOSpeed

- **Strengths:** IOSpeed had a business and clientele who were passionate about Art. Due to the pandemic and the lack of online presence, they lost a few clients and the artists due to competitors. However, the following are some of the strengths of IOSpeed:
  o IOSpeed has a good brand name and niche loyal clients
  o They have niche at master pieces and artists creating them. This differentiates them from competitors into similar products or market
  o IOSpeed had established an excellent leadership team to focus on strategic transformation
  o They have a board of directors and investor support

Table 8.1 Michael Porter's five forces strategic model

Strategic force	Stakeholders	Rating
Bargaining power of suppliers	Multiple NFT platform providers and more are upcoming and have created and established platforms and products for NFTs. Some of the examples of the NFT marketplace were discussed in Chapter 1. The suppliers of the platform and also products to enable the platform can have a high level of bargaining power.	HIGH
Bargaining power of buyers	Buyers of NFT platforms or services also have a high level of bargaining power due to gaps in the maturity of the platform and also risk of regulatory changes. Unless an organisation create and manage their own NFT platform, they need to select an appropriate platform provider and negotiate with them. As discussed in Chapter 1, there are multiple providers of NFT platforms, and the list is continuously growing. This provides flexibility to the buyers with options. Creating our own platform to establish an NFT-based art marketplace can be expensive, so the organisation needs to decide on using the available NFT platform or creating those on their own. This decision needs to be based on risk and reward.	HIGH
Threat of new entrants	Although not impossible, creating and managing NFT platforms is very expensive. There are already multiple platforms like Opensea.io, who have high adoption of customers using the platform to buy/sell NFTs globally. It will be difficult for new entrants to enter the market. IOSpeed will be classified as a new entrant within the NFT market. We will discuss the best way to disrupt the market as part of strategy formulation.	LOW
Threat of substitute products or services	There are other products and platforms that can be used to buy/sell art. The traditional digital channels based on the web/ mobile user interface and payment getaways to carry out end-to-end transactions and transfer of the art work are still well adopted. However, NFT provides additional features against the traditional web-based platform to transact art online. The threat of a substitute is therefore low. IOSpeed needs to evaluate all options before executing on the most appropriate solution.	LOW
Rivalry among existing competitors	Competition among suppliers of NFT platforms, products and services is very HIGH. The market is already full of online digital art marketplaces, and many more are launching NFT features. The rivalry among existing competitors of NFT marketplaces is high. IOSpeed needs to factor this during strategy formulation.	HIGH

- **Weaknesses:** IOSpeed leadership was slow in adopting innovation and to take proactive strategic measures to be competitive in the market. As a result, business had an impact on revenue, staff turnover, and also loss of a few loyal customers. Even after the leadership changes, they still have some weaknesses that need to be taken into account during strategy formulation.

The following are some of the weaknesses of the IOSpeed as an organisation:

o A negative impact on the brand image due to old leadership and slowness in adoption of new technology

o Loss of knowledge and experience due to organisation restructuring

o High overheads due to physical only presence of Art exhibitions

o Lack of resiliency as proven during the pandemic. The organisation has only one value chain to carry out business, that is, physical brick and mortar

o Lack of capital allocation for innovation as well as spare budget allocation for unpredictable risks

o High turnover of staff, artists, and also customers due to the lack of liquidity and customer service.

- **Opportunities:** Post the restructure of the senior management, IOSpeed has the potential to be more competitive and create value addition for investors, customers, and staff.

  The following are some of the opportunities the company has to disrupt the market going forward:

  o Analyse the geographical markets globally to look out for financial and regulatory assistance to innovate products and platforms for Art

  o IOSpeed is registered in UK and can benefit from Government assistance through Corporation tax cut and additional benefits/ subsidy for Fintech and Art/Media sectors

- **Threats:** Every business needs to assess the resiliency against external threats due to macro-economic and natural disaster factors.

  The following are some of the threats that have potential impact on IOSpeed:

  o IOSpeed has already been impacted by the COVID-19 pandemic due to the lack of resiliency. The natural disasters can still impact the business if there are not sufficient steps put into the strategy going forward.

  o IOSpeed can have an impact from global taxation rules if they go global in future. This needs to be factored into the strategy and has sufficient spare budget to accommodate for taxation changes.

  o IOSpeed can also be impacted by the lack of artists in a specific country or loss of artists to competitors.

  o IOSpeed can also have an impact on minimum wages of employees as the local employment rules need to be followed. This needs to be factored into the strategy.

  o They can hit with supply chain issues related to import/export of the physical art pieces if the future strategy is to have digital as well as physical art business (Figure 8.1).

SWOT on IOSpeed use case

Factor	Description	Impact on IOSpeed Blockchain adoption
Strengths	Highlights its capabilities, uniqueness and niche to differentiate itself from competitors, using internal and external data.	• IOSpeed has a good brand name and niche loyal clients as well as artists • IOSpeed had established an excellent leadership team to focus on strategic transformation • Support from Board of directors and investors support
Weaknesses	Weaknesses are the factors that can lead to stop or slow down an organisation to perform at its optimum level.	• Negative impact on Brand image • Brain drain due to organisation restructuring • High overheads due to physical only presence of Art exhibitions • Lack of resiliency • Lack of capital allocation for innovation • High turnover of staff, artists and also customers
Opportunities	Opportunities refers to external factors that can be favourable to the organisation to have competitive advantage.	• Analyse the geographical markets globally to look out for financial and regulatory assistance to innovate products and platform for Art • IOSpeed is registered in UK and can benefit from Government assistance through Corporation tax cut and additional benefits/subsidy for Fintech and Art/Media sectors
Threats	Threats refers to external factors that have potential to harm an organisation or have a negative impact.	• IOSpeed has already been impacted by Covid-19 pandemic due to their lack of resiliency. • IOSpeed can have impact from global taxation rules if they go global in future. • IOSpeed also can be impacted by lack of artists in a specific country or loss of artists to competitors • Supply chain issues related to import/export of the physical art pieces if the future strategy is to have digital as well as physical art business.

Figure 8.1 SWOT.

Strategy formulation

The strategy formulation process can begin once a deep dive has been completed about the organisation, that is, IOSpeed in this case. We will review all the work completed as part of IOSpeed organisational analysis through various strategic models and start the strategy formulation process.

The following are the steps in strategy formulation. These were also explained in detail in Chapter 6.

Setup vision and mission for IOSpeed

Throughout the organisational analysis, it was decided to set the following vision and mission of the IOSpeed organisation.

Vision

Make affordable ART reachable to anyone globally.

Mission

Connect artists and customers globally through Blockchain technology, providing efficient, secure and transparent marketplace.

Vision and mission are required to define the existence of IOSpeed in the society. The strategy should be in alignment of vision and mission statements of IOSpeed. The next steps are to assess how external and internal environments could affect IOSpeed and what measures are required to transform the organisation to be competitive.

Understand the external environment and our position

IOSpeed faces multiple challenges as well as some favourable factors against the competitors in the market. To become more competitive in the market, it is essential to have a deep insight into the external environment and carry out an assessment of the IOSpeed current position. The following is a list of some of the external factors that might impact the strategic goals:

- Blockchain regulatory and legal frameworks are still not mature and continuously changing. Regulators are still educating themselves and reviewing the impact of blockchain and how it will impact the current financial system. The financial sector is already very complex; however, the regulation to control them have matured throughout multiple decade journeys. IOSpeed needs to watch the regulatory rules for blockchain very closely and also make relationship with local regulators to make sure that they get a chance to review and contribute towards draft regulatory papers. IOSpeed also needs to be flexible in adopting the regulations as and when they get finalised promptly, meeting regulator requirements. This becomes more complex based on the IOSpeed strategy to launch the platform in multiple countries.

- IOSpeed needs to review political policies towards blockchain before deciding on to launch a platform in a specific country as it can impact the timelines of the launch as well as becomes a bottleneck.
- On top of political policies of a government, it is a good idea and also recommended to assess the political stability of the country before targeting it for business launch.
- It is recommended to review existing as well as upcoming tax policies towards blockchain in a country that is under review for the business launch. A review might highlight taxation policy to be against the strategy or in favour.
- It is recommended to review the employment laws in the country before targeting it for business launch. Some countries have strict employee unions or employment laws that might be against the strategic goals and might slow down the strategy execution.
- IOSpeed had a business in United Kingdom and so are well verse with UK laws, the political system, and employment laws; however, they need to do a deep dive for other targeted countries. It will involve budget allocation and time to do a thorough assessment on external factors before the launch of the business in those countries.

Understand the internal environment and our position

A good understanding of the internal environment and where IOSpeed stands is as important as knowing about the external environment. As part of the IOSpeed organisation analysis, there are several factors that need to be reviewed before formulating the strategy and strategic outcomes. The following are some of the factors that are strengths and others that are opportunities to improve for IOSpeed.

- As part of the IOSpeed organisation assessment, it was highlighted that there was a high turnover of staff and artists and also loss of some customers. IOSpeed must define some strategic objectives within the upcoming strategy to retain existing employees, artists and customers as well as attract new ones.
- IOSpeed went through restructuring, and one of the main elements that have already been accomplished was to change the leadership team. The new strategy should include capability uplift of the leadership team to educate the new management about the historical weaknesses/gaps, so new strategic programmes could be well defined as part of the strategic objectives.

- IOSpeed were slow in adopting the new technological innovation and way of working. It had a huge negative impact on its brand, loss of customers, artists and employees and made them less competitive in the market. The new strategy must have strategic objectives to transform the whole organisation adopting innovative technologies including blockchain.
- IOSpeed still have some loyal artists for creating ART and also loyal customers. This can benefit them to grow and launch new value businesses and channels.
- IOSpeed only had a presence in UK. The new strategy needs to factor in other external and internal challenges.
- IOSpeed lost time due to less effective leadership team and slow decision to adopt innovation as compared to their competitors. The new strategy needs to factor in loss of opportunity cost and have additional budget allocation to innovate quickly and launching the business in appropriate countries.

Articulate long-term objectives and goals

This is the right time to review the long-term goals and objectives for IOSpeed as we have already done a deep dive on internal and external environmental factors and IOSpeed position against its competitors. These will be the factors contributing towards strategy formulation.

- Improve Brand image of the IOSpeed in United Kingdom post the negative impact that caused loss of customers, artists and staff
- Integrate innovation in the core of the IOSpeed strategy
- Retain existing staff and hire new, aligned to new strategic objectives
- Establish a capability uplift programme to train all staff across the organisation to deliver the strategic objectives effectively
- Transform existing business processes to make them more digital whilst keeping the existing business process. This will provide benefit of retaining existing business and also gain a competitive advantage through launching new platforms/products in existing and new markets
- Create and launch ART marketplace using blockchain technology in UK followed by other countries

Prospective solutions

As we have already gone through strategy in Chapter 6, we will focus this section on launching a new platform for a digital ART marketplace for IOSpeed.

The following are the prospective solutions to launch blockchain-based solutions for the ART marketplace. The solution will depend on IOSpeed position, such as the following:

- Budget
- Skills to develop the platform from scratch
- Timelines to launch the marketplace
- Regulatory approval to use the platform in a specific country

Launch the IOSpeed ART Marketplace Using the Existing NFT Platform

The first option for IOSpeed is to use an existing established platform for the ART marketplace. There are advantages and disadvantages of this approach like any other. In this section, we will go through the process of evaluating a few options and how actually it will work for IOSpeed.

In Chapter 1, we explained various NFT platforms. We will select two of the NFT platforms for this case study and provide recommendations.

- **Option 1: opensea.io (https://opensea.io/):** Opensea (https://opensea.io) is the world's first and largest NFT marketplace. We can literally sell or buy anything digital here. IOSpeed will be able to create its own portfolio within the Opensea eco-system. Usually, IOSpeed can create a digital art marketplace on its own website, and the transaction can be facilitated by the Opensea platform. The transaction needs to be through Crypto currency. Opensea supports two blockchains, that is, Ethereum and Polygon. Both charge a fee for a successful listing and transfer of the digital assets from the IOSpeed wallet to customer wallet.
- **Option 2: crypto.com (https://crypto.com/):** Crypto.com (https://crypto.com/nft) has recently also launched the NFT marketplace on top of a successful Crypto wallet and exchange. Crypto.com provides a whole eco-system ranging from debit card, Crypto wallet and Crypto exchange to buy and sell major Crypto currencies and also has its own Crypto currency called CRO. They recently launched the NFT marketplace. It has been a major success as they validate and vet the artists before they can use the platform to sell their ART on the platform. Although the NFT platform is smaller than Opensea, they offer artists to list the items to sell them for Fiat currency (dollars). The customers can pay for the digital art through credit/debit cards or Crypto currency.

Advantages of the third-party NFT platform

The following are the advantages of using a third-party NFT platform provider such as crypto.com:

- Using a third party, the NFT platform can provide quick time to market to launch a business globally. IOSpeed will not have to spend time to deploy and maintain an NFT platform, which can take substantial time.
- IOSpeed will not have to spend budget to deploy and maintain the platform that can be very costly.
- The regulatory approval to launch the NFT platform can be lengthy. IOSpeed can launch the digital marketplace without spending time on regulatory approval.
- Designing, creating and deploying an end-to-end NFT marketplace require a variety of technology skills. Some of those skills are rarely available in the market due to supply of candidates with Blockchain experience. It would be advantageous for IOSpeed to use an already established NFT platform to launch a digital art marketplace.

Disadvantages of the third-party NFT platform

Using a third-party platform also has some disadvantages. The following are the disadvantages of using a third-party NFT platform provider such as crypto.com:

- The IOSpeed brand name will not improve by using a third-party NFT platform, although the third-party brand name can flourish.
- IOSpeed will be limited to make a decision and execute changes on a third-party platform as per their own strategic objectives.
- IOSpeed needs to carry a risk of cyber security and rely on third-party cyber security policies. Recently, crypto.com was hacked. These kinds of cyber-attacks can ruin the brand image of IOSpeed and impact customer trust towards IOSpeed. This can lead to loss of artists and customers.
- Using third-party services and platforms can be expensive in a longer term. The third party will charge for their services, and that service fees could have been invested in IOSpeed's own platform.

Recommendations

- One of the IOSpeed strategies could be to acquire a start-up offering an NFT platform and rebrand them.
- IOSpeed could use the third-party platform to launch a digital art marketplace in the short term whilst working on their own platform in parallel. This would give them quick time to market to retain the business and also work on strategic outcome to develop their own NFT platform.

- The other strategic move for IOSpeed could be to make a partnership with a third party to develop the IOSpeed NFT platform. This will provide an advantage to develop a platform using third-party experience and skills as they already launched a platform for the NFT marketplace.
- IOSpeed can also hire a third-party consulting/blockchain development company to assist them in the delivery of the NFT marketplace. This will provide benefits of quick time to delivery and quality products along with reasonable budget.

Architecture diagram

The following is an architecture diagram to create an NFT platform using the Opensea platform (Figure 8.2).

Create a brand-new NFT platform to launch an IOSpeed ART marketplace

Rather than utilising a third-party NFT platform to launch a digital art marketplace, IOSpeed could design and deploy its own digital marketplace using NFT technology to connect artists and customers. In this section, we will go through the end-to-end process to launch an NFT-based marketplace providing a variety of unique features, gaining a competitive advantage.

The following is the process to launch a digital art marketplace.

- Hire a leadership and technical teams to design, create and run the platform. The essential roles will be the following:
  - o Chief Technology Officer
  - o Chief Financial Officer

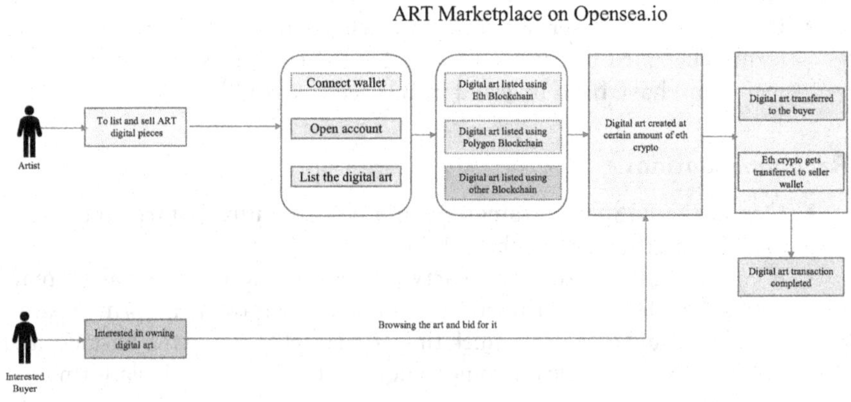

Figure 8.2 ART marketplace on crypto.com or opensea.io.

- o Chief Marketing Officer
- o Head of Engineering
- o Head of Legal
- o Head of Procurement
- o Head of HR (Human resources)
- o Head of Cyber Security
- o Head of Blockchain
- o Team beneath each of the above roles
- Design an end-to-end architecture of the NFT-based ART marketplace
- Review the architecture internally and also through external parties under NDA (non-disclosure agreement). Some examples of external parties can be blockchain SMEs (subject matter experts) and blockchain consulting firms
- Create functional and non-functional requirements
- Review external blockchain and other technology products and services required as per the prospective architecture. Some of the products could be as follows:
  - o Hosting the provider preferably cloud providers like AWS, Azure or Google.
  - o Virtual machines (VMs) to provide compute power and also to install the software. Cloud providers offer various choices of VMs.
  - o Load balancers (LBs) to improve performance of the product based on its design. There are various choices of LBs offered by cloud providers.
  - o Disaster recovery (DR) solution. Again, cloud providers have multiple offerings for DR.
  - o Relational database for off-chain storage. It can be an open-source database or a licensed product provided by the cloud provider.
  - o A digital vault to store passwords, identity, secrets and certificates. It can be hashicorp vault or a Vault service provided by cloud providers.
  - o A messaging queue product like Redis.
  - o DevOps product (hosted on Cloud) to set up the development eco-system.
  - o Identity and authentication service like active directory. Mostly all cloud providers offer a service for identity management as well.
  - o Storage. All cloud providers offer various storage services based on the use cases.
  - o Blockchain products.
- Set up workshops and meeting for vendors to provide more details of their products in line with the high-level requirements.

- Ask the vendors to provide a formal quotation for the product license and support cost.
- Go through the initial evaluation process based on the vendor profile, leadership, location, support, benefits, cost and alignment with the architecture.
- Select a minimum of three prospective products that meet the requirements of the business and are aligned to the architecture.
- Start the process to ask the prospective vendors of those products to showcase the functionalities through POC (proof of concept).
- Go through an unbiased process to evaluate the final product.
- Ask vendors to send license agreement for IOSpeed to legal and procurement teams, so they can review it.
- Sign the contract with the vendors of the selected products.
- Once the hosting provider, blockchain product and other technology stacks have been selected, the real development work for the platform starts.
- The development methodology should be Agile, so a small portion of the product can be developed in parallel by multiple developers. The advantage of this approach is that each agile sprint will produce a feature that can be tested. This also provides a benefit to rule out the feature if it is not appropriate or will not work, without impacting the whole development project. In other words, IOSpeed will adopt the Agile method of development and the whole architecture will reply on micro services.
- The product development will go through various lifecycles of testing to create POC and minimum viable products (MVPs).
- Once the end-to-end functionality has been tested through MVP, it needs to go through Dev and UAT before the launch of the product.
- There are various steps that need to be adhered to before launching the product as general release (GA) or mainstream. The following is a high-level list:
  - o Carry out a thorough cyber security review and get certified from a recognised third-party cyber security company as well as other associations to improve the confidence level of regulators and customers.
  - o Get approval from the regulators to launch the platform. Usually depending on the jurisdictions of the regulator and in what country the platform will be consumed, there are various regulators to get approval from. The recommendation here is to start the process early enough, so the launch timelines do not get impacted.

- o Train employees and set up support functions to manage the platform and provide real-time incident response as well as customer support.
- o Set up SRE (site reliability engineering) functions to effectively manage the technical environment.
- o Setup SLAs (service level agreements) for the service availability and quality.
- o Set up regulatory engagement and reporting functions.
- o Set up monitoring and alerting to detect the problem proactively and improve MTTR (mean time to recover) in the case of a major incident.
- o Kick off a marketing plan to publicise the platform and attract customers as well as artists to use the marketplace.
- o Launch the IOSpeed digital ART platform in appropriate countries as per the regulatory approval.

Advantages of the IOSpeed-owned NFT platform

- IOSpeed will have more control over the design and functioning of the platform
- Their brand name can be significantly improved
- IOSpeed will have potential to disrupt the market of the digital marketplace to connect the buyer and seller through their platform
- It can be easier for IOSpeed to grow by expansion in different markets
- IOSpeed can have positive ROI in a longer term by creating and establishing its own branded platform
- There is more possibility to attract artists and customers by getting their feedback and improve the functionality of the platform promptly
- Reducing the reliance on a third party for core functionality is beneficial in a longer turn. It can also retain employees and make them loyal towards the company. This would reduce staff turnover and improve their productivity
- IOSpeed can increase the value of the company and also increase its chances to go public through IPO (Initial Public Offering)

Disadvantages of the IOSpeed-owned NFT platform

- IOSpeed can find it difficult to deliver the platform under tight timelines due to limited skills in the market for blockchain and upcoming innovative technologies.

- Creating and maintaining our NFT-based marketplace can be very expensive. IOSpeed might face difficulty to raise money to sponsor the programme and deliver the platform.
- There can be delay in platform delivery due to a requirement for regulatory approvals, depending on the country IOSpeed would like to launch the platform.

Recommendations

- IOSpeed should launch its own NFT-based Digital ART marketplace. They should start small initially to have a *quick to market* advantage for their solution. As IOSpeed already had a business in UK, my recommendation for them is to launch in the UK first and expand to other countries as a staged approach.
- They should have a clear roadmap of releases of the platform along with high-level features along with timelines.
- They must hire an experienced leadership and technical team who have had experience in the delivery of similar blockchain platforms or products.
- It is also important to have a member in the team who has experience in engaging with regulators as it is crucial to get regulatory approval to launch the platform in various countries.
- IOSpeed needs to carefully plan and forecast for the budget, required to launch and platform as well as maintain it. They must avoid the situation of forecasting for under-budget and facing the problems during or after the launch of the platform.

Architecture diagram

The following is an architecture diagram to create a IOSpeed-owned NFT platform.

Solution selection

A selection of the solution based on the fact and data points would be easier. In previous two sections, potential solutions to establish an NFT-based digital marketplace were discussed. The recommendation for IOSpeed is to create and maintain its own NFT marketplace rather than using an already established third-party solution. This decision is aligned to the IOSpeed vision and mission.

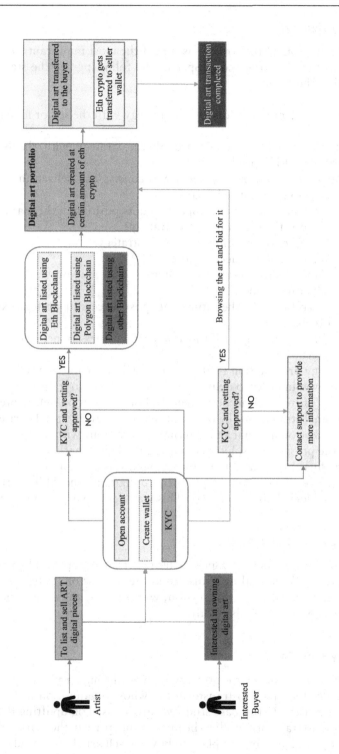

Strategy sign-off

Getting a sign-off of the strategy is one of the most important steps in the transformational journey of IOSpeed. The following are the steps to get approval of the strategy:

- Review the presentation for the strategy with the senior management of IOSpeed
- Set up workshops to go through the strategy with the Board of Directors of IOSpeed
- The presentation must be clear and concise and deliver an impactful message to the IOSpeed Board
  o Current state of the company and its position in the market
  o What is the need for a new strategy?
  o What are the benefits of the new strategy?
  o What are the budget requirements?
  o Timelines to execute the strategy
  o What would be the ROI?
  o What would be the future state post successful strategy execution (To-Be state)
  o What is the impact if the new strategy does not get signed off and executed?
- Strategy presentation is like a sales pitch for a start-up to get budget approved in order to deliver strategic outcomes to transform the company. There needs to be a great deal of preparation before presenting the final strategy to the board of the company. IOSpeed carried out a deep dive on internal and external factors along with detailed analysis of the prospective solutions to launch a digital marketplace for ART.
- The final outcome of the strategy pitch was a full approval of budget to deliver the brand-new platform to digitalise the ART marketplace using blockchain technology. This was a good win for IOSpeed.

Strategy execution

The excitement starts for IOSpeed after the strategy approval by the Board of Directors. We have already discussed the process of strategy execution in Chapter 6; however, in this section, we will apply the same concepts on IOSpeed as part of this case study.

Strategy planning

The first step to execute the strategy is to go through a planning exercise. A full-fledged strategy to transform the whole organisation usually takes around 3–5 years. In this case study, we are focused on uplifting IOSpeed's capabilities to transform itself to be more competitive in the market through the blockchain-based marketplace to buy and sell art. This is a subset of the overall strategy and will deliver the strategic outcome in 2 years timelines.

The following are the steps of strategic outcome planning for IOSpeed:

- Review and create strategic initiatives to deliver strategic objectives
- Review and confirm the high-level requirements to deliver the objectives. This can include the following:
  o Leadership team selection
  o Technical, HR, business, legal, sales, marketing and finance resource hiring requirements
  o Internal and external human resource demand
  o Engagement with vendors, consulting partners and regulators to set the objectives and timelines to deliver the objectives
  o Budget allocation for each initiative
  o Set deliverable timelines for each initiative
  o Establish RACI (Responsible, Accountable, Communicate and Informed) against each strategic objective

Communication of the objectives and goals

Communication is an important part of the successful delivery of the strategic objectives and goals of IOSpeed. The following are some of the steps to communicate IOSpeed objectives and goals successfully as part of the communication strategy:

- Discover a list of stakeholders on various levels and those that are directly/indirectly involved in the strategy execution.
- Categorise the stakeholders in various categories as follows:
  o Internal stakeholders
    – Business, technology, human resources, procurement, Employee Unions and legal
  o External stakeholders
    – Consulting firms, vendors, societies like British blockchain association and British Banking Association (BBA)
  o Regulators
    – Regulators of the countries where IOSpeed wants to launch the business
- Design a communication template and content for various types of stakeholders
- Get approval from sponsors and senior management on the communication template and content
- Establish communication channels (paper, digital, advertisement, workshops, roadshows, etc.)
- Frequency of the communication
- Set up a feedback channel for the communication. The feedback channel is important to improve the communication strategy of IOSpeed
- Once all the administration and governance of the communication strategy are complete, IOSpeed can launch the communication initiative and kick off the execution.

Create strategic and transformational programmes aligned to the strategic plan

At this stage, all the prerequisites have been completed to establish transformational programmes aligned to the strategy. Creation of the programmes and project underneath is a lengthy process. The following are the steps to establish a programme and start the execution:

- Create programmes to deliver strategic objectives. All programmes must be aligned to the strategy and contribute towards IOSpeed vision.
- Create a business case for individual programmes and start the approval process.
- Get business case approval.
- Once the business case has been fully approved, start establishing the programme and make it ready for execution.
- Create projects to deliver the business outcomes, contributing to the programme.
- Set up milestones and KPIs (key performance indicators) for each programme and project.
- Launch the programme officially. Milestones must have quantitative and qualitative measurements along with outcome delivery timelines.

Realignment of human resources to strategic programmes

Human capital is an important part of a successful programme delivery. As IOSpeed goes through the execution of the programmes, it is essential to align the right resources, where it is needed as per the programme requirements and employee skills. This is to make sure that they are all aligned and fit for purpose. The following steps are recommended to align the right skilled employees to appropriate initiatives:

- As mentioned in Chapter 6, IOSpeed needs to create a database of existing employee job roles, locations, departments, existing skills and the career goals.
- Create a consolidated list of all projects and initiatives underpinning the programme strategic deliverables.
- Carry out an exercise with managers of the departments to match and align the skills of the employees to the initiatives.
- Formalise the alignment and move of the employee inter-department. Get approval from managers and HR.
- Communicate it to the employees and get their buy-in for the new alignment and job role.
- Once all realignment has been completed, an assessment can be done for requirements to hire external skilled employees.

Capability uplift

Capability uplift is essential to improve the productivity of existing and new employees. It is also required to continuously improve the skills of the employees as per the requirements of the new initiatives of the IOSpeed to deliver the strategic objectives. The following are high-level steps to set up a successful capability uplift initiative:

- Collect a list of all employees that were part of realignment as well as new hires from departmental managers
- Make a matrix of employees, job roles, skills required by job role and existing skills of employees
- Establish an experienced team across IOSpeed organisation, who are SMEs
- Assessment of internal skilled resources, who have experience on skills required by job roles and also who can teach or have mentorship skills
- Partnership with vendors and external training partners for the skills that are lacking internally. Create a team of SMEs and trainers who would assist the employees on skill uplift
- Design and finalise the training courses (theoretical and practical)
- Create training plans based on the job roles
- Work with HR and managers to adopt the training plans as part of employees' career goals and performance targets. Make sure that these become targets for each employee and part of performance reviews at the end of the year
- Communicate the finalised plan to targeted employees and their managers
- Launch the capability uplift programmes across IOSpeed organisation

Establish Centre of Excellence (COE)

As IOSpeed kick off the transformation journey across organisation to deliver strategic objectives, it is beneficial to set up a Community of Practice (CoP) or Centre of Excellence (CoE). There can be more than one CoP or CoE within IOSpeed as it depends on the business and technology themes being used as part of transformation. For instance, IOSpeed can have a CoP for blockchain architecture standards and good practices.

The following are some of the steps to establish a successful CoP or CoE:

- Collect feedback on the requirements for upcoming transformational projects, skill gap within the organisation and teams working on them.
- One of strategic objectives of IOSpeed is to design a fully automated payment system that can use Fiat currency (GBP, USD) and also Crypto

currencies to transact on digital ART. This requires using the best architecture, cyber and operational best practices. It would be beneficial to establish a CoP and CoE to exchange ideas and set up standards.

- Get sponsorship and buy-in from the senior management as COP and CoE require SME time and also budget for innovation.
- Select stakeholders for each CoP and CoE. It needs to be a panel with exceptional skills and also who can contribute towards setting up standards, analyse the existing business process and suggest improvements.
- Select an owner of the CoP and CoE. The owner needs to schedule recursive sessions with the stakeholders and capture minutes/actions.
- The sessions must have a clear agenda. Every session must have minutes of the meeting and actions assigned to stakeholders with a due date.
- Invite external industry experts as required on the CoP and CoE to provide the latest developments on innovative technologies like blockchain, cyber security and more.

Programme and milestone governance

Many programmes fail without delivering a business value, wasting time and money, without a tight governance. Hence it is important to spend time on setting up programme level governance to deliver strategic milestones successfully. In this section, we will walk through good practices to establish governance:

- Define appropriate milestones as part of the programme deliverables.
- Milestones can be monthly, quarterly or yearly depending on the complexity.
- Categorise milestones into levels to set up parent and child relationship. For instance, creating an interoperability with various blockchains can be level 1 (parent). Multiple child milestones can be classified as Level 2–4. All these milestones have a target to deliver programme level outcome.
- Each milestone must have quantitative and qualitative benefits associated with them.
- Milestones must be reviewed and measured on a weekly basis to assess the progress as well as highlight any risks/issues against them.
- Transparency, clarity and communication are essential for all milestones. An appropriate communication and reporting mechanism needs to be set up to provide updates to all stakeholders across the IOSpeed organisation.
- Every programme and milestone has risks and issues associated with them. It is essential to raise them on time.
- Budget allocation for the programme and individual milestones needs to be managed with caution. The potential of overspend or underspend

Governance model - framework	
Executive summary	
A high-level summary of the purpose of governance model and what are the benefits that can be delivered as part of the model	
Strategic initiatives	**RAG (Red, Amber, Green) status**
Includes list of strategic objectives and the purpose of them against organization vision and mission	Provide a RAG status against each initiative and the whole programme that has made up of multiple incentives
Strategic alignment of the initiatives	**Re-pivot of the initiatives Roadmap, timelines and budget**
Clear mapping of initiatives to strategy to make sure all initiatives are aligned to the strategy of the organisation	Provide a clear articulation of the initiatives that have to reset in terms of timelines, scope change and budget re-allocation. Each initiatives must have a risk or issues against it
Roadmap and timelines	to justify the re-pivoting.
Define a roadmap of the initiatives, their delivery timelines, setup KPIs, dependencies and business outcomes	**Deliverables and success stories**
Budget allocation and % of budget spend	Provide a list of any business success story through the initiative's delivery. Provide a list of any initiatives that has been completed successfully.
Align the budget against each initiative and measure the % of budget spend for each initiatives	**Bottlenecks and ask from Management**
Risks and Issues	Provide a list of any bottlenecks that has a potential to impact the delivery of the initiatives on time and budget. It should also have a clear ask from the management to support it.
Define a list of all potential risks against each initiative. If the Risks have become issue, provide details of the issues as well.	

Figure 8.3 Governance template.

of allocated budget needs to be highlighted to the sponsors of the programme promptly. A delay in highlighting the budget concerns can have an impact on the whole strategy of the company and can have disastrous outcomes.

- Every programme and milestone within it must create business value and align to the IOSpeed strategy (Figure 8.3).

Define the operating model

The operating model has a big role in establishing the structure to run the organisation business effectively. It defines how IOSpeed will operate the business. The existing operation model is called 'Operating Model', and if an organisation is going through strategic transformation, the future operating model is called 'Target Operating Model'. These terms are also classified as

- Operating model: How an organisation operates currently? – 'As-is model'
- Target operating model: How an organisation will operate in future? – 'Target Operating Model'.

The following are the steps to design and establish an effective operating model for IOSpeed:

- Create a baseline of the existing operating model for IOSpeed. It should include all functions of the organisation and how they operate to provide value to the end customer.
- Define requirement for the target operating model. This should define how the new functions will operate.

- The roles and responsibilities of each function should be defined for the target operating model.
- A leadership team to run the function should be clearly defined.
- There should be a clear definition of the business process for the target operating mode and interaction between each function. The goal must always be to create value for the customer.
- There should be clear definition of Change and Run budgets and what it will deliver. Change budget is for transformation of the organisation including innovation, developing new platforms/products, changing the business processes and so on and finally how to improve customer satisfaction and value. On the other hand, Run budget is to operate the Business-as-Usual (BAU) operations of the organisation to maintain and operate existing business.
- The following template is the best example of the IOSpeed operating model to launch a Digital ART marketplace based on blockchain technology.

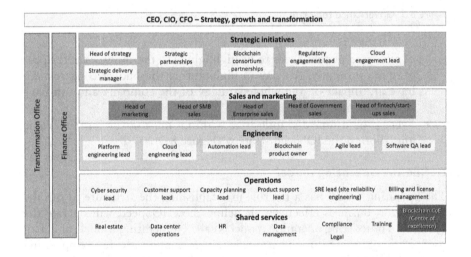

Evaluation of strategy execution

Evaluation of the strategy execution is necessary to showcase the delivery of the strategic outcomes and also to learn lessons from the whole journey. In a complex transformational programme, no one can achieve the outcomes without risks/issues and also mistakes. The recommendation is to assess the journey to design, manage and execute the objectives.

The following is the critical evaluation of the strategic execution:

- It is essential to evaluate if the programmes delivered strategic outcomes and also within allocated budget. Learning from past mistakes on missing targets as well as budget allocations is essential for future success of the strategy execution

- Evaluation of the employee's productivity and loyalty towards the strategic programmes is important. This can highlight the deficiencies about the leadership and how a programme should be managed in future
- Strategy evaluation should include assessment of strategic objective delivery. It is important to evaluate the gaps in executing the programmes, unpinning the strategic objectives and what more can be done to improve the governance to get final strategic outcomes
- The evaluation of the business outcomes and value addition aligned to the vision and mission of the company is essential to deliver successful strategy

Strategic outcome delivered

Transparency is crucial in evaluating whether the strategic outcomes have been delivered. The sponsor of the programme is accountable to report on the delivery of the outcomes to all stakeholders.

All deliverables should be evaluated against the set KPIs and the milestones set at the beginning of the strategy execution.

In this section, we will evaluate the strategic outcome for IOSpeed. The following is a list of outcomes delivered in this case study for IOSpeed:

- A fully digital marketplace to buy, sell and exchange ART master pieces
- Provide a secure and transparent platform to collect and sell ART such as paintings, photographs, animations, short films and so on.
- Provide a faster way to transact any kind of digital art
- Provide a complete audit of transactions and proof of ownership of the art pieces
- Platform launches in UK with regulatory approval for customer confidence and security
- Full ownership of the platform and customer data
- Full integration and support of most of the smart mobile phones, tablets and web browsers
- A mobile app with multiple functionalities to complete end-to-end transactions to buy, sell and exchange art collectibles
- Provide a wallet to store digital currency to be able to transact on the marketplace. The wallet is fully controlled by customers
- Launch of IOSpeed's own coin attached to Fiat currency (GBP)
- A full KYC (know your customers) as part of customer onboarding. This includes art collectors and also artists who design the art. This can also be called buyers and sellers
- A fully automated marketplace without a need for any intermediators. A secure and audited smart contract to facilitate end-to-end transactions
- 24/7 support team to manage the platform and assist customers
- Best-in-class leadership team
- A fully trained team to manage the day-to-day operations of the platform

Strategic outcome not delivered

Although the IOSpeed initial target was to go global and gain market in various countries through the use of digital technology, an executive decision was made to launch the product and platform in UK first and then look for opportunities in other countries.

The following is a list of strategic outcomes that were not delivered due to the decision made by the board of directors based on risk and rewards:

- Launch the platform in other countries than UK
- Support of multiple Crypto currencies to carry out a transaction on the platform
- Approval of other regulators than only the UK regulator for the platform

Benefits delivered to IOSpeed

The strategy was successfully executed to deliver most of the strategic outcomes. IOSpeed can now focus on onboarding existing customers to the new digital platform and also to gain more market share in UK to improve the revenues.

The following is a list of benefits delivered through the strategy execution:

- Launch of a digital art marketplace in UK based on innovative technology like blockchain
- Best-in-class product and platform development making it simple and easy to be launched in other countries in future
- Retain existing employees and attract new skilled employees to run the operations efficiently
- Appropriate allocation of budget for the innovation
- Retain existing customers and attract new customers
- Highly motivated and skilled employees
- Potential to gain an IP (intellectual property) for the marketplace product and platform. This can increase IOSpeed chances of a successful IPO in future
- Shift the substantial % of Run budget to manage the business-as-usual (BAU) activities, to change budget to support innovation and to transform the organisation to be more innovative, agile and deliver with speed
- Improvement of the IOSpeed brand image to make them a highly innovative company
- Growth in sales revenue
- Growth in customer number using the platform for Digital ART
- Growth in the artists using the platform to display and sell their digital art

- A high ROI. It is forecasted to recover initial investment within 2 years of the platform launch and be profitable from the third year
- Improvement on the potential to expand the marketplace to other countries and get regulatory approval post the successful launch in UK
- Gaining a competitive advantage over their competitors.

Lessons learnt

Every transformational and strategic initiative has complex interdependencies between multiple internal and external factors. Due to the complexity, it is often possible to make mistakes or be a victim of uncontrolled risks/issues. The most important step is to learn from them to make the strategic initiatives better controlled in future. This will also answer the question of what could have been done better?

The following is a list of lessons learnt from the IOSpeed transformation journey:

- IOSpeed could have reviewed their strategy on time to avoid damaging their brand image and losing customers and artists to their competitors.
- Balancing Run and Change budget is critical. IOSpeed should have allocated their budget more towards change. Change budget incorporates innovation and other transformational initiatives to be competitive in the market.
- Human capital is essential for any company trying to disrupt the market with innovative solutions. IOSpeed should have made more efforts to retain the employees by providing them skill uplift and also provide them benefits based on the performance targets.
- IOSpeed had to spend substantial time to train the existing employees on innovative technologies and also hire new employees from the market. This situation could have been avoided, or an impact could have been reduced by running a capability uplift programme to uplift employees' skills.
- The IOSpeed leadership team should have selected the option to build their own digital art marketplace rather than evaluating the third-party platform. This could have saved time and money.

Summary

Human brain remembers and learns quicker when knowledge is applied to create something real. This chapter was designed to exactly do the same thing. In this case study, we applied most of the knowledge learnt through this book and applied on a real use case through this case study.

This case study showcases how a struggling company tries to transform itself through innovation and gain a competitive advantage in the market. IOSpeed transformed itself by disrupting the market through innovative technologies including blockchain. IOSpeed went through a brand-new strategy and executed it successfully. They launched a brand-new digital marketplace to connect art collectors and art designers through blockchain technology called NFT.

IOSpeed recovered its brand image, improved revenue, grew its customers and artists using new digital platform and successfully created skilled and motivated human capital. They increased the allocation of its budget on innovation and most importantly became the most trusted digital art marketplace in the UK.

Chapter 9

Conclusion

Blockchain is on a journey to be adopted in every industry. The value addition of adopting blockchain is significant.

In this book, we have gone through the following topics:

- Basics of blockchain technology
- Technical architecture of blockchain
- Overview of Crypto currencies and how to transact them
- Overview of blockchain products and platforms
- Critical analysis of blockchain technology
- Use cases of blockchain in the industry to replace or improve existing business journeys
- Framework to assess the validity of blockchain adoption
- Strategy formulation and execution of strategic outcomes
- Business case creation to achieve budget allocation for strategic initiatives
- A case study to apply the knowledge earned in the whole book.

Although there is a lot of hype about blockchain, some of it is real as well. The adoption of blockchain is still on a journey to become mainstream, and the journey has just started. In my view, blockchain has real potential to disrupt all sectors due to its unique features including immutability, transparency and consensus mechanisms.

IS BLOCKCHAIN A HYPE OR A HOAX?

As the book title is *Blockchain: A Hype or a Hoax?*, it is essential to conclude the outcome of this book in this chapter. We discussed a lot of topics trying to focus on real-life use cases as well as critical analysis of adoption of blockchain within different sectors.

In this section, we will refresh and focus on articulating a conclusion. The following are the conclusive points to make an assessment on whether blockchain is a hype or a hoax:

DOI: 10.1201/9781003225607-9

Why blockchain is not a hoax?

- There has been a lot of hacking and scam about blockchain, especially on one of its first and most successful use cases, that is, Crypto currencies. Thousands of people lost their hard-earned savings through Crypto currency scams. High percentages of people who invested in Crypto currencies were hoping to become millionaires. The real problem was the lack of vetting and validation from investors before investing on the Crypto currencies.
- Multiple exchanges offering Crypto currencies were hacked, losing millions worth of real fiat currencies. This created a perception about blockchain technology being not secure. However, this perception is not valid. The hacking of Crypto exchanges and Crypto scams were successful due to the lack of education about technology as well as the lack of regulatory rules and standards. Blockchain technology is secure, transparent and immutable, but the hacking was successful due to the lack of skilled employees managing the exchanges, other technologies vulnerability, social engineering, regulations and gap in education.
- There are hundreds of new ICO (Initial Crypto Offering) projects are being launched every month. People invest into them by buying their coins to support the project delivery. They need to validate and assess the viability of the projects before investing their money into them. The assessment of the leadership team launching the ICO as well as project deliverables is very important. Having said that, not every ICO project is a scam or unsuccessful. Ethereum was also launched as an ICO, and people who invested into Ethereum ICO coins (Ether) have gained substantial capital returns now.
- Regulators around the globe are learning, upskilling and working on regulating the blockchain market. Once there is an established blockchain regulatory framework, customers and investors will gain confidence on blockchain technology including Crypto currencies.
- There are also multiple start-ups launching a blockchain smart contract security and audit solutions. This will reduce the fraud and hacking of the blockchain eco-system that relies on automation of business processes using smart contracts.

Why blockchain is not a hype?

Blockchain is disrupting fintech, heathcare-techs, supply chain, entertainment, estate and the majority of the other industries that need digital identity, financial transaction transparency, automation, decentralisation and immutable transaction records. There are so many start-ups and incumbent players in the market. They are all trying to gain a competitive advantage through the use of blockchain technology. However, not all of them get to deliver a successful blockchain solution due to use of the blockchain technology for wrong use cases.

The following are some of the important facts that provide insights on why blockchain is not a hype as well:

- Many organisations do not perform a proactive assessment before investment on blockchain use cases. They tend to fail, wasting money and time. As discussed in this book, organisations need to go through an assessment using blockchain fit-score assessment before starting a programme to solve a problem using blockchain.
- It is recommended to define a problem statement and requirements to solve the problem before directly making a decision to launch a programme to use blockchain technology. This way, there are no surprises of failure during or near the programme completion.
- It is recommended to try blockchain for small use cases that are part of a complex business problem. This way, an organisation can quickly prove the benefits of blockchain for specific business problems or fail fast to rule out the use of blockchain.
- An organisation should use an agile methodology to break down the complex use case into micro elements. This way blockchain can be applied for micro elements and re-prioritisation can be done before losing money and time.
- A deep dive on the business problems and assessment of technology stack to facilitate the resolution of the business problems can be beneficial in the longer term. The benefit would be a successful blockchain-based solution delivery.
- An end-to-end solution to solve a business problem requires multiple technologies. Blockchain is one of the parts of technology stack. An initial assessment to define the business problem, current architecture, business processes and gaps is critical before even starting the planning for the new solution. Most of the solutions fail due to the lack of gathering of initial requirements.
- Blockchain technology is still maturing to get adoption in real use cases and especially on production ready solutions. There is a lack of knowledge and skills in the industry with enough and relevant experience to assess and deliver a blockchain-based solution to solve the real-life use cases. Organisations need to uplift the employee's capability or hire external skilled resources to carry out blockchain use cases assessment before investing their budget on a solution that might not be fit for purpose.
- To conclude, blockchain technology is here to stay, and its adoption journey has just started to disrupt all industries. In order to get successful results from this unique and exciting technology, organisations need to follow the guidelines and recommendations discussed

in this book. The use cases can deliver business value addition for the organisation and customers if assessment and due diligence are followed from the start of the strategic formulation to deliver the strategic initiatives.

BEST PRACTICES TO ADOPT BLOCKCHAIN AND GAIN A COMPETITIVE ADVANTAGE

As concluded in the above sections, blockchain is a disrupting and unique technology to benefit business on multiple channels and scales. Organisations need to make use of blockchain technology on right and appropriate use cases to avoid failures.

In this section, we will discuss the best practices to use the blockchain technology for the right business purpose to deliver strategic outcomes.

- A solution needs to solve an existing or future problem within a business rather than finding a problem after creating a solution to justify investment. This should be a mantra for any strategic initiative.
- The above rule is also applicable for innovative technologies like blockchain. Any investment must be to solve a business problem or to support the business to be more competitive in the market to sustain and grow.
- A strategic level deep dive needs to be carried out on existing business processes, the way of working, external and internal forces and internal and external capabilities of the organisation. This step is most important to understand the forces supporting the organisation and set a baseline before going any further on strategy formulation.
- Once a baseline on the organisation has been established, the next natural step is to do go ahead with formulating a strategy based on organisation vision and mission.
- Part of the strategy formulation involves creating strategic initiatives to fix the existing gaps within the organisation and setting up strategic objectives to enable the organisation meeting its vision and mission.
- Strategy formulation should review the existing operating model of the organisation to enable them reducing the run budget and allocate more budget on change budget for innovation. This will also be part of the target operating model for the organisation as to how the organisation will look like after the strategy execution.
- Strategy formulation should define the strategic initiaives. Some of the initiatives would be to invest on disrupting technologies like blockchain, artificial intelligence, Cyber security and so on.
- As part of this section, we will now focus on blockchain technology that has been selected for strategic transformation. The following points are best practices to formulate a strategy for blockchain-based strategic transformation and a successful strategy execution to deliver the strategic objectives.

- During the strategy formulation process, use of blockchain technology needs to be focused on delivering solutions to business problems that are aligned to strategic outcomes.
- As discussed in Chapter 5, potential blockchain-based solutions should go through a blockchain fit-score and feasibility framework to make sure a right use case has been selected to use blockchain technology.
- Once an appropriate business problem or strategic initiative has been identified through the blockchain framework, the selected use case needs to go through strategy formulation and execution methodologies as discussed in Chapter 6. Any strategic initiative selected to use blockchain technology must deliver a strategic outcome and align to the organisation's vision and mission.
- Strategy execution should launch multiple programmes with key deliverables, roadmap, timelines and budget allocation.
- As discussed in Chapter 6, one of the main initiatives highlighted as part of the strategic formulation or execution was uplifting the skills of the organisation. To be more specific, the skills of all employees including the leadership team should be uplifted. Business and technical teams within the organisation should go through capability uplift on innovative technologies including blockchain. This will make sure that the organisation is ready to have a competitive advantage.
- Every programme aligned to strategic objectives must go through programme management guidelines and governance to make sure that the outcomes are on target and within allocated budget. This was also discussed in Chapter 6.
- Every programme needs to create a business case for each initiative to justify the budget allocation and also deliver the outcomes within budget and timelines. This also makes sure that each initiative within the strategic programme delivers an outcome that is aligned to the organisation strategy. This was discussed in Chapter 7.

SUMMARY

In this book, we have gone through a journey with a deep dive on technical, business and strategic value deliverables of blockchain technology. We appreciated the technical aspects of blockchain and how it is and will disrupt the industry. Blockchain technology's journey is going through unimaginable transformation and within about 5–10 years will become mature and establish mainstream adoption. As discussed in this book, blockchain will disrupt every single industry as long as it is adopted on an appropriate use case through appropriate due diligence.

References

101 Blockchains, 2021. *A strategist's guide to blockchain.* [Online]. Available at: https://101blockchains.com/blockchain-business-strategy/ [Accessed 28 05 2022].

99Bitcoins, 2022. *Dead coins from dead coins—1600+ cryptocurrencies forgotten by this world (2022 updated).* [Online]. Available at: https://99bitcoins.com/deadcoins/#nnbitcoins-deadcoins-list [Accessed 22 05 2022] (Digital, 2021) (Health, 2022)

Acord Solutions Group, 2022. *ADEPTTM (ACORD Data Exchange Platform & Translator) platform.* [Online]. Available at: https://www.acordsolutions.com/solutions/adept [Accessed 18 05 2022].

Bank of England, 2021a. *Digital currencies.* [Online]. https://www.bankofengland.co.uk/research/digital-currencies [Accessed 31 01 2022].

Bank of England, 2021b. *PS6/21 | CP29/19 | DP1/18 Operational resilience: Impact tolerances for important business services.* [Online]. Available at: https://www.bankofengland.co.uk/prudential-regulation/publication/2018/building-the-uk-financial-sectors-operational-resilience-discussion-paper [Accessed 28 05 2022].

BBC News, 2019. *Cryptoqueen: How this woman scammed the world, then vanished.* [Online]. Available at: https://www.bbc.co.uk/news/stories-50435014 [Accessed 22 05 2022].

BCG, 2022. *Corporate strategy.* [Online]. Available at: https://www.bcg.com/capabilities/corporate-finance-strategy/corporate-strategy [Accessed 28 05 2022].

Berkeley, 2022. *Our courses.* [Online]. Available at: https://blockchain.berkeley.edu/courses/ [Accessed 22 05 2022].

Bernard Marr & Co, 2021. *The 5 big problems with blockchain everyone should be aware of.* [Online]. Available at: https://bernardmarr.com/the-5-big-problems-with-blockchain-everyone-should-be-aware-of/ [Accessed 22 05 2022].

BigThink, 2021. *10 Emerging technologies that will change our world.* [Online]. Available at: https://bigthink.com/the-future/10-emerging-technologies-change-world/ [Accessed 22 05 2022].

Biometrics Institute, 2022. *Types of biometrics.* [Online]. Available at: https://www.biometricsinstitute.org/what-is-biometrics/types-of-biometrics/ [Accessed 22 05 2022].

BIS, 2020. Central bank digital currencies: *Foundational principles and core features*. [Online]. Available at: https://www.bis.org/publ/othp33.pdf [Accessed 31 01 2020].

Bitcoin, 2022. *Bitcoin*. [Online]. Available at: https://bitcoin.org/en/ [Accessed 22 05 2022].

Blockchain Council, 2022. *How blockchain can be used in regulatory reporting & how it works?* [Online]. Available at: https://www.blockchain-council.org/blockchain/blockchain-can-used-regulatory-reporting-works/ [Accessed 28 05 2022].

Blockchain Workbench, 2022. *Forge your blockchain skills*. [Online]. Available at: https://blockchainworkbench.com [Accessed 22 05 2022].

Boston Consulting Group, World Economic Forum, 2021. *Digital assets, distributed ledger technology and the future of capital market*. [Online]. Available at: http://www3.weforum.org/docs/WEF_Digital_Assets_Distributed_Ledger_Technology_2021.pdf [Accessed 18 05 2022].

Bouchrika, I., 2021. *7 Universities offering online blockchain, cryptocurrency and FinTech education*. [Online]. Available at: https://research.com/degrees/universities-offering-online-blockchain-cryptocurrency-and-fintech-education [Accessed 22 05 2022].

Brown, G., and Whittle, R., 2019. *More than 1,000 cryptocurrencies have already failed—Here's what will affect successes in future*. [Online]. Available at: https://theconversation.com/more-than-1-000-cryptocurrencies-have-already-failed-heres-what-will-affect-successes-in-future-127463 [Accessed 22 05 2022].

Builtin, 2021. *34 Blockchain applications and real-world use cases disrupting the status quo*. [Online]. Available at: https://builtin.com/blockchain/blockchain-applications [Accessed 22 05 2022].

Cabinet Office, 2019. *Digital identity: Call for evidence*. [Online]. Available at: https://assets.publishing.service.gov.uk/government/uploads/system/uploads/attachment_data/file/973979/Digital_Identity_-_Call_for_Evidence_V2.pdf [Accessed 18 05 2022].

Calista, 2022. *End-to-end, supply chain solutions platform*. [Online]. Available at: https://calista.globaltrade.services/CALISTAWEB/cusLogin/login.cl [Accessed 18 05 2022].

Cambridge University, 2022. *Bitcoin network power demand*. [Online]. Available at: https://ccaf.io/cbeci/index [Accessed 22 05 2022].

CargoSmart, 2022. *CargoSmart*. [Online]. Available at: https://www.cargosmart.com/en-us/ [Accessed 18 05 2022].

Carson, B., Romanelli, G., Walsh, P., and Zhumaev, A., 2018. *Blockchain beyond the hype: What is the strategic business value?* [Online]. Available at: https://www.mckinsey.com/business-functions/mckinsey-digital/our-insights/blockchain-beyond-the-hype-what-is-the-strategic-business-value [Accessed 28 05 2022].

Chandler, S., 2020. *Here are the worst uses for blockchain technology developed so far*. [Online]. Available at: https://www.cryptovantage.com/news/here-are-the-worst-uses-for-blockchain-technology-developed-so-far/ [Accessed 22 05 2022].

Chapman, L., and Kharif, O., 2021. *Biggest crypto coin sale fueled by 'Pump' scheme, research says.* [Online]. Available at: https://www.bloomberg.com/news/articles/2021-09-02/billionaire-backed-exchange-funded-by-alleged-scheme-to-pump-price [Accessed 22 05 2022].

China Banking News, 2019. *Chengdu launches blockchain cross-border trade platform to connect China and Europe.* [Online]. Available at: https://www.chinabankingnews.com/2019/10/30/chengdu-launches-blockchain-cross-border-trade-platform-to-connect-china-and-europe/ [Accessed 18 05 2022].

CIPS, 2022. *What is a supply chain.* [Online]. Available at: https://www.cips.org/knowledge/procurement-topics-and-skills/supply-chain-management/what-is-a-supply-chain/ [Accessed 18 04 2022].

CoinDesk, 2021. *The top universities for blockchain by coindesk 2021.* [Online]. Available at: https://www.coindesk.com/learn/2021/10/04/the-top-universities-for-blockchain-by-coindesk-2021/ [Accessed 22 05 2022].

CoinGecko, 2022. *Cryptocurrency prices by market cap.* [Online]. Available at: https://www.coingecko.com [Accessed 22 05 2022].

CoinMarketCap, 2022a. *All cryptocurrencies.* [Online]. Available at: https://coinmarketcap.com/all/views/all/ [Accessed 22 05 2022].

CoinMarketCap, 2022b. *In full—The complete ICO calendar.* [Online]. Available at: https://coinmarketcap.com/ico-calendar/ [Accessed 22 05 2022].

CoinMarketCap, 2022c. *Top cryptocurrency spot exchanges.* [Online]. Available at: https://coinmarketcap.com/rankings/exchanges/ [Accessed 18 05 2022].

Coinopsy, 2022a. *Coinopsy.* [Online]. Available at: https://www.coinopsy.com [Accessed 22 05 2022].

Coinopsy, 2022b. *Dead coins.* [Online]. Available at: https://www.coinopsy.com/dead-coins/scam/ [Accessed 22 05 2022].

Consensys, 2020. *ConsenSys acquires Quorum® platform from J.P. Morgan.* [Online]. Available at: https://consensys.net/blog/press-release/consensys-acquires-quorum-platform-from-jp-morgan/ [Accessed 18 05 2022].

Consensys, 2022a. *Access the Codefi assets sandbox.* [Online]. Available at: https://consensys.net/codefi/assets/sandbox/ [Accessed 28 05 2022].

Consensus, 2022b. *Blockchain in financial services.* [Online]. Available at: https://consensys.net/blockchain-use-cases/finance/ [Accessed 18 05 2022].

Consensys, 2022c. *GoQuorum enterprise ethereum client.* [Online]. Available at: https://docs.goquorum.consensys.net/en/stable/ [Accessed 18 05 2022].

Consensys, 2022d. *Quorum.* [Online]. Available at: https://consensys.net/quorum/ [Accessed 22 05 2022].

Consensys, 2022e. *Unlock Web3. Build on ethereum.* Collaborate worldwide. [Online]. Available at: https://consensys.net/blockchain-use-cases/social-impact/ [Accessed 22 05 2022].

Contour, 2022. *Contour.* [Online]. Available at: https://contour.network [Accessed 18 05 2022].

Conversation, 2019. *More than 1,000 cryptocurrencies have already failed—Here's what will affect successes in future.* [Online]. Available at: https://theconversation.com/more-than-1-000-cryptocurrencies-have-already-failed-heres-what-will-affect-successes-in-future-127463 [Accessed 22 05 2022].

Cornell, 2022. *Cornell blockchain.* [Online]. Available at: https://cornellblock-chain.org [Accessed 22 05 2022].

Coso, 2022. *Committee of sponsoring organizations of the treadway commission.* [Online]. Available at: https://www.coso.org [Accessed 28 05 2022].

Dale, O., 2018. *A look at 8 of the most successful ICOs of all time.* [Online]. Available at: https://blockonomi.com/most-successful-icos/ [Accessed 22 05 2022].

Disruptor, 2018. *40 Startups using blockchain to transform healthcare [market map].* [Online]. Available at: https://www.disruptordaily.com/blockchain-market-map-healthcare/ [Accessed 18 05 2022].

DP World, 2020. *DP world joins with TradeLens to digitise global supply chains.* [Online]. Available at: https://www.dpworld.com/news/releases/dp-world-joins-with-tradelens-to-digitise-global-supply-chains/ [Accessed 18 05 2022].

E&Enterprise, 2022. *UAE trade connect.* [Online]. Available at: https://www.etisalatdigital.ae/en/uae-trade-connect.jsp [Accessed 18 05 2022].

ECB, 2022. *Eurosystem launches digital euro project.* [Online]. Available at: https://www.ecb.europa.eu/press/pr/date/2021/html/ecb.pr210714~d99198ea23.en.html [Accessed 31 01 2022].

Economist, 2021a. *Govcoins.* [Online]. Available at: https://www.economist.com/weeklyedition/2021-05-08 [Accessed 31 01 2022].

Economist, 2021b. *What if bitcoin went to zero?* [Online]. Available at: https://www.economist.com/finance-and-economics/2021/08/02/what-if-bitcoin-went-to-zero [Accessed 22 05 2022].

Economist, 2022. *Economist.* [Online]. Available at: https://www.economist.com/ [Accessed 31 01 2022].

eCornell, 2022. *Blockchain essentials.* [Online]. Available at: https://ecornell.cornell.edu/certificates/technology/blockchain-essentials/ [Accessed 22 05 2022].

Ethereum, 2022a. *Ethereum.* [Online]. Available at: https://ethereum.org/en/ [Accessed 31 01 2022].

Ethereum, 2022b. *Ethereum DeFi.* [Online]. Available at: https://ethereum.org/en/defi/ [Accessed 31 01 2022].

Ethereum, 2022c. *Ethereum networks.* [Online]. Available at: https://ethereum.org/en/developers/docs/networks/ [Accessed 28 05 2022].

Ethereum, 2022d. *Ethereum upgrades.* [Online]. Available at: https://ethereum.org/en/eth2/ [Accessed 22 05 2022].

eTradeConnect, 2022. *eTradeConnect.* [Online]. Available at: https://www.etradeconnect.net/Portal [Accessed 18 05 2022].

European Commission, 2022a. *Blockchain strategy.* [Online]. Available at: https://digital-strategy.ec.europa.eu/en/policies/blockchain-strategy [Accessed 28 05 2022].

European Commission, 2022b. *Legal and regulatory framework for blockchain.* [Online]. Available at: https://digital-strategy.ec.europa.eu/en/policies/regulatory-framework-blockchain [Accessed 28 05 2022].

FCA, 2020. *Digital regulatory reporting.* [Online]. Available at: https://www.fca.org.uk/innovation/regtech/digital-regulatory-reporting [Accessed 28 05 2022].

FCA, 2022a. *Global financial innovation network (GFIN)*. [Online]. Available at: https://www.fca.org.uk/firms/innovation/global-financial-innovation-network [Accessed 28 05 2022].

FCA, 2022b. *Regulatory sandbox accepted firms*. [Online]. Available at: https://www.fca.org.uk/firms/innovation/regulatory-sandbox/accepted-firms [Accessed 28 05 2022].

Finance Magnates, 2020. *Blockchain: Is it all hype?* [Online]. Available at: https://www.financemagnates.com/fintech/blockchain-is-it-all-hype/ [Accessed 18 05 2022].

Financier Worldwide, 2018. *The emergence of the ICO*. [Online]. Available at: https://www.financierworldwide.com/the-emergence-of-the-ico#.YYgq2S-l2J9 [Accessed 22 05 2022].

Gartner, 2019. *Gartner reveals seven mistakes to avoid in blockchain projects*. [Online]. Available at: https://www.gartner.com/en/newsroom/press-releases/2019-06-12-gartner-reveals-seven-mistakes-to-avoid-in-blockchain [Accessed 22 05 2022].

Gartner, 2022. *Blockchain platforms reviews and ratings*. [Online]. Available at: https://www.gartner.com/reviews/market/blockchain-platforms [Accessed 18 05 2022].

GFIN, 2021. *The global financial innovation network (GFIN)*. [Online]. Available at: https://www.thegfin.com [Accessed 28 05 2022].

GSBN, 2022. *GSBN—Our platform*. [Online]. Available at: https://www.gsbn.trade/our-platform [Accessed 18 05 2022].

Harvard Business Review, Nanda, R., and Bussgang, J., 2018. *The hidden costs of initial coin offerings*. [Online]. Available at: https://hbr.org/2018/11/the-hidden-costs-of-initial-coin-offerings [Accessed 22 05 2022].

Harvard Business Review, Tapscott, D., and Vargas, R. V., 2021. *Blockchain is changing how companies can engage with customers*. [Online]. Available at: https://hbr.org/2021/01/blockchain-is-changing-how-companies-can-engage-with-customers [Accessed 22 05 2022].

Harvard Business School, 1985. *The value chain*. [Online]. Available at: https://www.isc.hbs.edu/strategy/business-strategy/Pages/the-value-chain.aspx [Accessed 18 05 2022].

Harvard Business School, 2022. *Strategy explained*. [Online]. Available at: https://www.isc.hbs.edu/strategy/Pages/strategy-explained.aspx [Accessed 28 05 2022].

Harvard, 2022. *Best in free blockchain courses*. [Online]. Available at: http://tech.seas.harvard.edu/free-blockchain [Accessed 22 05 2022].

Homeland Security, 2021. *Biometrics*. [Online]. Available at: https://www.dhs.gov/biometrics [Accessed 22 05 2022].

Hyperledger Fondation, 2022a. *Case studies—Browse various use cases powered by Hyperledger technologies*. [Online]. Available at: https://www.hyperledger.org/learn/case-studies [Accessed 18 05 2022].

Hyperledger Fondation, 2022b. *Hyperledger foundation*. [Online]. Available at: https://www.hyperledger.org [Accessed 18 05 2022].

Hyperledger Foundation, 2022c. *Hyoerledger sawtooth*. [Online]. Available at: https://www.hyperledger.org/use/sawtooth [Accessed 18 05 2022].

Hyperledger Foundation, 2022d. *Hyperledger fabric.* [Online]. Available at: https://www.hyperledger.org/use/fabric [Accessed 18 05 2022].

Hyperledger Foundation, 2022e. *Hyperledger indy.* [Online]. Available at: https://www.hyperledger.org/use/hyperledger-indy [Accessed 18 05 2022].

Hyperledger Foundation, 2022f. *Hyperledger quilt.* [Online]. Available at: https://www.hyperledger.org/use/quilt [Accessed 18 05 2022].

Hyperledger Foundation, 2022g. *Hyperledger transact.* [Online]. Available at: https://www.hyperledger.org/use/transact [Accessed 18 05 2022].

IBM, 2022a. *IBM blockchain.* [Online]. Available at: https://www.ibm.com/uk-en/blockchain [Accessed 22 05 2022].

IBM, 2022b. *IBM value package 2.0 sandbox.* [Online]. Available at: https://www.ibm.com/partnerworld/program/benefits/value-package-sandbox [Accessed 28 05 2022].

ICO Rating, 2022. *ICO rating.* [Online]. Available at: https://www.crypto-rating.com/ico-rating/ [Accessed 31 01 2022].

ICODrops, 2022. *Active ICO.* [Online]. Available at: https://icodrops.com/category/active-ico/ [Accessed 31 01 2022].

ICOHolder, 2022. *Hot and trending blockchain companies.* [Online]. Available at: https://icoholder.com [Accessed 22 05 2022].

IMF, 2019. *Central bank digital currencies: 4 Questions and answers.* [Online]. Available at: https://blogs.imf.org/2019/12/12/central-bank-digital-currencies-4-questions-and-answers/ [Accessed 31 01 2022].

Infosys, 2018. *Press release.* [Online]. Available at: https://www.infosys.com/newsroom/press-releases/2018/pioneers-blockchain-based-trade-network.html [Accessed 18 05 2022].

InstaDapp, 2022. *InstaDapp.* [Online]. Available at: https://defi.instadapp.io/ [Accessed 31 01 2022].

Instarem, 2018. *8 Most successful ICOs of all time with the highest ROI.* [Online]. Available at: https://www.instarem.com/blog/8-most-successful-icos-of-all-time/ [Accessed 18 05 2022].

Insurwave, 2022. *Insurwave.* [Online]. Available at: https://insurwave.com [Accessed 18 05 2022].

Investopedia, 2022a. *Best crypto exchanges.* [Online]. Available at: https://www.investopedia.com/best-crypto-exchanges-5071855 [Accessed 18 05 2022].

Invetopedia, 2022b. *Supply chain.* [Online]. Available at: https://www.investopedia.com/terms/s/supplychain.asp [Accessed 18 05 2022].

Investopedia, and Reiff, N., 2022. *How to identify cryptocurrency and ICO scams.* [Online]. Available at: https://www.investopedia.com/tech/how-identify-cryptocurrency-and-ico-scams/ [Accessed 22 05 2022].

IOTA, 2022. *An open, feeless data and value transfer protocol.* [Online]. Available at: https://www.iota.org [Accessed 28 05 2022].

ISO, 2022a. *ISO 31000 risk management.* [Online]. Available at: https://www.iso.org/iso-31000-risk-management.html [Accessed 28 05 2022].

ISO, 2022b. *ISO/IEC 27001 information security management.* [Online]. Available at: https://www.iso.org/isoiec-27001-information-security.html [Accessed 28 05 2022].

Iyer, S., 2019. *8 Most successful ICOs of all time with the highest ROI.* [Online]. Available at: https://www.instarem.com/blog/8-most-successful-icos-of-all-time/ [Accessed 22 05 2022].

Joshi, N., 2019. *Alternatives to blockchain that businesses must consider.* [Online]. Available at: https://www.allerin.com/blog/alternatives-to-blockchain-that-businesses-must-consider [Accessed 28 05 2022].

Kenton, W., 2022. *PEST analysis.* [Online]. Available at: https://www.investopedia.com/terms/p/pest-analysis.asp [Accessed 28 05 2022].

Komgo, 2022. *Komgo.* [Online]. Available at: https://www.komgo.io/about [Accessed 18 05 2022].

Marco Polo Network, 2022. *Why marco polo network.* [Online]. Available at: https://www.marcopolonetwork.com [Accessed 18 05 2022].

Martin, K., and Nauman, B., 2021. *Bitcoin's growing energy problem: 'It's a dirty currency'.* [Online]. Available at: https://www.ft.com/content/1aecb2db-8f61-427c-a413-3b929291c8ac [Accessed 22 05 2022].

MAS, 2022. *Sandbox.* [Online]. Available at: https://www.mas.gov.sg/development/fintech/sandbox [Accessed 28 05 2022].

Mauborgne, R., and Kim, C., 2022. *What is blue ocean strategy?* [Online]. Available at: https://www.blueoceanstrategy.com/what-is-blue-ocean-strategy/ [Accessed 28 05 2022].

McKinsey & Company, 2008. *Enduring ideas: The 7-S framework.* [Online]. Available at: https://www.mckinsey.com/business-functions/strategy-and-corporate-finance/our-insights/enduring-ideas-the-7-s-framework [Accessed 28 05 2022].

McKinsey & Company, 2015. *Beyond the hype: Blockchains in capital markets.* [Online]. Available at: https://www.mckinsey.com/industries/financial-services/our-insights/beyond-the-hype-blockchains-in-capital-markets [Accessed 18 05 2022].

McKinsey Digital, 2018. *Blockchain beyond the hype: What is the strategic business value?* [Online]. Available at: https://www.mckinsey.com/business-functions/mckinsey-digital/our-insights/blockchain-beyond-the-hype-what-is-the-strategic-business-value [Accessed 22 05 2022].

McKinsey Digital, 2021. *How to launch a new business: Three approaches that work.* [Online]. Available at: https://www.mckinsey.com/business-functions/mckinsey-digital/our-insights/how-to-launch-a-new-business-three-approaches-that-work [Accessed 28 05 2022].

Minehub, 2022. *Minehub—Global supply chains.* [Online]. Available at: https://minehub.com [Accessed 18 05 2022].

MIT Technology Review, 2019. *Once hailed as unhackable, blockchains are now getting hacked.* [Online]. Available at: https://www.technologyreview.com/2019/02/19/239592/once-hailed-as-unhackable-blockchains-are-now-getting-hacked/ [Accessed 22 05 2022].

MIT, 2022. *Blockchain technology and cryptocurrency courses by the digital currency initiate.* [Online]. Available at: https://dci.mit.edu/courses#mitstudentcourses [Accessed 22 05 2022].

Nakamoto, S., 2008. *Bitcoin: A peer-to-peer electronic cash system*. [Online]. Available at: https://www.ussc.gov/sites/default/files/pdf/training/annual-national-training-seminar/2018/Emerging_Tech_Bitcoin_Crypto.pdf [Accessed 18 05 2022].

Office for National Statistics, 2022. *GDP output approach—Low-level aggregates*. [Online]. Available at: https://www.ons.gov.uk/economy/grossdomesticproductgdp/datasets/ukgdpolowlevelaggregates [Accessed 18 05 2022].

Orion, 2022. *Your single point of access to the crypto market*. [Online]. Available at: https://www.orionprotocol.io [Accessed 18 05 2022].

Ovum, 2022. *Market landscape: Blockchain for telecoms*. [Online]. Available at: https://www.oracle.com/a/ocom/docs/corporate/analystrelations/ovum-blockchain-for-telecoms.pdf [Accessed 18 05 2022].

Oxford Learner's Dictionaries, 2022. *Strategy*. [Online]. Available at: https://www.oxfordlearnersdictionaries.com/definition/english/strategy [Accessed 28 05 2022].

Paiementor, 2019. *Trade finance basics*. [Online]. Available at: https://www.paiementor.com/trade-finance-basics/ [Accessed 18 05 2022].

Palm, 2022. *What is PALM?* [Online]. Available at: https://palm.io/get-palm/ [Accessed 28 05 2022].

Payments Canada, 2018. *New report from Payments Canada, the Bank of Canada, TMX group, Accenture and R3 proves that distributed ledger technology can enable equity settlement*. [Online]. Available at: https://www.payments.ca/about-us/news/new-report-payments-canada-bank-canada-tmx-group-accenture-and-r3-proves-distributed [Accessed 22 05 2022].

Peachey, K., 2021. *'We lost our life savings in a cryptocurrency scam'*. [Online]. Available at: https://www.bbc.co.uk/news/business-57983458 [Accessed 22 05 2022].

People's Bank of China, 2021. *Progress of research & development of E-CNY in China*. [Online]. Available at: http://www.pbc.gov.cn/en/3688110/3688172/4157443/4293696/2021071614584691871.pdf [Accessed 31 01 2022].

Porter, M. E. *Competitive Advantage: Creating and Sustaining Superior Performance*. Export Edition Ed. S.l. New York: Free Press, 2004.

Porter, M. E. *On Competition: Updated and Expanded Edition (Harvard Business Review Book)*. Export Edition, S.l. New York: Free Press, 2004.

PWC, 2016a. *Blockchain in the capital markets*. [Online]. Available at: https://www.pwc.co.uk/financial-services/fintech/assets/blockchain-in-capital-markets.pdf [Accessed 18 05 2022].

PWC, 2016b. *Blockchain in the insurance sector*. [Online]. Available at: https://www.pwc.co.uk/financial-services/fintech/assets/blockchain-in-insurance.pdf [Accessed 22 05 2022].

PWC, 2019. *Estonia—The digital republic secured by blockchain*. [Online]. Available at: https://www.pwc.com/gx/en/services/legal/tech/assets/estonia-the-digital-republic-secured-by-blockchain.pdf [Accessed 22 05 2022].

PWC, 2021. *PwC CBDC global index*. [Online]. Available at: https://www.pwc.com/gx/en/industries/financial-services/assets/pwc-cbdc-global-index-1st-edition-april-2021.pdf [Accessed 31 01 2022].

R3, 2022a. *Build multi-party solutions for a digital-first world.* [Online]. Available at: https://www.r3.com/customers/ [Accessed 18 05 2022].

R3, 2022b. *Digital currency accelerator.* [Online]. Available at: https://www.r3.com/digital-currency-sandbox/ [Accessed 28 05 2022].

R3, 2022c. *Direct digital collaboration.* [Online]. Available at: https://www.r3.com/corda-platform/ [Accessed 18 05 2022].

R3, 2022d. *r3.* [Online]. Available at: https://www.r3.com [Accessed 22 05 2022].

REIFF, N., 2022. *The Collapse of FTX: What Went Wrong with the Crypto Exchange?.* Available at: https://www.investopedia.com/what-went-wrong-with-ftx-6828447 [Accessed 20 11 2022].

Ripple, 2022a. *Cross-border payments settlement in seconds, not days.* [Online]. Available at: https://ripple.com/solutions/cross-border-payments/ [Accessed 18 05 2022].

Ripple, 2022b. *Ripple.* [Online]. Available at: https://ripple.com [Accessed 18 05 2022].

Ripple, 2022c. *XRP—Utility for the new global economy.* [Online]. Available at: https://ripple.com/xrp/market-performance/ [Accessed 18 05 2022].

Robinson, N. J., 2021. *Why cryptocurrency is a giant fraud.* [Online]. Available at: https://www.currentaffairs.org/2021/04/why-cryptocurrency-is-a-giant-fraud [Accessed 22 05 2022].

SandDollar, 2022. *Digital bahamian dollar.* [Online]. Available at: https://www.sanddollar.bs/ [Accessed 31 01 2022].

Selfkey, 2020. *A comprehensive list of cryptocurrency exchange hacks.* [Online]. Available at: https://selfkey.org/list-of-cryptocurrency-exchange-hacks/ [Accessed 22 05 2022].

SITA, 2020. *SITA and key industry partners launch MRO blockchain alliance.* [Online]. Available at: https://www.sita.aero/pressroom/news-releases/sita-joins-industry-partners-to-launch-mro-blockchain-alliance/ [Accessed 18 05 2022].

Skuchain, 2022. *Skuchain.* [Online]. Available at: https://www.skuchain.com/ec3/ [Accessed 18 05 2022].

Stellar, 2022. *Stellar.* [Online]. Available at: https://www.stellar.org/?locale=en [Accessed 18 05 2022].

Terra, 2022. *Terra 2.0.* [Online]. Available at: https://www.terra.money [Accessed 29 05 2022].

Thomas Reuters, 2020. *Blockchain 2020: The hype may be over, but the tech is here.* [Online]. Available at: https://www.thomsonreuters.com/en-us/posts/news-and-media/blockchain-2020-future-look/ [Accessed 18 05 2022].

Trade Finance Global, 2020. *12 Companies using blockchain to rewire trade and trade finance.* [Online]. Available at: https://www.tradefinanceglobal.com/posts/12-companies-using-blockchain-to-rewire-trade-and-trade-finance/ [Accessed 18 05 2022].

Trade Finance Global, 2022. *Trade finance without barriers.* [Online]. Available at: https://www.tradefinanceglobal.com [Accessed 22 05 2022].

TradeFinex, 2022. *Empowering trade finance ecosystem.* [Online]. Available at: https://www.tradefinex.org [Accessed 18 05 2022].

TradeLens, 2022. *Better visibility and control of your containers.* [Online]. Available at: https://www.tradelens.com [Accessed 18 05 2022].

TradeWaltz, 2022. *Create the future of trade*. [Online]. Available at: https://www. tradewaltz.com/en/ [Accessed 18 05 2022].

UCL, 2021. *UCL blockchain rules online programme*. [Online]. Available at: http:// blockchain.cs.ucl.ac.uk/blockchain-rules-online-programme/ [Accessed 22 05 2022].

UCL, 2022. *Introduction to blockchain and distributed ledger technology (DLT)*. [Online]. Available at: https://www.futurelearn.com/courses/demystifying-blockchain [Accessed 22 05 2022].

University of Oxford, 2022a. *Blockchain for managers (online)*. [Online]. Available at: https://www.conted.ox.ac.uk/courses/blockchain-for-managers-online [Accessed 22 05 2022].

University of Oxford, 2022b. *Blockchain software engineering*. [Online]. Available at: https://www.conted.ox.ac.uk/courses/blockchain-software-engineering [Accessed 22 05 2022].

University of Oxford, 2022c. *Oxford blockchain strategy programme*. [Online]. Available at: https://www.sbs.ox.ac.uk/programmes/executive-education/online-programmes/oxford-blockchain-strategy-programme [Accessed 22 05 2022].

Virtual Reality Society, 2022. *What is virtual reality?* [Online]. Available at: https://www.vrs.org.uk/virtual-reality/what-is-virtual-reality.html [Accessed 18 05 2022].

Wanguba, J., 2021. *How many cryptocurrencies have failed in 2021?* [Online]. Available at: https://e-cryptonews.com/how-many-cryptocurrencies-have-failed/ [Accessed 22 05 2022].

XinFin, 2022. *XDC protocol*. [Online]. Available at: https://www.xinfin.org/ xdc-protocol.php [Accessed 18 05 2022].

Yaga, D., Mell, P., Roby, N., and Scarfone, K., 2018. *NISTIR 8202—Blockchain technology overview*. [Online]. Available at: https://nvlpubs.nist.gov/nistpubs/ ir/2018/NIST.IR.8202.pdf [Accessed 28 05 2022].

Youngblom, R., 2020. *The top universities for blockchain—Methodology*. [Online]. Available at: https://www.coindesk.com/markets/2020/10/06/the-top-universities-for-blockchain-methodology/ [Accessed 22 05 2022].

Index

Note: **Bold** page numbers refer to tables; *Italic* page numbers refer to figures.

51% attack 9, 11, 105

Altcoins 5
alternative currencies overview 5
anti-money laundering (AML) 17, 90,
    136
artificial intelligence 70, 116, 135, 143,
    174, **178**, 246
audit/compliance concerns 136, **139**,
    145, **151**
augmented/virtual reality 116

Bank of England 41, 42, 55, 141,
    174
benefits of strategy execution
    evaluation 194
Binance (BNB) 54
biometrics 116
Bitcoin 1–3, *4*, 5, 8, **9**, 10, 11, *13*,
    15–16, 41, 47, 48, **49** 51,
    52, 55, **56**, 57, 63, 97–111,
    119–121, 124, 130, 131, 177
block's header 7
blockchain adoption 84, 88–89, 133,
    135, 137, 138, *139*, 144,
    145,147, 148, 149, 150, *151*,
    155, 161, 168, 175, **178**, 181,
    183, 197, *208*, 220, 243
blockchain as a service platform 54
blockchain education 1, 137, 138
blockchain interoperability issues 138
business strategy 164, *165*
Byzantine generals' problem 9–10

C-Suite buy-in 138, 150
chain of blocks 1
CoE 117, 150, 189, 191–193, 196, 212,
    235–236, *238*
CoinDesk 15, 117–118
coinmarketcap 3, 97
competitive advantage 1, 63, 71, 132,
    143, 144, 150, 154, 163–164,
    166, 170, 175, 177, 179, *182*,
    183, 190, 195-196, 199,
    204, *208*, 210–211, 217, 220,
    223, 226, 241, 244, 246–247
consensus 5, 8, 9–12, **48–50**, 56, 57,
    59, 111, 130, 138, 152, 154,
    159–161, 198, 243
Consensys Quorum 48, **56**, 58, 69, 172
Consortium blockchain 8, 158
corporate strategy 163–164, *165*
cost leadership strategy 166
crowdfunding 5, 20, 57, 109
cryptography 2, *4*, 8, 55, **60**, 119–120
Cryptoqueen 101
cyber strategy 144

DAO 16–17, 46, 136, 199
dApps 12, *13*, 15–16, 20, 22, 28, 46,
    50, 53, 56, 57, 125
data protection regulation concerns 136
dead coins 112
decentralisation 3, 18, 86, 116, 244
decentralised exchanges (DEXs) 15, 20
decentralised finance 1, 12, **48**, 53, **56**,
    88, 136, 199

Delegated PoS (dPoS) 11, 50
DEX 15, 18
difficulty in establishing a consortium 137
difficulty to establish a blockchain eco-system 137
digital assets 15, 17, 39–40, 50, 53, 61, 84, 88, 154–155, 158, 161, 198, 224
Directed Acyclic Graph (DAG) 12, *13*
distributed ledger 1, 45, 52, 59–60, 65, 93–94, 119, 121–122, 130, 148, 153
divisibility 3
DLT 1, 4, **45**, 52–53, 65–66, 122, 148, 153

Economist 41, 45, 98
EHR 75, 77
energy 10–11, *13*, **56**, 61, 80–81, 87, 174, 177, *178*, 183
EOS *13*, 50, *55*, 104, 111
Ether 5, 24, 27, 34, **48**, **51**, 109, 244
Ethereum 2.0 11, **48**, 57

fake platform 115
Financial Conduct Authority (FCA) 141
free courses 119–122, 124
FTX 102

genomic data 78–79
GovTech 61, 81, 87

hash 7–8, 105
hashing 4, 8
healthcare 61, 75–79, 81, 87, 134, 140, 170
Holding User's Private Keys 115
hybrid blockchain 8, 68, 86, 88, *95*, 137, 158–159
Hyperledger 11, *13*, **48–49**, **51**, **56**, 58, **59–60**, *67–69*, 72, 77–78, 124, 170

ICO 7, 46, **51**, 54–55, 58, 97, 105, 109–115, 131, 244
Ignatova, Ruja 101
immutability 1–3, 15, 22, 116, 243
immutable 1–2, 8, 15, 22, 39, 52–53, 65, 80, 83, 92, 130, 153–155, *156*, 157, 159, 244

important business services (IBS) 140–141
intellectual property concerns 137, *139, 151*
internet of things (IoT) 55, 75, 110, 116
interoperability 15, **49**, 89, 138, *139,* 148, *151,* 170–173, 202–203, 236
IOSpeed Limited 17

lack of governance 138, *139,* 149, *151*
lending platforms 16
limited supply 3, 114
list of blockchain sandboxes 197

Massive Premine 114
media and entertainment 94–95
Metamask 17, 23–28, 31
miners 3, *4, 5,* 10–11, **48**, 99, 105, 130
mining 3, 11, 68, 99, 105, 114, 130, 177
Mt Gox 103, 107–108

Nakamoto, Satoshi 2, *55,* 63, 97

OneCoin 101

paid courses 117, 119–124
performance issues 137, *139,* 148, *151*
permissioned blockchains 8, *13*
PEST 173–174
Porter, Michael 71, 164, 168, 169, 217, 218
    cost leadership strategy 166
    Five forces strategy model 168
    Generic strategy 165
    value chain model 71
practical byzantine fault tolerance (PBFT) 11
predictive markets 16
private blockchain 8, *13,* 65, *91, 92,* 124, 158–159
processors 3
programmability 15
Proof of Authority (PoA) 11, *13, 154*
Proof of Elapsed Time (PoET). 11, *13*
Proof of History (PoH) 12, *13*
Proof of Reputation (PoR) 12, *13*
Proof of Stake (PoS) 11, *13,* 57, 154
Proof of Work (PoW) 10, *13,* 154
Prudential Regulatory Authority (PRA) 141

pseudonymity 3
public blockchain 2, 8, 15, *93*, 94, 158
Pump and Dump 113

quantum computing 116, 135, 138, 143

R3 Corda *9*, **48**, **51**, **56**, 61, 67–68,
    170, 172
regulatory rules uncertainty 135, *139*,
    145, *151*
Requirements for Strategy Execution
    Evaluation 193
resiliency and concentration risks
    133, 143
robotics 116, 135, 138, 143, 174, **178**

sandbox 197–199
Satoshi 3
scalability issues 137
Scammers/Tricky People 114
serverless computing 116
skill gap 131, 138, 150, 235
smallest unit of Bitcoin 3
social impact 78, 85, 90, 92, 93, *94*

Solana blockchain 12
stablecoins 15–16, *19*, 100
static registry **51**, 53
storage strategy 144
strategic models 1, 168, 173, 183, 199,
    217, 221
successful ICOs 55, 110–111, 131
SWOT 173, 175, 179, *182*, 183–184
    217, *220*
synthetic assets 20

telecommunications 61, 74, 87
Terra blockchain 103
tokenisation 20, 65, 136, 154
trade finance *9*, *52*, 61, 66–69, 85
trust issues amongst parties 137

university ranking *118*

wallets 3, 15, 17, 23, 28, 41, **45**,
    104–108
Web3 22

yield farming 16, 19

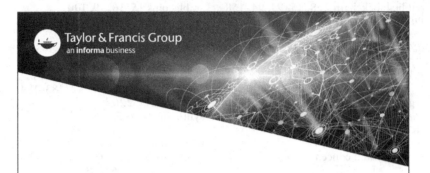

Printed in the United States
by Baker & Taylor Publisher Services